EXPLORING THE
OF SOCIAL P

G000135379

An International Approach

Michael Hill and Zoë Irving

P

First published in Great Britain in 2020 by

Policy Press
University of Bristol
1-9 Old Park Hill
Bristol
BS2 8BB
UK
t: +44 (0)117 954 5940
pp-info@bristol.ac.uk
www.policypress.co.uk

North America office:
Policy Press
c/o The University of Chicago Press
1427 East 60th Street
Chicago, IL 60637, USA
t: +1 773 702 7700
f: +1 773-702-9756
sales@press.uchicago.edu
www.press.uchicago.edu

British Library Cataloguing in Publication Data
A catalogue record for this book is available from the British Library

Library of Congress Cataloging-in-Publication Data
A catalog record for this book has been requested

978-1-4473-3499-6 hardback
978-1-4473-3500-9 paperback
978-1-4473-3501-6 ePub
978-1-4473-3503-0 ePdf

Cover design by Clifford Hayes
Front cover image: iStock/lambada
Printed and bound in Great Britain by CMP, Poole
Policy Press uses environmentally responsible print partners

Contents

Contents

List of figures, tables and boxes

Boxes

Preface

This book emerged from our desire to provide a resource for advanced students that reflected a shift in the discipline of social policy from a focus on advanced welfare states in the OECD 'world' to wider interest in social policy development beyond the 'welfare state'. A commitment to taking an international approach to analyzing social policy across different countries involves not merely an interest in comparative work but also a recognition of a need for global perspectives.

Zoë Irving's interests in reconciling comparative and global analytical interests began while completing a PhD in comparative social policy supervised by Bob Deacon, whose prescient conviction regarding the notion of 'global social policy' in the mid-1990s has shaped it as a field, and without whom global actors and institutions would be conceived of much less confidently in terms of their social politics. In putting these interests into practice, Zoë has since taught comparative and global social policy at several UK universities, co-founded and convened the International and Comparative Group of the Social Policy Association 2004–11 with Nicola Yeates, and with Kevin Farnsworth is co-founding editor of the *Journal of International and Comparative Social Policy*. Following its launch in 2012, this journal aims to bridge the gap between global and national social policy, and its acquisition by the UK Social Policy Association in 2019 is a positive consolidation of this professional and disciplinary aim. Zoë's current research centres on two strands of interest – the social politics of crisis and austerity (with Kevin Farnsworth), and the relationship between national population size and the possibilities for social policy development.

Michael Hill is at the end of a career that may be described as twin-tracked. On the one hand, there has been his engagement in very explicitly policy-oriented research on key issues of UK social policy – race relations, unemployment, social work, housing benefit, rent control – that has led to textbooks committed to detailed accounts of UK policies. On the other hand, he has developed an expertise in the study of the policy process, and explored ways to develop the diverse literature from the US and continental Europe. This has led to fruitful collaborations with scholars from the Netherlands, Belgium, Germany and Scandinavia, and particularly writing on policy implementation with Peter Hupe. Michael has taught in several UK universities over the course of his career and has also been a visiting lecturer in many countries outside the UK including Hungary, Sweden and Taiwan. He continues to advise on research and publications, mostly from home but with visits to Denmark and Brazil in 2018–19.

Some time has passed between developing an initial idea and this book's publication, and for their patience and support in the process we offer our sincere thanks to Alison Shaw, Catherine Gray, Vaarunika Dharmapala and all the team at Policy Press. In developing the book, it is also important to acknowledge the support of the publishers (Blackwell and later Wiley-Blackwell) of Michael

Hill's earlier work, *Social Policy in the Modern World*, which informed some of the content in this book, and of eight editions of *Understanding Social Policy*. Co-authoring the eighth edition (2009) of the latter provided the impetus for our writing partnership on this book.

As most authors acknowledge, their work is also dependent on the goodwill and encouragement of family, friends and colleagues, and we also thank them for their support. Zoë Irving would like to acknowledge the University of York MA students on the 2018–19 Global Social Problems and Global Social Policy module. Many of the chapters here were refined in learning and teaching with this superb group of students, who brought their knowledge of, and experiences from, countries in all world regions, and whose insights and engagement with most of the issues discussed in the book were very much valued. Table 7.1, which was the topic of a particularly productive and memorable teaching session (and with regret for the 'missing data'), is dedicated to them. Our thanks too, to the anonymous reviewers who took the time to comment on the full text. We recognize our limitations in 'exploring the world of social policy'; retaining the strengths of regime theory while attempting to step outside of this framework is a work in progress. Nevertheless, we hope that the book makes a worthwhile contribution to a widening and deepening internationalization of social policy study.

Social policy and social progress:
how can we explore the world?

This book builds on an approach adopted in the eight editions of *Understanding Social Policy* (most recently Hill and Irving, 2009) and also in the book *Social Policy in the Modern World* (Hill, 2006). The former was essentially an analysis of policy in the UK while the latter represented a comparative review of developed welfare states across a number of policy domains and dimensions of disadvantage, with an approach embedded in the traditions of cross-national comparison. In one sense this book represents some continuity in the analysis of social policy development and its cross-national comparison. However, it also represents a broadening shift of perspective in response to changes that have occurred in the discipline of social policy and the scope of field of study. Although since the 2010s many countries now seek to turn inwards politically, economically and socially, it remains the case that momentum for global and world regional social policy has gathered pace, and that three decades of economic globalization means that no policy now emerges or exists in national isolation. That implies a need to combine a global perspective with a comparative one, accepting that, while there are many shared influences on national policy, responses vary considerably from country to country in ways that comparative analytical frameworks can help to explain.

Worlds of social policy

The title of the book deliberately has a triple meaning, explored in this and the next two sections. First, it looks at the *worlds of social policy* in the comparative sense established by Esping-Andersen (1990) – that there are different welfare *regimes*, ways of arranging and organizing welfare provision based on different welfare relations, principles and mechanics. This approach to categorizing national welfare systems has dominated comparative study for a quarter of a century, providing insight and provoking further investigation in equal measure. While the ubiquity and impact of the 'three worlds' approach is undoubtedly sensed in general reading of international and comparative scholarship, in metric terms the study of 'welfare regimes' is indicated as the 'leading topic' in citation classics among key social policy journals (Powell, 2016). Since the 1990s, a significant critique and elaboration of this approach has contributed to its further embedding as a valid foundation for comparative research. Recent three worlds anniversary collections in the journal *Social Policy and Society* (2017) and *Social Policy Review 27* (Irving et al., 2015) attest to the continuing influence of welfare state typologization as an analytical mainstay in comparing national welfare states and determining the factors that produce similarity and difference between them.

The welfare regime approach has, however, two important weaknesses. First, its limitations are most apparent where it is stretched beyond advanced welfare states (see Gough and Wood, 2004). Second, as an analytical approach it is more comfortably applied within some areas of social policy, particularly income security, than others. While it indicates essential parameters for the study of social policy around the world, these are most useful where the idea of regimes is used to suggest political and cultural characteristics that cluster and seemingly suggest determinants of change, rather than as an analytical prison that reduces debate to the accuracy of the typologies produced. This is particularly the case when attention is directed beyond countries with established welfare state architectures.

The world of social policy

The second way in which the book looks at the *world* of social policy, is in the geographical sense, drawing on examples and systems from across the globe. In the twenty-first century, while it is possible to evidence many claims that the world is a better place than it has ever been – that human rights are more protected, that there are fewer social and geographical divisions and that more people have more power to determine the course of their lives than ever before – this has been an uneven development, and potential setbacks are only too evident today. Where global social progress has occurred, social policy has been central to its achievement, but because analysis of social policy is often restricted to the realm of established welfare state institutions, its wider arrangements and contribution outside of formal structures are less recognized, or at least less well integrated into policy debate and discussions of social politics centred in the global North. Because social policy is associated with recognizable administrative structures, distinctions often made between national categories, such as 'mature' welfare states, 'emerging economies' and 'low-income countries', carry the assumption that nation states remain the most important socio-political and policy units, an assumption that is challenged in the contemporary global circumstance.

The significance of the nation state has been a matter of debate within the globalization literature since the 1990s (for example Ohmae, 1990; McGrew and Lewis, 1992; Rhodes, 1994; Mishra, 1998; Pierson, 2001). The perceived strength or weakness of national actors divides perspectives in international political economy, and contrasts perspectives on the state as a 'zombie category' (Beck and Beck-Gernsheim, 2002) in the new forms of governance, with those that see the state as an enduring locus of government. The focus on 'methodological nationalism' has similarly vexed some analysts of social policy where comparative analysis of *worlds of welfare capitalism* (Esping-Andersen, 1990) and *families of nations* (Castles, 1999) has been argued to neglect both the transnational character of Western welfare state development and the rising influence of global actors, organizations and collectives on contemporary welfare evolution across the world.

In considering countries themselves, there is debate regarding the porous borders of welfare state development in the global North, and contestation of the idea that developed welfare states were ever 'national' or formed and managed within national borders (Clarke, 2005). This is not only because national borders themselves are subject to change, as secession, independent statehood, annexation and state formation shape and reshape countries geographically. The movement of people also means that 'national' populations have always been fluid, with consequent differentials in (welfare) citizenship. Additionally, however, as Clarke (and others, for example Williams, 1995) points out, the welfare states of advanced economies have been built on the labour and contribution of migrants. In Europe in particular, its place in the history of colonialism combined with the post-war expansion of a regionalist supranational organization, the European Economic Community, to become the European Union, has created a further European context for social policy development which sometimes overrides, sometimes follows and otherwise interacts with the 'national'.

Analyzing 'welfare states' rather than social policy necessarily drives attention to the 'state' itself, and relatedly to the focus on 'national' units as the subject of study. Historically, this has made sense as national political events since 1945, such as the strength of national labour movements, their capacities in formal politics and their alliances with other interest groups such as the parties representing the middle classes or farmers, have shaped what are now the formally established systems of welfare provision in the global North. In the balance of provision within these systems, the roles and responsibilities of the state emerged as most influential in the achievement of social welfare, and a focus on state intervention therefore often overshadowed the activities of other non-state actors. From the 1970s, a backlash against state intervention began to gain political and popular support, leading to much greater interest in the activities of market actors, families and non-governmental ('third-sector') organizations and their place in the mixed economy of welfare.

There has been a more sustained contemporary academic critique of the problem of 'methodological nationalism' which characterizes comparative social policy scholarship and treats states (and their welfare arrangements) as stable, easily defined units of comparison. It is argued that this approach omits the increasingly important transnational and global influences, interests, actors and activities which, in many countries, have greater significance for welfare outcomes than those which are nationally confined (see Yeates, 2002, 2007; Wimmer and Schiller, 2003; Deacon, 2005, 2007). 'International' social policy is equally prone to this national categorization, especially where 'international' simply means the discussion alongside each country's welfare arrangements and applies international in the sense that the countries described stretch beyond Europe (for example Alcock and Craig, 2001). The development of the subfield of global social policy (Deacon, 1997) was thus an important break from a scholarly focus on national actors to shift attention to the extremely powerful but under-researched interests and influences that operate in the global and transnational sphere. In this sphere, the ideas, desires and influences of political and economic actors, including international governmental organizations (IGOs) such as the World Bank, International Monetary Fund (IMF) and United Nations (UN) as well as transnational businesses, aid organizations and activist networks, are all significant in shaping not only the general tone of social policy debate at the world level but also the development and implementation of social policies in individual countries and across world regions. The regionalization of social policy has itself become of much more direct significance and consequently of academic concern in the 2000s (Kaasch and Stubbs, 2014).

This is not to say that the role of interests beyond formal state institutions have been neglected. Historical analyses are clear that they also have their part to play – the medical profession in the emergence of the British welfare state for example, or the role of business actors in lobbying and shaping developments to minimize their costs or maximize their power. However, the operation of these interests was somewhat less complex in the mid–twentieth century than it is today. Even though borders have always been porous to some extent, certainly ethnically and culturally but also economically and even politically, in the 2020s the influences shaping mature welfare states are supranationalized, and the economy is globalized. For those countries where welfare state development is in its early stages (emerging economies such as India and Brazil), where it has yet to gain a stable institutional and bureaucratic foundation (such as Honduras and Nigeria), where conflict has devastated social systems (El Salvador, Syria, Somalia) or where society has been subject to a significant political intermission that has halted one trajectory and left the door open to an onslaught of possibilities (such as in Central and Eastern European countries), the traditional comparative understanding of 'how' welfare arrangements are brought to life and subsequently sustained is challenged. In this context, hierarchical categorizations based on whether a country has more or less of something – public spending as a proportion of gross domestic product (GDP), public administrative bureaucracy or social democratic cabinet seats, for example – are not only bound to emphasize difference rather than commonality, but in focusing on state-level institutions are also unable to capture the complexity of social policy actors and interests and their interaction amid and beyond the state. An approach which attempts to view social policy from a global perspective therefore requires a recognition that not all national social policies involve the state, and that not all social policies within states are state policy. It also reflects a looser understanding of the mixed economy of social policy and directs attention to a range of often unconnected programmes and projects with welfare objectives (see Deacon, 2007) as much as the overarching policy environments in which they exist (see Seelkopf and Starke, 2019).

One of the difficulties in mapping a world of social policy in this way, however, is the availability of data and, where data are available, the scope and scale of its detail. The picture provided by international comparative data is very mixed, and biased towards the richer nations. Data on 'welfare states' relating to levels of spending, participation in markets such as labour and housing, and indicators of outcomes, inequalities and diswelfare are accessible through international organizations such as the Organisation for Economic Co-operation and Development (OECD) and the European Union statistical service (Eurostat). The databases managed by these organizations provide important sources of information for comparative research among countries in the global North, that is, Europe (Eurostat) and the OECD – high- and middle-income countries which have passed the membership tests relating to economic and political values. OECD data routinely cover the current thirty-six member countries, although not all data are available for all countries because the databases rely on national statistical office submissions (Coicaud and Zhang, 2011). Outside of the richest states, Mexico and Chile are OECD members and both Colombia and Costa Rica are progressing with membership applications. While the scope of OECD data is considerable, and the organization is a prolific publisher of working papers and annual reviews of economic and social issues, OECD data clearly also have a geographical disadvantage in attempts to present a global perspective.

To answer questions about the worldwide state of welfare, 'global' social policy-related data are therefore generally drawn from the key IGOs: the World Bank; the agencies of the UN; the International Labour Organization; and sometimes the IMF. This 'official' data can be supplemented by so-called grey literature such as survey reports from international non-governmental organizations and private organizations that undertake mainly economic research. As a result, analysis that aims to produce global comparisons is limited in two key ways. Firstly, in databases that hold data for all nation states, depth is traded for breadth. Many countries with limited resources for data collection are only able to meet the collection of headline data targets and missing data are prevalent at the more granular level and across time. More importantly, in terms of robust analysis, international organizations such as the World Bank do not operate in a political vacuum and are themselves policy makers. As scholars of global policy making have shown, data collection is itself a political process, as issues are constructed and defined and the ways in which they are subsequently measured are determined by these organizations and their results feed into the wider policy agendas of both the IGOs and their member countries. In this way the IGOs have 'social construction power' (Barnett and Finnemore, 2004) and are able to assert 'cognitive authority' (Broome and Seabrooke, 2012) in relation to the social problems faced around the world, how they should be understood and what kind of responses are required.

Reflecting on the capacity for assessing the world of social policy, therefore, it is necessary to accept that due to limitations of data, depth of knowledge, sources of evidence and breadth of coverage, in practice scholars tend to work towards a global-comparative perspective rather than achieving like for like comparison wherever analysis goes beyond headline counts of key socio-economic indicators. To some extent, due to space constraints, qualitative depth is traded for quantitative breadth in this book too, and the balance of evidence in the chapters to follow also tends towards the use of statistical data rather than evaluation of the rich and significant qualitative research that informs social policy study.

The world of academic social policy study

In a third meaning, this book draws upon the world of *social policy* scholarship in the sense of exploring the parameters of the discipline (or field of study, as some scholars prefer). This is not to claim that the book is comprehensive in its range of analysis, or that it offers a definitive approach to social policy as an academic subject. The aim here is not to provide an encyclopaedia of international social policy (see Fitzpatrick et al., 2010 for such a publication) or a reference work (see Castles et al., 2010 and Greve, 2013). Instead the chapter contents aim to present an international analysis of the essential concerns of social policy, an examination of the policy domains generated to address these concerns and discussion of the contemporary challenges to policy makers in the twenty-first century brought by social and economic change.

The book is thus a contribution to the expansion of study in social policy and its understanding as an international and global endeavour. As noted earlier, the shape of social policies beyond established welfare states is often subject to influences that are neither 'national' nor 'state'. This is highlighted in many of the chapter discussions, but in focusing on particular themes and challenges in areas of policy it is not possible to also do justice to the depth of insight drawn from analyses in global social policy that provide a more forensic examination of the politics and practices of international actors and organizations. This can be found both in more generalized accounts of social policy at the global level (for example Deacon, 1997; Deacon and Stubbs, 2013; Kaasch and Martens, 2015) and in work which is focused on specific policy areas in a global context (for example Kaasch, 2015; Verger et al., 2018). Similarly, while the policy domain chapters, in particular, aim to consider the subject matter beyond the concerns of advanced economies, space restricts detailed integration of the full breadth of perspectives from development studies on these concerns. Such integration of traditional social policy approaches with those from social development studies is emerging, both in academic research and in the work of organizations such as the UN (for example Mkandawire, 2016). The work of James Midgley has been particularly influential in establishing these disciplinary connections (Midgley, 1995; Hall and Midgley, 2004), which are further elaborated by others (Surender and Walker, 2013; Copestake, 2015), and they extend to more recent work on world regionalism and its emergent forms of social policy making (Deacon et al., 2010).

All these literatures help to inform the overarching analytical approach of this book, which recognizes the ways in which history, politics and economics matter, not just in terms of how institutions develop, but also in how national and global historical processes affect the way that people treat each other in bounded locations and across boundaries, the variety of ways in which policy operates vertically and horizontally and the kinds of material concerns that shape collective responses. The analysis also recognizes questions about whether and how all these dimensions are comparable, and which theoretical frameworks enable us to understand them better. Thus, although the comparative dimensions are important in all of the chapter analyses presented, an open understanding of social policy underpins the book, which recognizes that comparative frameworks developed in the context of advanced welfare states in the global North can do no more than assist in constructing better ways to explore social policy elsewhere in the world.

In view of this, social policy here concerns purposeful collective actions that influence the distribution of resources. Its analysis is very often, as in this book, driven by concerns about disadvantages and the structures of inequality, and therefore aims to improve welfare conditions and to contribute to social progress. This implies a particular focus on policies with self-evident welfare goals (such as those with respect to income support, health and social care) but also has regard (as for example in the discussions of employment, education and environment issues in this book) to the wide range of policies which have an impact on human welfare.

Social policy and social change

Examining the relationship between social policy and social change assists in delineating some key concepts used to analyze social policy in a way that detaches them from the specific concerns of mature welfare states. The purpose of this approach is to demonstrate the human commonalities that drive social policy development, and to emphasize that the answers to questions of when, how and why people seek to meet their needs collectively take us beyond the concern of 'policy' in any formal sense. The discussion will show that welfare is thus dependent upon a mixed economy and a combination of personal and collective efforts, describable in terms of the activities of households and families, localities and communities, and the economy and the state. Concerns about the extension of welfare, its desirability and the means by which it is achieved are matters of philosophical and ideological debate and political action. Social progress occurs as human needs are increasingly met, and human welfare is expanded. Social policy is not entirely responsible for delivering these kinds of improvements to the quality of people's lives, their health and well-being, but without social policy improvements they are unlikely to occur, and where they do occur they are unlikely to be patterned in a way that promotes social justice.

It is tempting to look back through decades or centuries and make claims that, compared to the world of the early twentieth century for example, contemporary conditions of life such as those in work, habitat, prosperity and security are far removed from the privation experienced before the 1940s and the arrival of the 'golden age' of welfare capitalism (although see Wincott, 2013). The 1940s are generally regarded as the decade that propelled the instruments of rapid progress: welfare states, decolonization, international cooperation and economic growth on a continuous upward trajectory which has raised standards of all human life. This is argued to apply, even despite the intervening economic crises, civil and international conflicts and political upheavals. There is evidence to support this claim. In 2010 the UN Human Development Report (UNDP, 2010) included an assessment of changes in the indicators of the Human Development Index (HDI) (using measures of life expectancy, years of schooling and per capita income) from 1970, to show that taken together, all countries showed 'impressive' improvements and that the gap between developed and developing countries had narrowed by approximately 25 per cent in forty years.

Despite these claims of human progress, and the real benefits that this has brought to millions of people, the world remains a highly unequal place, and particularly since the global financial crisis in 2008, this inequality has increased along many dimensions. The UNDP report (2010) also presents many examples of failures and reversals in progress which 'remind us that progress is not linear' (2010, p. 30). Not only is this the case, but the world regional differentials have not changed either, with sub-Saharan Africa disproportionately represented in countries with reversals in progress, and in the lowest-ranking countries using the HDI measure. As economists (including two previously leading officials of the World Bank) have shown, inequalities of wealth and income began to rise in the decade before 2008 (Piketty, 2014; Atkinson, 2015; Milanovic, 2016; Stiglitz, 2016), but in the post-crisis world many of the equalizing welfare gains made in previous years have been reversed (Ortiz et al., 2015). The evaluation of social progress therefore clearly becomes less certain when further questions are asked regarding who has progressed and what the nature of that progress might be. It is also important to recognize that historical comparisons seeking to remind us how far we have come, especially those based on generalized quantitative measures, also require more context-heavy comparative, qualitative reflection as a counter-balance to the drawing of simple conclusions that progress necessarily accompanies the passing of time.

Where the analysis of social policy is concerned, there is much to consider in terms of social change that can be considered 'progress'. The example of life expectancy (which is often used as a measure of social development) illustrates well the competing conceptions of 'progress', 'welfare' and 'need' that characterize the analysis and evaluation of social policy. Broadly speaking, it is clear that outside the effects of generalized military conflict in the early and middle periods of the twentieth century, people's expectations of years of life have increased considerably. However, as research continues to highlight, the level of differentiation in the social distribution of these expectations is striking. Some of these differences are presented in Table 1.1.

Thus, while general trends for longer life, even in the poorest countries, do indicate, as the UNDP (2010) has suggested, that progress has occurred, the beneficiaries of this progress can easily be contrasted with those whose life expectations, both in years lived and the possibilities during those years, remain little different to those of a century ago. What is also apparent is that differences in expectations are shared transnationally, stratified across groups and geographies and not simply the problem of particular countries or regions. A second important theme emerges from the example of life expectancy, which is that progress may

Table 1.1: Differentiated life expectancy at birth

Black or African American women in the US (2016)	77.9	White women in the US (2016)	81.0
Women and men born in Central African Republic (2017)	52.9	Women and men born in Hong Kong (2017)	84.1
Women in Sierra Leone (2017)	52.8	Women in Australia (2017)	85.0
Boys born in the north-east of England (2012–14)	78.0	Boys born in the south-east of England (2012–14)	80.5
Increase between 1970 and 2010 in Norway	7 years	Increase between 1970 and 2010 in the Gambia	16 years

Sources: UNDP (2010); US Centers for Disease Control and Prevention, https://www.cdc.gov/nchs/hus/contents2017.htm#Figure_001; UNHDP, http://hdr.undp.org/en/composite/HDI and http://hdr.undp.org/en/composite/GDI; Office for National Statistics, https://www.ons.gov.uk/peoplepopulationand community/birthsdeathsandmarriages/lifeexpectancies/bulletins/lifeexpectancyatbirthandatage65by localareasinenglandandwales/2015-11-04#regional-life-expectancy-at-birth.

not necessarily be a good in itself. Living longer presents its own challenges for maintaining health, income and social participation. Thus the extension of life, both a desire and an outcome associated with development (in human and economic terms), is accompanied by the emergence of related needs. A substantial body of literature exists on the subject of 'need' (see Dean, 2010, for a summary of the debates), and what the basis should be for the provision of guarantees that needs are met. From the psycho-social hierarchy developed by Abraham Maslow and conditions of social citizenship outlined by T.H. Marshall in the mid-twentieth century, to the Sustainable Development Goals (SDGs) agreed by the UN in 2016, the answer to the question of what is needed for a decent human existence centres on the development of social policy.

In its tracking of trends in human development, the UNDP (2010) identified improvements in health and education as being the key drivers of progress.[1] On a practical level, the notion that health and education are essential propellants for human development has underpinned the emergence of social provision throughout history, driving household strategies, the actions of social collectives and public intervention in state development. In theory and research, the significance of health and education is at the core of generalized theories of 'need' (for example Doyal and Gough, 1991) and in expanded debates on basic/human needs and capabilities (for example Sen, 1985), as well as measures of need satisfaction developed to improve and expand on the HDI (see Klugman et al., 2011, for a discussion of these). Education and health represent the core of the earliest welfare measures in the longest-established welfare states (i.e. those whose welfare arrangements have become determined by formal national politics and institutionalized bureaucratic structures). In the nineteenth and early twentieth centuries, public sanitation and compulsory schooling, alongside health insurance to meet needs related to illness and incapacity, laid the foundations of modern

Western welfare states. In countries such as Brazil, South Korea and South Africa, publicly funded provision for health and education is similarly significant. These two needs represent an obvious intersection between conditions ('health' and 'understanding') that are essential for human flourishing, and potential ('capacity' and 'ability') that are essential to economic growth (and where national interests are concerned, competitiveness). What this intersection highlights, is the way in which social progress is coupled with both economic development and the role of the state.

There is an additional element of need that is directly associated with the interests of states: that of security. Security as a condition is usually conceptualized as concerning the absence of harm or the threat of harm. In broad terms, security incorporates physical, psychological and social dimensions of harm and extends beyond the personal security of individuals to the collective interests in security that pertain to states and, at their most universal, global security. For social policy, the significance of civil rights in guarantees of 'security' are essential (although they still remain only partially realized from a global perspective), but guarantees of security of livelihood are far more political. In essence, this difference has its roots in philosophical beliefs around the nature of human rights and freedoms, and while freedom from harm has gradually been recognized formally as something that sovereigns have the duty to protect over many centuries, the freedom to participate fully in society is much more contested. As industrialization – and, in the advanced economies, deindustrialization – takes place, pre-existing systems of householding and exchange are supplanted or reshaped, and this socio-economic change generates new needs, new demands for meeting those needs and the expectation, if not the reality of new responses to those demands.

The emergence of citizenship in the global North has rendered states important guarantors of both the rights and the freedoms associated with autonomy, health and security, the last of which Doyal and Gough (1991) argue is a prerequisite for the first two. However, even in countries that are regarded as well-established democracies in the global North, these rights and freedoms are fragile, and currently in both Europe and North America they are threatened by retrograde political forces (Szikra, 2014; Buzogány and Varga, 2018). Looking back less than a century, it is clear that even in established democracies, states also have the capacity to oppress people, limit freedoms and rights and control populations. Historically social policy has been an important tool by which social harm has been inflicted as well as a means to achieve social progress (King, 1999). There are instances where social policy has been used to deliberately disadvantage certain groups, but it is also the case that even where social policy is intended to guarantee rights, it operates in a world structured by many forms of social division, and while policies may seek to redistribute resources and opportunities, there are always risks that policy will effect no change, displace advantage or aggravate existing inequalities.

The many international declarations which now exist to commit states to guaranteeing rights in the realms of health, labour standards, gender equality and the treatment of citizens, refugees and children for example, act as both the political acceptance of need, and the basis for legitimate claims on collective resources. Nevertheless, while the world's welfare is better served by having them than not, being a signatory of an international declaration is a relatively soft option for national governments, which weigh the political costs of meeting obligations against other competing interests. States can therefore be unreliable actors, irrelevant in practice and, at worst, destructive powers that produce greater diswelfare than welfare.

Given that states have a relatively short history as purveyors of welfare progressivity, and one that is also, globally, relatively limited in terms of geographical expanse and depth of intervention, it is not surprising that the provision of welfare is largely undertaken by non-state actors, even in countries with the longest-established formal institutions. The mixed economy of welfare characterizes all provision in all countries; what differs is the balance of activity, responsibility and obligation attributed to informal, state and market actors.

There is a substantial body of literature which explores 'the family' within the welfare mix, how families interact with wider informal means of welfare support and, related to this, the gendered operation of these activities in households, communities and the third sector. In the context of advanced economies, these studies necessarily account for the interaction between citizens and states, while in a development context the state is far less present and therefore the role of informal actors in care and welfare support is bound up with a focus on wider 'household strategies'. Non-governmental welfare actors, agencies and organizations also have far greater involvement in modelling the welfare arrangements in the global South than the North, and the private sector too has a different shape depending on the extent to which states have the capacity to engage in regulatory and enabling policy making. It is well established that the boundaries between the state/market and third-sector actors are often blurred in practice, and in the contemporary global policy context these distinctions are becoming less and less clear. The CEOs of corporate giants such as Microsoft and Amazon, for example, are able to channel billions of dollars to charitable ventures which directly influence the nature of welfare provision and the 'informal' formation of policy goals in areas of health and security.

Discussion in this chapter has considered some of the universal themes which bind human commonalities in relation to welfare needs. It is clear that, as Titmuss (1974, p. 22) proposed when social policy study was in its academic infancy, social needs and problems are common, but they are approached differently in different times and places. The remaining chapters in this book seek to explore these commonalities and differences and to offer explanations for differentiation drawing on theoretical insight from a range of disciplines.

Structure of the book

The chapters to follow are divided into two parts. The first part sets out three key frameworks of analysis used to understand and explain the shape (that is the design, development and outcomes) of social policy within the global context. These chapters draw on social scientific theories, concepts and themes developed across sociology, political science, political economy and economics that apply to the concerns of social policy and welfare states. Chapter 2 focuses specifically on the key historical problematic of social policy: inequality. This is because it is the existence and impact of inequalities and the political approach to these that shape the variety of policy responses to welfare needs. Chapter 3 considers ways of assessing difference and similarity in welfare arrangements in order to understand better their heritage, principles and survival. The final chapter in this section explores the mechanics of policy making in order to explain how things have been, and can be, done in the world of policy design and development.

The concerns of these chapters are also reflected in Part II. Here, not all chapters follow the same structure and they do not provide a systematic assessment across policy domains. This is because each chapter attempts to highlight key themes and issues that are most salient to the area, and most illustrative of the ways in which particular ideas, problems and processes affect policy development.

Part II focuses on a series of policy domains. These policy domains include what are sometimes referred to as the 'five giants' of post-war reconstruction, as identified by William Beveridge when he was tasked with assessing the provisions of the British welfare state in the early 1940s. This includes chapters on income security, work and employment, education, housing, and health. In addition to these domains of policy and service provision, we include two other areas of policy which are crucial to human welfare and social progress, but for various reasons are not always considered 'core' to the welfare state. There is a chapter on social care, which although not considered by British policy makers as a key element of societal rebuilding after the Second World War, is viewed through a very different lens in the twenty-first century. The term 'social care' is adopted for this chapter to distinguish the discussion of policy and provision from a wider consideration of the myriad dimensions of obligation and reciprocity in human relations that are inherent to the wider concept of 'care'. Of course, these elements are also central to the operation of social care, but our distinction is one of perspective – the chapter is concerned with the mixed economy of care, that is, the ways in which the state, the market and people interact in the provision of care services. The final chapter in this section concerns environmental policy. Again, this is a policy domain which has been more generally associated with 'public' rather than 'social' policy, but again, the convergence of environmental concerns and social policy concerns in the modern world is such that the two areas are now inseparable.

The final chapter in this book has two purposes. Within a framework which foregrounds consideration of social change and continuity, the discussion draws together conclusions from the preceding chapters to identify the dominant themes. In addition to this, however, the chapter also reflects on the universal and particularistic dimensions of social policy and how these can shape a global understanding that assists in better exploring the world. It considers the general challenges and opportunities in the contemporary policy-making context and what they imply for the future development of social policy. There is much to be pessimistic about where the survival of state-supported welfare arrangements are concerned: the seeming triumph of markets over political processes; worsening inequalities within and between nations; a lack of welfare commitment on the part of governments; and the deterioration in public services through lack of funding and investment. What is clear from all the chapters is that the contemporary global 'state of welfare' is unsustainable for political, economic and moral reasons. However, even in ostensibly negative circumstances there is always possibility, and glimpses of this can also be discerned in many of the policy developments explored in the discussions to follow.

Part I

THEMES AND PERSPECTIVES

2

Inequalities and why they matter

This chapter expands on the themes in Chapter 1, exploring the particular importance of concerns about inequality and social justice for ideas of social policy. This represents a key theme for comparative analysis in that the salience of ideas about inequality in political debate influences differences between social policies across countries. The chapter will examine global and regional trends in inequality as well as the ways in which these spatial dimensions intersect with other forms of structural inequalities and social divisions in key areas of need satisfaction and measures of welfare. The chapter will consider the idea of inequality as it informs the range of policies in practice, and in policy discourse at national and supranational level, and will discuss the association of discourse and practice with the politics of welfare.

Introduction

Discussions of the origins of social policies treat concerns about inequality and social justice as not necessarily tied to explanations of policy development. Interpretation of social policy origins is a matter of some intellectual controversy, often driven by ideology, in which it seems impossible to arrive at definitive conclusions. This point is revisited at the end of the chapter, as a link to the chapters that follow. Inequality is given primary attention here since one of the challenges to comprehensive social policy analysis involves the assertion that it is primarily concerned with exceptional casualties of society, in a context in which it is economic policy that is crucial for overall social progress. Such a view, of course, largely excludes the possibility that market systems have a role to play in the production of social casualties, and it is not the view that is taken in this book. On the contrary, discussions in this and following chapters are presented from the position that the need for social policy arises largely because of the inadequacies of market societies. Such a view takes social policy analysts deep into many aspects of economic policy, and in so doing widens rather than narrows the range of issues that social policy is expected to address.

However, it is appropriate to mention briefly the alternative point of view and to highlight its limitations. The view that social progress emerges from good economic policy ensuring a strong and growing economy tends to embrace two propositions. One of these is that economic institutions work best when constraints upon the market are minimized. The other is that economic progress produces social progress inasmuch as 'a rising tide lifts all boats'. The first of these is contestable within economics in terms of the range of issues that markets do not handle very effectively. Welfare economics literature, for example, emphasizes externalities and monopolistic forces that are hard to restrain. Furthermore, it is contestable that it is any longer feasible to protect vigorously competitive markets in the face of powerful global monopolistic tendencies. With regard to the second proposition, there is now a great deal of evidence that it is not working. First, the boat-lifting image is misleading. When a real tide rises it does of course lift all boats indiscriminately, but in the context described here some boats are lifted much faster than others, and this is true both within individual countries and across world regions. This is demonstrated in Figure 2.1, which presents data on changes in the distribution of increasing global wealth between 2000 and 2016, indicating limited gains in wealth accumulation in Africa, India and Latin America in comparison to those in other regions.

In the starkest terms, wealth inequality has been calculated as ninety-two individual billionaires holding as much wealth as the poorest half of the world (Oxfam, 2015). Second, in reality, the rising of the tide is very slow in many of the so-called advanced economies, and this has been the case particularly since the global financial crisis when economic growth measured in GDP has barely reached its lowest pre-crisis points, and is predicted to slow even further up to 2020 (IMF, 2017a). This unequal distribution of world assets and opportunities, combined with limited capacity for any meaningful wealth creation, suggests not only difficult questions for economists but also a need to look more closely at the social fallout from the market economy.

Figure 2.1: Regional and selected country percentage of global total wealth (US$ trillion), 2000 and 2018

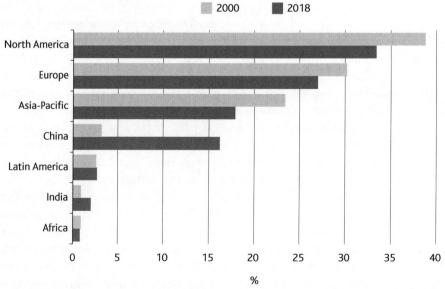

Note: Calculation from smoothed exchange rates, i.e. five-year moving average exchange rates.

Source: Authors' calculation from Credit Suisse (2018, p. 154, table 6.3)

Embedded particularly in writings that generalize about the rise of 'the welfare state' is the idea that social policies emerged in the twentieth century to curb the rampant inequality produced by capitalism. This argument, it may be noted, is given currency as much in terms of the need to protect capitalism as in terms of the recognition of inequality as a social problem. Indeed, the role of social policy in the reinforcement of the status quo led socialist movements in the nineteenth and twentieth centuries to see reforms as distracting attention from the fight against capitalism. In that respect welfare provision may be seen as a means to 'buy' votes for the status quo in the context of universal democracy, a theme continued in scholarly presentations of the Marxist interpretation of social policy (O'Connor, 1973). Moreover, the strongest impetus towards the reduction in wealth inequality is shown to have occurred around the two world wars (Piketty, 2014).

Questions about social policy's egalitarian goals have become particularly significant because of the evidence of increases in income and wealth inequality across the industrialized nations during the twentieth and early twenty-first centuries, often framed as a more combative question of whether this implies a failure of the so-called welfare state project (see discussions in Taylor-Gooby, 2013 and Gamble, 2016). Inasmuch as rising inequality embodies a fightback by economic elites against equalization, it implies a need to give attention to the *structural* factors determining achieved income before, as well as after, any direct state interventions with respect to taxes and benefits. It is here that a particular justification for a perspective on social policy that embraces much more than income-related interventions can be found. The weakening of redistributive action may need to be explained not merely in terms of policy 'retrenchment' but also by deindustrialization, globalization and demographic change. There are complex interactions here, which cannot be addressed satisfactorily in any analysis that separates issues about social policy from those about economic policy. These issues are explored further in the next two chapters.

Problems such as these have been highlighted especially by the advocates of 'basic income' or 'citizens' income' schemes. Their arguments coalesce around a need to detach a concern with the relief of poverty from the labour market assumptions characteristic of social protection schemes established from the mid-twentieth century in advanced economies (see the discussion in Chapter 6). The rise of conditional cash transfer systems of social assistance as a means of poverty relief in low-income countries is indicative of how this policy problematic is emerging. In countries where administrative systems and formal labour markets are not so well established, the idea that income support may be made conditional on participation in other forms of welfare-related behaviour aiming to improve health and education outcomes and ultimately human capital development has been attractive to governments. But the arguments for resource transfers implicit in both these universal basic income and conditional cash transfer schemes cannot side-step the question of the relationship between those who pay their costs and those who receive their benefits, even though this division is in many ways artificial (Farnsworth and Irving, 2018a). The implicit 'universalism' (whether categorical, that is, based on membership of a particular social group, or not) has to rest upon some notion of deductions to support payments. In that sense the fundamental proposition of this chapter remains relevant: that social policy analysis needs to address the wider distribution of resources as a whole.

Finally, the recognition of intimate connections between social policy and inequality is given additional support from research that identifies the extent to which the most unequal societies have inherent problems even for those who are advantaged within them. That point is explicitly addressed in, for example, the work of Wilkinson and Pickett (2010), in which they show the relationship between, on the one hand, economic inequalities and health inequalities, and on the other, the relationship between the latter and other social problems. In summary, they argue that even the better off are disadvantaged (in terms of health and other problems) in unequal societies. Hence specific ameliorative interventions in societies (even the provision of universal health services) will be undermined where economic inequalities are not addressed.

Such a view has more recently found echoes in some unexpected places. Christine Lagarde, managing director of the IMF, for example, argued in a speech in May 2014 that rising income inequality was one of the 'leading economic stories of our time'. After three decades where economic orthodoxy had embraced inequality as a motivating factor propelling growth, under Lagarde the IMF has been much more vocal on the negative consequences of inequality for economic development, for example in the October 2017 issue of its flagship publication *Fiscal Monitor*, entitled *Tackling Inequality* (IMF, 2017b). Other international organizations have also begun to publicly question the costs of inequality. The OECD has a Centre for Opportunity and Equality, and published an important report with a revealing subtitle, *Why Less Inequality Benefits All*, indicating the organization's shift in thinking (OECD, 2015). After several years in development and negotiation (Deacon, 2013), the International Labour Organization (ILO) successfully adopted a universal Social Protection Floor in Recommendation (No. 202, 2012) and through Convention (No. 102, 1952). 'Reduced Inequalities' is also the tenth of the seventeen explicit SDGs adopted by the UN in 2015. With these issues in mind the next section goes on to address the evidence about inequality.

Inequality between and within nations

The two central topics for this discussion of inequality concern both inequality between nations and inequality within nations. There are various sources for data on incomes and wealth across the world,[1] and the picture generated by these data sources is very predictable. With respect to wealth per head, Switzerland tops the list at $537,600, followed by Australia at $405,600 and the US at $388,600. The figure for the UK is $278,000 (Credit Suisse, 2018, p. 80). At the other end of the scale, wealth per head is below $5,000 in much of Africa and South Asia.

Similar evidence emerges if the focus is on annual income rather than wealth. The term income refers to a flow of money across a specific period of time, while wealth refers to the holding of assets (including, for example, property) which may, or may not, contribute to that income. Of course, holdings of wealth affect inequalities, but it is important to be aware what sorts of data are being compared. Among the richer member states of the OECD, 2015 data on GDP (per head) range between $100,000 (Luxembourg) and $18,000 (Mexico), with the US at $56,000 and the UK at $41,000. The OECD average is $40,000. The figures for many countries are much lower, at less that $1,000 per head. Looking at the combination of between- and within-country inequality, Bourguignon summarizes that:

> The gap between the standard of living of the richest 10% of the world and the poorest 10% was above 90 in 2008. In absolute values, the poorest 600 million have an average of $270 in disposable income per year, while the richest have a standard of living above $25,000. (2015, p. 22)

The best comparative measure for within-country inequality is the Gini coefficient, 'a single-number summary index of inequality ranging from 0 to 100 per cent', which converts a whole distribution to a single number (Atkinson, 2015, p. 17; see also there his further exploration of its use). Atkinson's country comparison of coefficient scores shows inequality to be lowest in Sweden, Norway, Iceland and Denmark. A range of European and East Asian nations feature in the middle of his list, including Taiwan, Japan and South Korea. Higher inequality is found in the UK and the US, with scores comparable to that of Russia. The poorest OECD member country, Mexico, is also the most unequal in that group. Below Mexico in Atkinson's list are various Latin American countries, China and South Africa. One obvious pattern, evident in Atkinson's data, is that, as far as the richer nations are concerned, distinctions between countries have much in common with the ordering of 'welfare regimes' (discussed in Chapter 3). However, what is also significant are the high levels of inequality within many low-income countries, which is another factor in the recent adoption of 'inclusive growth' as a key element of policy discussion for international organizations. The precarious growth of a 'middle class' in African countries in particular (AfDB, 2011) has a direct impact on both median incomes and the shape of social policy development.

An alternative to examination of nations in terms of Gini scores is a comparison using a poverty measure. There has been a long-running debate about how to define poverty, in which absolute measures have been challenged by alternatives that take into account national contexts (Townsend, 1970, 1993; and more recently Anand et al., 2010). It is still feasible, at the extremes, to identify poverty so severe that a quantitative label can be used, and countries can be compared in that way (such as an updated version of the $1 a day standard adopted by the

World Bank in 1990). However, this can be an inflexible approach that pays little attention to social and cultural variations. Moreover, it does not reflect the substantial disadvantages that are suffered by those on low incomes in many richer countries. The problem, however, about responding to this critique is that in applying a simple measure that can be deployed comparatively it has to be accepted that such a measure is open to the allegation that it is merely 'relative' – that to describe someone in Sweden as poor has a very different resonance to describing someone in Mozambique as poor. Comparative statistics tend to use a relative measure of poverty (a percentage of median income) which provides an indication of differences within nations. It is important, however, to move beyond this and the Gini coefficient approach which focus on the overall income distribution to consider the more revealing question of 'whether countries can achieve low rates of poverty at the same time as having high top income shares' (see Atkinson, 2015, p. 25).

A concern of much contemporary analysis of inequality has been with shifts over time. Again, there is a need to be aware of a combination of changes between nations as well as within them. As far as the between nation relationship is concerned, the large gap that characterizes much of the world today is a product of a divergence that began as the industrialization process 'took off' in Europe and other nations in the global North. This increasing divergence continued until near the end of the twentieth century (Bourguignon and Morrisson, 2002). At that point a sharp reversal became evident both in the data on the Gini coefficient and on poverty rates, but this was a product of population growth in several key countries, not a reduction in the total numbers of those in poverty (Bourguignon, 2015, pp. 26–8). Much of this change was a product of exceptional economic growth in East Asia.

A different perspective is possible on contemporary events if changes that have occurred within the industrialized nations in the twentieth and twenty-first centuries are considered. Here, two phenomena have been highlighted. One is the strong impact of the two world wars, and their immediate aftermaths, when equalization processes occurred both with respect to the distribution of gross incomes and in the impact of taxes and benefits to further that effect upon net incomes. This trend was reversed from the early 1980s (see Piketty, 2014, for a general analysis, particularly featuring developments in France, the US and the UK). For contemporary advanced economies, Atkinson (2015, pp. 66–7) specifically notes 'the role played by the welfare state in reducing income inequality and preventing any rise in market income inequality from feeding into inequality in disposable income' in the period after the Second World War, and the weakening of that effect after the end of the 1980s (see also Förster and Tóth, 2015).

A pertinent OECD study of differences in levels of inequality across its member nations in the 2000s indicated that tax and benefit systems have become less distributive, but noted that net incomes are distributed less unequally than market incomes. The report (OECD, 2011a, p. 36) suggested that:

Public cash transfers, as well as income taxes and social security contributions, played a major role in all OECD countries in reducing market-income inequality. Together, they were estimated to reduce inequality among the working-age population (measured by the Gini coefficient) by an average of about one-quarter across OECD countries. This redistributive effect was larger in the Nordic countries, Belgium and Germany, but well below average in Chile, Iceland, Korea, Switzerland and the United States.

This is particularly important in the context of another key point also accepted by the OECD, that when the lowest income deciles fail to gain any benefit from economic growth, 'the social fabric frays and trust in institutions is weakened' (2015, p. 21). At the broadest level, research on widening inequality leads to general agreement that not only does it reduce economic growth, measured for example by GDP, but that it also presents serious social and political challenges that are societally unsustainable.

In national studies of inequality, attention is often given to the interplay between economic inequality and inequalities of gender and ethnicity (as well as other social divisions such as age and sexuality, for example). In the case of ethnicity a key generalization is drawn from the massive gap that opened up between the early industrializing nations and the rest of the world, noting that the gainers were European countries plus a number of nations with strong connections to Europe – the US and those countries of the British Empire where large-scale colonization from the UK took place. The impact of imperialism on structuring contemporary divisions of ethnicity is an important factor in explaining the significant and sustained economic disadvantage of the countries excluded from this process in the eighteenth and nineteenth centuries. Echoes are also present in the emergence and operation of institutional racism experienced by minority ethnic populations in advanced economies such as the UK (EHRC, 2016), as well as in the policy discourse on migration which is driven by economic rather than humanitarian concerns (see Chapter 6).

In the case of gender, the fundamental fact is marked inequalities between men and women across the world in all dimensions of life, including income and wealth. Since the groundbreaking Fourth UN Conference on Women held in Beijing in 1995 (United Nations, 1995), discussion of women's poverty has wrestled with methodological problems about measuring income and wealth and the disaggregation of more widely available household data to account for gender distributions within households. UN Women, the UN agency established to promote gender equality, highlights more revealing inequalities in access to economic resources that 'keep women poor'. This includes less access to credit than men, restricted rights to hold land and more limited rights to social protection. This last form of inequality has been the subject of important social security and workplace reforms since the 1970s in advanced economies, but globally, although over the half of the world's women are in waged employment, the gender gap in employment participation has hardly changed since 1995. Women continue to be more likely to be unemployed, more likely to be in vulnerable employment and consequently are overrepresented among those who lack pension and other social protection entitlements (ILO, 2016). Progress in reducing economic gender inequality has, in fact, stalled since the 2008 financial crisis (World Economic Forum, 2018), and in the intersection with race and ethnicity divisions have also been deepened through austerity measures (Bassel and Emejulu, 2018). There are, in addition, other dimensions of inequality that are often blurred or omitted in public debate, such as the notion of inequality of opportunity and inequalities between generations, but which are also central to policy outcomes. The next section will consider these issues sequentially, while acknowledging connections between them and the broader agenda about inequality.

Persistence and change in inequality

As far as inequality of opportunity is concerned, the fundamental question of whether and to what extent some degree of inequality is acceptable and/or justifiable is of more than philosophical interest in the social policy context. Inasmuch as there is widespread acceptance of the case against extreme inequality, this is often supplemented by a concern about inequality of opportunity. The position that tends to capture general agreement is that while some inequality of outcome as a consequence of differences in individual endeavour is tolerable, it is desirable that individuals start life equal. Nevertheless, even were this to be a generally agreed principle, there is substantial evidence that this ideal is not realized in practice. Piketty's (2014) examination of the distribution of capital explores the importance of its transmission between generations. Studies in the US and the UK have provided extensive evidence that individual life chances are affected by parental wealth. A particular UK contribution to this has been cohort studies following people from birth (Pearson, 2015). It has been shown that upward social mobility is heavily dependent upon increases in job opportunities (Goldthorpe, 2013), although even where occupational mobility is possible it is argued that a 'class ceiling' linked to 'cultural capital' continues to operate (Friedman and Laurison, 2018). Deindustrialization, the automation and precarity of much work and the effects of the 2008 crisis on incomes, savings and debt have led to a considerable deterioration in the generation of new opportunities. Upward mobility is thus only feasible if there is equivalent downward mobility, which is limited given that family advantages among the better off are generally preserved.

The implications for social policy are that the most commonly accepted social mobility policy – increasing educational opportunity – only works at the margins and mostly simply increases the effort needed to reach the same point as one's predecessors. More radical options then require a focus on limiting privileges. Here again, while educational privileges offer obvious targets, to go further implies the reduction of economic advantage. With respect to relationships between the generations, the taxation of the transfer of wealth such as inheritance tax is practised to a modest degree in various countries in the world. Scheve and Stasavage, in *Taxing the Rich* (2016), show that high rates of inheritance tax, like high rates of income tax on high incomes, were only developed across the period of very high state expenditure occasioned by war in the twentieth century. Since then there have been reductions in inheritance tax, including its abolition in Australia, New Zealand, Austria and (more surprisingly given its Gini coefficient) Sweden.

The discussion in this chapter has considered data on the distribution of both income (measured in terms of money accrued in a specific period) and wealth (measured in terms of the longer-run holding of assets). Clearly in any consideration of inherited advantage the latter is important. Perhaps the most important contribution of Piketty's (2014) path-breaking study of inequality is that he shows that in the countries he studied – France, the UK and the US – in the nineteenth century there was a steady increase in inequality seen in terms of variations in the holding of wealth. The wars of the twentieth century, and some of the policies that followed after them (particularly immediately after 1945), led to some equalization. Then, as noted earlier with respect to income inequality, the last years of the twentieth century and all of the twenty-first (so far) saw a reversal of that equalization, and the contemporary economic climate is a period in which wealth inequalities are particularly likely to grow.

While the general implications of Piketty's analysis are evident, it is useful to draw attention to an aspect of the growth of wealth with specific social policy implications. While the increasing wealth of the super-rich is most significant (the top 1 per cent or 0.1 per cent, for example), there has been some spread of wealth among a much larger number of the better off, taking the form of wealth invested in housing. Lowe (2011, p. 238) sees here a clear

> stratification effect … a major intergenerational rift in most of the home owning nations. House price increases, the famine of mortgages arising from the credit crunch and the differential layering in of housing wealth have all impacted to create disparities and fractures in the housing landscape with major long-term impact.

The implication is that a 'property owning democracy' is also likely to be an inequality perpetuating society. Lowe's analysis is particularly applicable to countries such as the UK and the US where home ownership is the dominant model, but is also increasingly relevant for countries such as Denmark where the 'social ownership' model is under threat. Ultimately an underlying policy problematic has been greatly intensified by the financialization of property accumulation through mortgages, which sets the benefits of housing asset ownership for those on the lowest incomes against the power of financial elites to maintain their position (see Chapter 8). The development has implications not just for social mobility but also for the other two topics to be discussed in this section.

The two issues – inequality between young and old and inequality between the generations – are linked in that a realistic analysis of the former requires a recognition of the significance of changes over time. In the nineteenth-century studies of poverty in the UK carried out by Seebohm Rowntree, much was made of a life cycle effect. Working-class adults able to participate in the labour force enjoyed a period of relatively good income (stressing the 'relative' aspect here) while single. Starting a family had a significant downward impact upon resources. Eventually, once children became earners, the late middle aged might again enter a period of relative prosperity before retirement brought a return to poverty (see Rowntree, 2000). The identification of this life cycle effect contributed to arguments for establishing child benefits and for state-guaranteed pensions in the early twentieth century. Its emphasis supports redistribution via social policies within the life course and echoes the important point made by Barr (2001) that, in general, the welfare state can be regarded as a 'piggy bank' in the sense that much of what is individually contributed while of working age is reclaimed over a whole lifetime.

There may be little to cause concern here unless processes of economic or demographic change occur that alter the impact of state interventions. It is these that have, not surprisingly, occurred, giving new complexions to the relationships between the generations. Generalizing developments requires caution, but across the nations of the world a long view reveals patterns of changing advantages and disadvantages. It may be noted, for example, that the nations of Western Europe experienced successively: high unemployment before the Second World War, low unemployment but with deprivations associated with conflict during the war, then a period of low unemployment accompanied by major advances in social policies for around forty years after the war, followed by a succession of economic problems involving high unemployment and/or insecure employment and the adoption of austerity measures by governments. This implies very different life experiences across that period, embodying advantages (opportunities to save and make house purchases, for example) and disadvantages (difficulties in getting into education and employment, for example) that have long-term effects.

War between or within nations is a significant factor in shaping life chances, since it is accompanied by general deprivation of welfare, and this is a feature that continues to characterize many countries in the global South in the 2020s. The current period of austerity too, is likely to have significant scarring effects on the life chances of young people whose education and school-to-work transitions have coincided with reductions in public investment. It may be possible therefore, and notwithstanding structural sources of inequality, that there are 'lucky' and 'unlucky' generations. These variations bring opportunities for political defenders of the status quo to emphasize life chance differences that distract attention from wider sources of social problems and undermine general solidarity.[2]

In the Western European context it is clear that the treatment of older people presents particular issues. As pension policies developed, the alleviation of widespread poverty among older people became a high political priority, and in the early implementation of austerity, the protection of pension incomes was prioritized as non-discretionary spending. In the context of a dramatic increase in longevity, and in societies where birth rates are low and therefore age ratios across society are changing, unfunded transfers make steadily increasing demands upon government budgets, and thus potentially on a falling number of taxpayers. The OECD, in its report *Preventing Ageing Unequally* (2017f), for example, sets out both the cumulative effects of inequality over the life course and the implications of contemporary trends of rising inequality and ageing populations, both in the advanced economies and in countries such as Brazil and China. While it is risky to make predictions of future patterns, given the evidence on cumulative inequalities and the scarring effects of unemployment and other social and economic disadvantages, it is safe to assume that younger generations now face greater risks of income, health and age-related inequality than their parents' and grandparents' generations, complicated by differences in asset ownership (particularly housing). This adds further dimensions to social analysis and policy challenges to which subsequent chapters return.

Inequality and social policy

Returning to the question of unacceptable inequality, there is an extensive debate about poverty, a concept used to identify levels of income and structures of relations that are deemed to be unacceptable. These issues are subject to analysis using a variety of approaches, some of them rooted in philosophy and ethics, others identifying the consequences of excessive inequality. In considering policies to tackle inequality, discussion has been limited here for two reasons. One of these is that, while the argument here adopts a stance that social and economic policy issues cannot be simply disentangled, much of the thrust of policies to tackle inequality must involve economic developments. Economic development itself, as suggested earlier, does not result in reduced inequality. On the contrary, as international organizations from the World Economic Forum to the UN now explicitly recognize, economic growth *is* severely hampered by inequalities that restrict people's opportunities to participate in and contribute to social, political and economic life. The social commentary we can provide here is confined to pointing out the benefits and/or consequences that follow from approaches to inequality reduction based upon stimulating growth. The second is simply that later chapters contain more detailed discussions of some of the key policy areas and specific interventions within these. In addressing policy issues a distinction is again made between policies to address inequalities within countries, and policies to address those between countries, while noting connections between the two.

When looking within individual nations, the distinction between 'gross' income (before the application of taxation or provision of benefits) and 'net' income is important. Much of the European social policy discourse on this was developed in the era of full employment and (often) relatively strong trade unions. This led to an approach summed up by the kinds of measures, advocated in the Beveridge Report, concerned with the needs of those temporarily or permanently outside the labour market. In the UK the path-breaking work of Abel-Smith and Townsend (1965), identifying poverty among families where there was employment on the part of at least one member, started to change the terms of discussion. Yet even then, the ensuing debate about poverty tended to focus on children, with 'child benefit' as the crucial remedial measure.

In the UK in the 1970s means-tested benefits for those in work began to be developed. A consensus dating from the 1832 poor law reforms, that it was undesirable for the state to subsidize wages, began to be challenged. This has led to the development of an extensive (and confusing) system of benefits to subsidize low wages. The latest radical alternative to existing measures to combat poverty, noted earlier in the chapter – universal basic income – does not really depart from an approach that sees public action as focusing on issues outside the labour market.

But there are other policies, in many advanced economies including the UK, that address the problem of low wages by focusing on gross income: laws that specify minimum wages. These have the weakness that they target the very bottom of the wage distribution, and do not address the equally problematic issue of excessive earnings at the top (for wider discussion see Orton and Rowlingson, 2007). There are other policies of wider application that address themselves to many aspects of the contractual deals between employers and workers. Significantly, they have featured strongly in European Union social policies. Approaches to the reduction of inequality concerned with gross incomes inevitably rest upon the extent to which unemployment (or the related issues of part-time and insecure employment) can be avoided. Notably here, variations exist in the extent to which social goals are identified in discussions of economic policy. In much of the debate between advocates of neoliberal 'laissez faire' and Keynesian 'demand management' policies in the last years of the twentieth century, a key difference was between the argument, by the former, that minimization of inflation should be the dominant policy goal and the argument that, as in the early post-Second World War years, the central concern should be to aim for full employment. In the twenty-first century so far, high inflation has not been experienced in most industrialized countries while the definition of 'full employment' seems to have been adjusted downward in orthodox economic analysis. However, since the global economic crisis of 2008 the dominant emphasis on 'austerity' with respect to government policies has replaced the concern about inflation as an argument against active policies to promote employment (see Farnsworth and Irving, 2015; McBride et al., 2015).

However, while there remains a political consensus that the right economic policies (whatever they may be) offer the best approach to tacking inequality by means of growth, there are voices suggesting that the combination of technological and global economic change make that an increasingly difficult ideal to realize in the advanced economies (see Baldwin, 2016, 2019). In that sense the reduction of inequalities between countries is seen as offering a challenge to the conventional approach to reducing inequality in individual countries. We now shift attention, therefore, to the issues about inequalities between countries.

Inevitably the emphasis in development economics has tended to be upon facilitating economic growth in the poorer countries of the world. We will not explore here the questions that can be raised about the 'good faith' of the exponents of this view, inasmuch as international capitalist enterprise tends to involve concern with the low cost rather than the welfare gains of its workforce (Artaraz and Hill, 2016, Chapter 3). Rather, the questions applicable to this chapter are about the notion that growth will necessarily reduce inequality. It was observed earlier that much of the recent economic growth has been in countries in the region of Asia. In contrast, most nations in the central and southern African region have seen very little.

Optimistic statements about growth in the global South are tempered by recognition that two very large nations – China and India – have done particularly well. But there is a key question about the extent to which national growth has been accompanied by increasing internal inequality. Bourguignon (2015, p. 53) observes that inequality tends to go up with market reforms in economies in 'transition', and that this was particularly evident in China between the 1980s and the 2000s 'where the Gini coefficient for this period increased from 0.28 to 0.42'. Cook and Lam (2011, p. 139) report the Chinese response to the financial crisis post-2007 as involving a massive fiscal stimulus package, including 'a range of social policy instruments, including interventions aimed at boosting consumption and protecting the vulnerable'.

With respect to the smaller countries of the global South, commentators on development (Anand et al., 2010; Surender and Walker, 2013; Bourguignon, 2015) tend to stress the need for aid policies that are linked to efforts to steer support towards less advantaged people. Much discussion of development emphasizes the need for the countries of the global South to develop governmental institutions that can support economic development with progressive social policies. The special cases of rapid modernization – particularly South Korea and Taiwan – have involved strong governmental controls (Kwon, 1997), but also exceptional support from the US. What has been widely criticized as the 'Washington Consensus' with respect to aid policies dominated by the notion of growth depending upon open free markets, though perhaps less influential in the 2010s (Serra and Stiglitz, 2008), has, where it has succeeded, set up a dynamic in which inegalitarian forces in the global North reinforce those in the South. The potential for the use of capital from the former and labour from the latter has threatened to generate a global 'race to the bottom' in labour standards and social protection, a threat which has re-emerged in the years since 2008 (Milanovic, 2012; Sørensen, 2012).

There is one other route towards the reduction of inequality that must be briefly mentioned, which is the movement of people (see Chapter 6). Migration presents opportunities to reduce inequalities between countries in the global North and those in the global South, for example through remittances (see Figure 6.1), as well as the capital (economic, human and social) accrued by migrants and contributed to countries of origin via return migration. However, it also represents the opposite given the benefits to countries of migration which receive largely prime working-age, highly skilled individuals whose educational and training costs have been borne elsewhere, or particularly in the case of women migrants, where demand for their health and welfare work may contribute to the gender equalization of care work in advanced economies but leaves a care gap filled informally, and at a cost, in their countries of origin. Collier's (2013) analysis notes that the benefits of migration offered to countries of origin depend largely upon the permanence of the move. Restrictions on permanence, such as countries of destination making specific efforts to limit migrants to 'guest worker' status without security and without families, may thus benefit countries of origin while creating insecurity and diswelfare for those migrating. These examples highlight the complexity of global inequalities where policy may facilitate equalization in simple economic terms but does not represent social progress.

Conclusion

This chapter has considered a number of dimensions of inequality that are important to the concerns of the chapters that follow. However, there are many other dimensions that have not been captured here, as well as further nuances to the debates and questions that have been discussed which add further complexity to the policy challenges arising. As a general position taken here, the conclusion is that there are broad global forces at work encouraged by capitalist perspectives on how development should occur that give little attention to social issues.

Actual policy responses depend a great deal upon decisions by actors within individual nation states. In this respect there is, as mentioned in the introduction to this chapter, no simple uncontestable way of explaining how social policies have grown to such levels of importance in societies today. This account has concentrated upon the consequences of capitalist economic processes for the generation of inequalities. But, in passing, it has been noted that social policy development may also be explained by concerns to limit social unrest and win support for the status quo. These themes secure more attention in the next two chapters.

It has also been observed that the egalitarian thrust of some policies has been constrained by limitations that focus upon changes within individual life cycles (the welfare state as 'piggy bank'). Moreover, when attention turns, as it will in Part II of this book, to specific policy areas, it will also be seen that, for example, health policies may be viewed as ways of dealing with risks for individuals rather than as generically redistributive. If treated as 'universal' in scope they cope with unexpected problems regardless of the original economic status of patients. Similarly, education policies can be seen as driven by economic concerns, and as noted they are unlikely, on their own, to have egalitarian outcomes. Finally, environment policies address societal risks alongside individual risks, and this is particularly illustrative of the limits of international equalization across unequal nations and the peoples within them. An important feature of the development of the study of social policy since the mid–twentieth century has been a recognition of the need to limit global generalizations (generally based on the experiences of the richest economies in the global North) and to recognize variations in national responses. This is particularly manifested in the development of comparative analysis, explored further in Chapter 3.

3

Varieties of welfare

Introduction

In trying to offer an account of social policy that takes a world view rather than one centred upon one country, it is essential to make use of ideas developed in comparative studies. Even if many of the world's smaller, poorer and less powerful countries are left out, any account organized country by country would resemble a dictionary, with brief unrelated comments on each country mentioned. Comparative studies uses typologies to explore the extent to which there are clusters of countries with commonalities, and the extent to which differences between those clusters or between individual countries within them can be explained.

It was always a matter of urgency that social policy studies should break away from a narrow preoccupation with single countries. Some of the early attempts to do this simply drew upon information from a narrow sample of countries, putting accounts of policies alongside each other in separate chapters in a way that announced 'other places are different and that is interesting'. The rise in interest in the spread of policies from country to country in the frame of 'policy borrowing' or 'policy transfer' (Rose, 1993; Dolowitz and Marsh, 1996, 2000) also stimulated attention towards similarities and differences between countries in the form of questions about why some transfers worked and some failed (or involved radical transformations). But there is a more fundamental reason why a systematic approach to comparison is important. The testing of hypotheses using the experimental methods favoured by natural scientists is largely ruled out for the study of policy processes, as researchers cannot control the variables and political processes themselves, making experimentation inappropriate. Hence, as Durkheim argued in his classic book on comparison in the social sciences (1982, p. 141):

> We have only one way of demonstrating that one phenomenon is the cause of another. That is to compare the cases where they are both simultaneously present or absent, so as to discover whether the variations they display in these different combinations of circumstances provide evidence that one depends on the other.

Of course, taking the lead suggested by Durkheim depends on what one wants to explain, but if, as intended in this book, the objective is not to explore and test the efficacy of specific policies but rather to provide an informed account of policy variation and the explanations for its occurrence, then it needs to be accepted, as Higgins (1981, p. 223) suggests, that 'Comparison, as a technique or method, is so crucially a part of any form of evaluation that one might wish to argue that comparative social policy is the parent discipline and any methodology not employing comparisons is of a lower order.'

The origins of comparative studies

Comparative approaches to the examination of social policy emerged from challenges to theories that saw its development as part of a modernization process in which economic, urban and demographic change were seen as explanatory variables producing policy convergence across the world. These challenges replaced this approach with typologies, recognizing the varied nature of social policy growth. 'Regime theory' has tended to dominate this work, first seeing political and economic variables as important for the varied features of social policy, and then becoming supplemented by examination of wider cultural and social factors and even by notions of the importance of ideas, factors which take comparative analysis far beyond a more crude assessment of public spending.

A simple comparison of social policy expenditure by different nations shows, not surprisingly, that high levels of such expenditure only occur in the richer nations of the world. The OECD average for social spending is around 20 per cent (OECD, 2019), but similar data are of limited reliability outside the OECD group of nations. Put simply, there is a relationship between high levels of GDP per head and high social expenditure, but this is a very imprecise relationship. This is particularly evident at the lower end of the spending ranking, where very prosperous nations such as the US, Australia, the Netherlands and Switzerland are relatively low spenders (OECD, 2019). Furthermore, as suggested in Chapter 2, it should not be taken for granted that high state social expenditure is necessarily a good indicator of effective use of that spending to reduce inequality.

Hence, the starting point for comparative analysis was a quest to explain the combination of evidence of a loose association between national prosperity and social policy expenditure with the other factors which might explain variation in that association. The evolving relationship between economic market systems and the state was an important driving force (Wilensky and Lebaux, 1965). Industrialization was seen as the generator of distributional changes in society and a source of demands for new ways of dealing with consequential disadvantages (Rimlinger, 1971). To then explain the expanding role of the state, arguments from welfare economics were applied. Firms recognized that meeting the health, educational and other welfare needs of their workforce imposed costs, which could make them uncompetitive by comparison with firms which did less. Hence, there was an increased tendency to look to the state as a means of enforcing the 'socialization' of those costs, sharing them more widely through society while lessening demands on private businesses.

The Marxian version of that argument was most forcefully presented by O'Connor (1973) and Gough (1979). This saw industrial capital as facing two kinds of problems. One of these, already set out in Chapter 2, is that the efficient operation of capitalism required attention to be given to the maintenance of a fit and trained labour supply. It was in the interests of individual capitalists that the cost of doing this should be 'collectivized', that is, taken on by society as a whole. This function was most readily performed by the only overarching body – the state. The other problem facing capital was unrest in a society in which employment was insecure, rewards from employment were low and age and ill health created particular vulnerability to hardship. Marxist theory proposes that capitalism needs a 'reserve army of labour' as a means to keep wages low, and that workers are regarded by capitalists as 'factors' of production to be employed as cheaply as possible, and with no regard to their nuclear or extended family responsibilities. These are inherent characteristics of capitalism which, for Marx, will contribute to its ultimate downfall. However, if the state can deal with some of these problems, without at the same time undermining the basic economic relationship between capital and labour, then the otherwise gradually accumulating discontent about the system can be reduced.

Both the non-Marxist theory and the Marxist theory are largely functionalist in character given their assumption that these developments are the necessary consequences of industrialization, and have thus been criticized as deterministic, paying little attention to the choices made by actors or to variations in response from place to place (Ashford, 1986). Nevertheless, these theories contributed to generalizations about welfare development, taking the discussion away from naïve emphases upon 'progress' or the growth of compassion. Industrialization was of course recognized as making an important contribution to increases in the standard of living, and with higher levels of personal income comes the possibility for the state to raise high levels of taxes to pay for social policies. Some exponents of the modernization thesis went on to consider the demographic effects of industrialization, urbanization and high levels of income, specifically lowered birth rates and raised life expectancy (for example Wilensky, 1975).

These emphases upon modernization were challenged by others who either sought to examine the quantitative evidence more carefully, recognizing the absence of a simple correlation between, for example, social expenditure and national prosperity (Flora and Heidenheimer, 1981; Pampel and Williamson, 1989), or sought to add qualitative considerations (Higgins, 1981; Ashford, 1986; Flora, 1986). These studies, and particularly the latter group, recognized that even if there were broad general influences to which countries were responding, there was a diversity of ways of doing this. This diversity might arise because of the varying strength of the influences on social policy development from country to country. Hence, attention shifted very much to the varieties of welfare arrangements, stimulated by the increased recognition of the complex influences upon policy change and also perhaps by the evidence that the convergence predicted by some of the earlier theorists was not occurring. It was from this that the approach that now dominates comparative social policy studies – regime theory – arose.

Esping-Andersen's regime model

The origins of Esping-Andersen's argument about how distinct types of welfare systems may be distinguished lie in work by Titmuss (1974; reproduced in Alcock et al., 2001), which suggests that three models may be distinguished according to their principles of redistribution:

- The institutional redistributive model, which provides services regardless of market participation and is based on the principle of need.
- The industrial achievement model, which holds merit (interpreted as productivity) as the determinant for meeting welfare needs.
- The residual welfare model, which assumes the private market and the family to be the main sources of welfare, with the state only coming into play temporarily when these institutions break down.

Taking his lead from these ideas, Esping-Andersen's (1990) approach to comparative analysis is rooted in the notion that some social policy systems may reflect and contribute to social solidarity. It also derives from arguments which have seen social policy development as an important element in the alleged 'truce' between capital and labour within democratic societies, in which social policies may be concessions to the latter that contribute to the preservation of the capitalist order (Streeck, 2014). The concept of 'decommodification' is used by Esping-Andersen to define the extent to which some policy systems achieve a universalism which treats all sections of society alike. Decommodification is used to describe the extent to which individuals' social entitlements are relatively independent of their positions in the labour market.

Esping-Andersen (1990, pp. 26–7) identifies what he describes as three regime types:

1. The 'liberal' welfare state, in which means-tested assistance, modest universal transfers or modest social insurance plans predominate. This indicates low levels of 'decommodification'. The word 'liberal' in the definition refers to liberal economic ideas which see the free market as the ideal device for allocating life chances, and the primary role for the state being to enhance economic efficiency. Esping-Andersen puts Australia, the US, New Zealand, Canada, Ireland and the UK (with some qualification) in this category.
2. Nations which Esping-Andersen labels as 'conservative', where state-led development significantly shaped the evolution of social policy institutions. In these societies neither strong pro-market ideologies nor democratic movements were important for this development. Instead, a strong state sought to incorporate interest groups to ensure their support for the regime, hence the use of the term 'corporatist' to also describe the welfare character of these nations. The consequence was welfare systems in which 'the preservation of status differentials' is more important than either 'the liberal obsession with

market efficiency' or 'the granting of social rights'. This second category includes Italy, Japan, France, Germany, Finland, Switzerland, Austria, Belgium and the Netherlands.

3. The 'social democratic' countries, those 'in which the principles of universalism and decommodification of social rights was extended also to the middle classes'; in these places 'the social democrats pursued a welfare state that would promote an equality of the highest standards'. Denmark, Norway and Sweden are the nations in this category.

The decommodified systems of the Nordic countries are thus contrasted with conservative and liberal systems which more clearly reflect labour market divisions and market ideologies. These are attempts to classify national systems as a whole; the inclusiveness of the Nordic system is seen relative to other systems. But it is important to bear in mind that in this approach the nations in the 'conservative' group are not simply identified as middle ones, with levels of spending between the other two. They may indeed be high spenders; the key point is that such spending will tend to be distributed proportionately across the socio-economic spectrum in ways which are likely to reflect Titmuss' idea of 'merit, work performance and productivity'. The method Esping-Andersen adopted to develop his regime model involved comparative statistical analysis of the extent to which some key social security benefits delivered extensive social support without making labour market participation a crucial qualifying condition. Decommodification is thus a variable, systems being placed along a commodification–decommodification continuum.

Esping-Andersen justifies his approach in two ways. First, he argues against the 'simple class mobilization theory of welfare state development' in which welfare development can be seen as coming from the growth of demands by less advantaged people through an emergent democratic political process. Instead he sets out a more complex theory which can be seen as built upon that idea. He presents a picture of regime development in which historical forces are interactive. Political coalition formation is seen as contributing in distinctive ways to 'the institutionalisation of class preferences and political behaviour' (1990, p. 32). Empirically, Esping-Andersen explores the influence of selected independent variables – a measure of the share of Left parties in government, a measure of the share of Catholic parties and 'absolutism' alongside measures of GDP per head and GDP growth – and shows that these political variables have a key influence on the dependent variable: decommodification. This part of his enterprise may be seen as focusing on the explanation of regime difference. The theory suggests, in Arts and Gelissen's (2002, p. 139) words, alternative 'regime-types, each organized according to its own discrete logic of organization, stratification and societal integration'.

Second, Esping-Andersen makes claims for the predictive capacity of his model, arguing that 'a theory that seeks to explain welfare-state growth should also be able to understand its retrenchment and decline' (1990, p. 32). That is a challenge taken up in his later edited work (1996), emphasizing differences in the ways the different regimes have responded to global economic challenges, giving attention to issues about family arrangements (a point of criticism for its neglect in his 1990 work) to predict responses to demographic change and increasing female labour market participation (1999), and exploring future scenarios (2002). The claim that the model has a predictive value will be explored further in Chapter 4.

Developments of regime theory

Esping-Andersen's work has spawned an enormous literature (see Emmenegger et al., 2015) and poses the question as to why a study conducted in the 1980s using a limited sample of OECD member countries (when that organization itself was much smaller) should be so influential in shaping scholarship. Inevitably, some of the responses to his work criticize his methodology. Bambra (2005) and Scruggs and Allan (2006) have even found errors in his original work. Studies have been developed with alternative indices and other methodologies (see Arts and Gelissen, 2010, table 39.1, for a summary of these).

Much discussion has centred on the implications of using a typology. As indicated above, this approach has been presented as advancing a superior approach to the analysis of welfare state development to theories that postulate uniform or unidimensional processes. Esping-Andersen (1999, Chapter 5), in an answer to his critics, makes the case for parsimony and questions whether the presence of ambiguous cases matters for the strength of the overall approach. A less defensive response could be that while arguing against a multiplication of types, the recognition that ambiguities can throw up important questions about what is happening in specific countries is productive in theory development.

Clearly there is an alternative response to the inadequacies of global generalizations. This is to stress the unique characteristics of each individual system (see Schubert et al., 2009). But there is a midway point between these alternative perspectives. Comparisons may be made between detailed developments in individual countries, developing 'middle range' theories. There is a good case to be made for this approach, recognizing that social policy 'systems' are complex mixtures of policies than may bear relatively little relationship to each other (see Kasza, 2002).

Arts and Gelissen (2002, pp. 138–9) provide a valuable discussion of reasons to be cautious about the use of a typology for theory development. Their starting position is as follows:

> Do typologies based on ideal types have theoretical and empirical value … ? The conclusion emerging from the philosophy of science literature is clear: not if ideal types are goals in themselves, but only if they are a means to a goal; namely, the representation of a reality, which cannot yet be described using laws (Klant, 1984). This means that typologies are only fruitful to an empirical science that is still in

its infancy. In contrast, a mature empirical science emphasizes the construction of theories and not the formulation of typologies.

They, not surprisingly, see the 'sociology of welfare states' as in its infancy. In this sense, typologization is 'a means to an end – explanation – and not an end in itself' (Arts and Gelissen, 2002, p. 140). In a similar vein, van Kersbergen and Vis (2014) point out that Esping-Andersen confuses his typological method with 'ideal type' analysis, but they go on to argue for the use of typologies as way to 'reduce complexity for analytical and comparative purposes'. Their argument is that reducing complexity through typologization is the purpose of the exercise rather than a flaw in the approach per se (van Kersbergen and Vis, 2014, pp. 67–74). Simplification, therefore, inasmuch as it is located in the ideas and evidence important for the explanation of differences, is significant in propelling further research. Here lies the answer to the question posed at the beginning of this section about why Esping-Andersen's work is so important.

It is long time since Esping-Andersen's original book was published, and the central issue is surely that regime theory aims to go beyond simple typification to make suggestions about how to explain differences. In that sense it may be used in ways that are not bound by Esping-Andersen's theory. The development of regime theory can be separated into two kinds of work. One of these is work that – using essentially the countries featuring in Esping-Andersen's original theory – suggests alternative ways of identifying regimes. The other is work that explores issues and problems about extending 'worlds of welfare' outside the original sample of nations (or those closely similar to them). While these tend to be mixed up together, particularly in the first of Arts and Gelissen's incisive reviews (2002), some of the issues, notably those concerning gender divisions, arise under both headings, and are considered here in separate sections.

Reshaping the original regime types?

Esping-Andersen's underlying explanatory approach involves the suggestion that decommodification has been a goal of social democratic parties. He thus correlates the political strength of social democracy in various countries with decommodification. This is a proposition that is challenged in Castles' and Mitchell's work (see Castles, 1985; Castles and Mitchell, 1992). In describing Australia and New Zealand as perhaps belonging to a 'fourth world of welfare capitalism', Castles and Mitchell (1992) draw attention to the fact that political activity from the Left may, in some places, have focused not so much on the pursuit of post-income equalization through social policy, as the achievement of equality in pre-tax, pre-transfer incomes. Hence the authors challenge what they term 'the expenditure-based orthodoxy', which assumes that only higher social spending will lead to more and better distribution of income. Castles' (1985) earlier work also drew attention to the particular emphasis on protecting wage levels in Australian and New Zealand Labour politics. Castles and Mitchell also make a second point, again about Australia but also with relevance for the UK: that the Esping-Andersen approach disregards the potential for income-related benefits to make a very 'effective' contribution to redistribution. Australian income maintenance is almost entirely means tested, but potentially challenges the liberal principles of this mechanism because it is not simply concentrated on redistribution to those with the lowest incomes.

Mitchell (1991) brings to the argument an interest in exploring the relationships between income differences in societies before and after government interventions, suggesting that it is the size of the 'gap' between rich and poor, and the extent to which policies close that gap, that needs to be the object of attention, rather than simply aggregate expenditure. She examines income transfer policies in terms of their contribution to both the reduction of inequality and the eradication of poverty – alternative social policy goals which need to be interpreted in their wider political contexts. She also compares income transfer systems in terms of efficiency (the relationship between outputs and inputs) and effectiveness (the actual redistributive achievement of systems).

This work, and that of Mitchell in particular, while offering what is perhaps now a historical account of Antipodean public policy (recently economic liberal trends in these countries have been strong), is important for raising questions about the wide range of influences on incomes, and the variety of policy options available to political actors who want the state to try to manage income distribution. Arts and Gelissen (2002), in their survey of alternatives to the Esping-Andersen model, identify an additional category that some authors have distinguished within the 'liberal' regime group, which is called 'radical' (see Kangas, 1994) or 'targeted' (Korpi and Palme, 1998). Its characteristic is an absence of social insurance, but some evidence of the use of means tests to effect substantial redistribution. It bears some resemblance to the fourth world identified by Castles and Mitchell, and may include the UK and Ireland.

Esping-Andersen's strong emphasis upon mainstream political processes has been challenged by those who see other ideologies and sources of power as important for the determination of income maintenance policies. Particularly important in this respect have been writers who have been concerned about the lack of analysis of relationships between men and women, and of family ideologies, in Esping-Andersen's work. There is now a significant literature on this, including early edited collections such as Sainsbury (1994) and Lewis (1993, 1997b), monographs (O'Connor, 1996; Sainsbury, 1996; Daly, 2000; Daly and Rake, 2003), and articles (Lewis, 1992, 1997a; Orloff, 1993; Sainsbury, 1993). Attempts to retypologize welfare states according to women's interests, such as Lewis (1992), remind us that the 'solidarity' of the Swedish model rests upon an expectation that there will be high labour market participation by women, and that this has implications for the state in terms of provisions for care services as well as gender equality in social security entitlements and employment protection. There is much differentiation in the extent to which women's employment is supported by these provisions, producing and reinforcing patterns of employment, reward and entitlement that are disadvantageous to women both in and out of the labour market (see Chapters 5 and 6 for further discussion).

Gender analyses recognize the political choices being made about how social relations between women and men are translated into policy, including the role the state will play in supporting family life and whether this will manifest itself in the direct provision of care or the provision of cash benefits to enable people to buy care. The answers to these questions have, in practice, considerable implications for the labour market participation of women. The high female labour market participation rates in the Nordic countries have partly been generated by a willingness of the state to pay women to carry out caring tasks which elsewhere have to be carried out by (generally female) parents and relatives themselves. While this approach has benefits for women, it has not significantly influenced the overall gender division of labour (Irving, 2015). A second point of significance that has emerged from the retypologization of welfare states, has added further empirical evidence to the argument that women's political participation is crucial to the development of social policies in women's interests. Early on, Siaroff's (1994) typology of welfare states identified a group of 'late female mobilisation' countries (Southern European nations plus Ireland), which were otherwise dissimilar but lacked gender equality across a range of indicators. This critique of Esping-Andersen also draws attention to the importance of familist ideologies in influencing the politics of social security and determining the expectations embedded within it, and more recently has had particular pertinence for analyses of welfare politics in Mediterranean Europe and in East Asia (Sung and Pascall, 2014; Papadopoulos and Roumpakis, 2017). Esping-Andersen's original sample only featured Italy and Japan from these regions.

The need for geographical extension is taken up in the following section, but it is also important to highlight that it is not just the range of countries which has prompted elaboration of welfare regime theory. One of the core elements of the feminist critique of mainstream welfare regime theory is that it privileges class over other structures of inequality. The absence of other dimensions of social relations is significant in comprehending the distributive drivers of welfare states, and crucial to understanding both development and change in social policy. The work of Ginsburg (1992) and Williams (1995) addressed these gaps, but as Williams has since argued (2016), the methodological and theoretical strengths of comparative analysis in foregrounding political forces came at the cost of neglecting much of the critical social policy scholarship around gender and race that had emerged in the 1980s. Thus, notwithstanding the gender critique of welfare regime theory, Williams argues (2016, p. 632) that there has been a lack of 'any *systematic* engagement with the multiple social relations of gender and race in themselves or in their relation to class'. Analyses and typologization of 'migration regimes' (Castles, 1995; see also Castles and Miller, 1993, 2003) have offered an alternative lens through which the social relations of race and ethnicity can be seen in the comparative operation of citizenship, while Green and Janmaat's (2011) specification of 'regimes of social cohesion' explores comparatively more abstract ideas of societal diversity and commonality. Williams (2015) has elsewhere argued for the need for more 'conceptual alliances' in social policy study that connect the political economy both with different 'organizational settlements' in welfare provision, and 'all those social, moral and cultural practices in which the social formation consolidates, fragments and reconstitutes itself – through conceptions of nationhood, citizenship, religion, moral worth, and so on' (p. 101). This highlights the sociological thinness of regime theory, which also becomes more obvious when its geographical boundaries are stretched.

Other regimes

To return to the geographical concerns, as noted previously, Esping-Andersen's original work was limited to the study of eighteen OECD countries. Arts and Gelissen's second review of regime theory (2010) identifies the Mediterranean (or Southern Europe), East Asia, Latin America and Eastern Europe as places where alternative or 'emergent' welfare regimes may be found. To these regions, Gough and Wood (2004) elaborate regime theory to add countries where, broadly speaking, welfare regimes are absent. This extension of regime theory beyond the original OECD worlds, and particularly to countries where political and industrial structures and policy actors are shaped very differently to advanced economies, presents some important tests for regime theory.

Attention has been drawn by those who examined the issues about gender in regime models to the extent to which there is a Roman Catholic and/or Southern European (see also Ferrara, 1996; Siaroff, 1994) approach to the design of social security – alternatively to be seen either as more 'protective' of women outside the labour market or as increasing their 'dependency' within the family. Ferrara argues that the income maintenance systems of the Southern European countries are fragmented and ineffective and often characterized by 'clientelism', in which political patronage is important. His view is supported by others. It is implicit in the regime categorizations developed by Bonoli (1997), Leibfried (1992) and Trifilletti (1999). Castles (2004, p. 179) adds a 'Southern European' category to his four-part identification of 'families' of nations, stressing the extent to which the states in this category are what he calls pensioners' welfare states with high levels of state expenditure on middle-aged and older people and low levels of fertility. Hence there is a quite widely identified different 'world' in Mediterranean Southern Europe which includes Italy, Greece, Spain and Portugal. But there may be others among the countries where social policy is more 'emergent': Turkey and some of the countries of the Balkan peninsula for example.

A similar theme of family ideologies is raised in the literature on the East Asian countries. Here the theoretical question is whether the highly industrialized Eastern economies (Japan, South Korea, Taiwan, Singapore, Hong Kong) can be fitted into Esping-Andersen's typology, at least as later 'arrivals'. There does seem to be a case for seeing the first three in that list (Singapore and Hong Kong have been more influenced by British colonial policies) as joining Esping-Andersen's corporatist–statist conservative group. This is a view that has been given support in Ramesh's (2004) examination of social policy in the last four of the five nations listed in this paragraph. An alternative is to see them as having features which are more specifically 'Eastern', which explain areas of limited development. The main argument along these lines has been the suggestion that 'Confucian' family ideologies lead to a greater delegation of welfare responsibilities to the family and extended family (Jones, 1993). The problems with this argument are that (a) in any underdeveloped income maintenance system the family will, *faute de mieux*, have to take on greater responsibilities, and (b) the use of 'Confucian' ideologies as a justification for inaction by the political elite cannot be regarded as evidence that political demands can be dampened down in this way, in the absence of other evidence demonstrating popular acceptance of that ideology.

Kwon (1997) seems to take a relatively agnostic stand on these issues. He does, however, point out another dimension in the policy processes in South Korea and Taiwan: the importance of state-led policies initiated in an era of authoritarian government. The groups who first secured social protection in these societies were the military and civil servants. Support for the military as a precursor to wider income protection measures is not a differentiating feature of East Asian countries, however, as Skocpol (1995) has shown this to have been an important factor in US developments. Measures to extend some insurance-based benefits to industrial workers followed next in South Korea and Taiwan, and securing the support of the emergent industrial 'working class' was important for the state-led growth which is regarded as so significant in these societies (Ku, 1997; Kwon, 1999). More universalistic policies only really got on to the political agenda with the emergence of democracy in these countries in the 1980s.

At the same time, Castles and Mitchell's argument about other ways in which states may promote social welfare may also be relevant for East Asian societies. Over much of the period between the Second World War and the severe financial crisis which shook East Asia in 1997, these societies experienced substantial growth with minimal unemployment. Hence, inasmuch as governments secured social support, they did it through their success in generating rapid income growth for the majority of the people. Data showing relatively low income inequality in South Korea and Taiwan offer additional evidence in support of this proposition (Ramesh, 2004, pp. 21–2).

Holliday has developed an alternative approach to the analysis of the special characteristics of East Asian societies, describing them as belonging to a 'regime' type characterized by 'productivist welfare capitalism' (Holliday, 2000, 2005), in which the orientation towards growth has been of key importance for social policy development. This point is relevant beyond East Asia given the argument that global economic forces make it increasingly difficult to defend the 'social democratic' version of the 'truce between capital and labour', or to extend it to later developing welfare systems. In this sense there are grounds for arguing that the 'liberal' regimes in Esping-Andersen's theory are also 'productivist'. But Holliday (2005, p. 148) suggests that the state has taken a more positive role in

East Asian societies: 'In a productivist state, the perceived necessity of building a society capable of driving forward growth generates some clear tasks for social policy, led by education but also taking in other sectors.' While Holliday is making some important links here with discussions of these societies as exemplars of state-led growth, it is worth noting that in emphasizing education policy he is citing a policy area not considered by Esping-Andersen in his formulation of regime theory (see Chapter 7 for further discussion on this point).

An important reservation about the suggestions that East Asian societies are following a trajectory not envisaged in Esping-Andersen's theory, is that it is important in comparative studies not to lose sight of the extent to which policy learning takes place over time and between nations. The newly industrialized Asian economies have had the opportunity to observe the strengths and weaknesses of the policies adopted earlier in other places and to learn from them selectively. They have, inevitably, been engaged with the new global debate about the economic costs of generous welfare benefit systems but have drawn their own conclusions on the value of social spending.

There is another kind of contribution to the debate about East Asia which goes further than questions about whether nations can be slotted into Esping-Andersen's regime typology or whether there are other types of regime. This is an argument that the whole regime approach embodies 'Western' ethnocentric assumptions about the role of the state and about welfare development as a product of the 'truce' between capital and labour (see Walker and Wong, 2004). The early comparative analyses of East Asia, while elaborate, were focused on a number of (relatively) small East Asian states with little attention to China. More recently, and particularly since the 2008 crisis, interest in the development in social policy in China is increasing (Cook and Lam, 2011) as its global influence has transformed. In their earlier analysis, Walker and Wong (2004, p. 124) observed that China had not been considered a 'welfare state' because it

> lacks a Western-style political democracy and is not a fully capitalist economy. In spite of these two institutional 'anomalies' from the perspective of the Western construction, it had managed and is still able to provide sufficient social protection to its urban population, albeit with enormous difficulties at the present moment.

They note that 'a poverty line, with its accompanying benefit provisions, was first promulgated in 1993 in Shanghai and now covers all urban areas', and contrast this with their previous analysis of provision in the pre-reform era (prior to 1978) when 'comprehensive welfare was provided through the "work-units" (that is, state-owned enterprises, government bureaux and so on) which could mirror the central idea of "from cradle to grave" welfare of the classic perception of the idealized Western welfare state' (Walker and Wong, 2004). This reference to the earlier model of work-unit-based welfare (also sometimes called the 'iron rice bowl', Leung, 1994) reminds us that up until the late 1980s the Soviet Union (and its satellites) offered a similar challenge to comparative theorists (see for example Deacon, 1983), while at the time of writing only Cuba and North Korea remain as societies that may claim to follow a centrally planned economic model. An interesting challenge here for the Esping-Andersen approach is whether these cases represented extreme commodification or extreme decommodification: the former since the key link to welfare was with work, the latter because work-unit protection extended to families rather than individuals.

This leads us on to consideration of Russia and the former Soviet-dominated countries of Eastern Europe. With significant trends towards privatization, Russia may be seen as moving into the 'liberal' camp, while in Central and Eastern Europe there is a continuing struggle between both internal and external pressures to adopt the liberal model (sold forcefully by bodies like the World Bank, see Deacon, 1997) and the vestiges of pre-Soviet conservative models. Comparative study of social policy in countries in this region within the regime typology framework has increased considerably since the 1990s (see for example Pascall and Manning, 2000; Cerami, 2006), facilitated by their similarity in core features with the original OECD countries studied by Esping-Andersen.

Walker and Wong's challenge reminds us, however, that the efforts to classify welfare regimes actually discounts much of the world, including Islamic Middle Eastern and North African countries, South Asia, sub-Saharan Africa and (to some extent) Latin America. Gough and Wood (and their associates) (2004) engaged in a bold attempt to deal with this problem in their exploration of ways to analyze welfare systems (including of course their absence) in the poorer countries of the world. They take as their starting point Esping-Andersen's regime theory, noting that while the original concern was with explaining 'welfare state regimes', in Esping-Andersen's later work (1999) this shifts into the simpler form of 'welfare regimes'. They argue that Esping-Andersen is generalizing about societies with two crucial characteristics: the presence of predominantly capitalist employment and a democratic nation state. Hence the significance of the idea of the welfare state as a product of state intervention to secure a 'truce'. Therefore, for Gough and Wood it is important to see welfare state regimes as one 'family' of welfare regimes in a world in which there are others, where those defining characteristics are not present. These others are identified as 'informal security regimes' in which families and communities may play key roles as providers of welfare, and 'insecurity regimes' in which even these do not provide effective welfare. Hence, regime theory is used by Gough and Wood and extended in important ways to contribute to the analysis of welfare worldwide (see also Sharkh and Gough, 2010, for their use of cluster analysis to extend this approach).

Important elements in Gough and Wood's analysis of regimes include exploration of the implications of an absence of secure formal employment, of states that function ineffectively or even exploitatively, of weak or absent communities and even of families that do not protect their members. Attention is also given to various respects in which welfare outcomes depend heavily on actions outside the regimes – not just the impact of global capitalism and of aid via governments and non-governmental organizations, but also the extent to which welfare in many societies depends upon contributions from family members living and working elsewhere in the world.

As noted earlier, while countries in Latin America did not figure in early regime theory, as with post-Soviet Europe, there has been increasing interest in the welfare state characteristics of the richer Latin American countries in particular. Barrientos' contribution to Gough and Wood's book explores the way in which Latin American regimes have shifted from being rudimentary conservative ones (within the Esping-Andersen 'family' of regimes) to liberal ones. Among these countries it is possible to see choices being made between these options, most notably in Chile, which has had a special role in shaping the global pensions debate. Chile has experienced oscillations in this respect, with the period of Pinochet's dictatorship enabling North American neoliberal economists to make the country a testing ground for free market theories. The important point in considering both Latin America and Central and Eastern Europe, is the extent to which it is possible to talk of states making choices between regime models. These choices are not 'free' in the sense that they are constrained by countries' positions in relation to parameters of global politics and global markets. The contemporary evolution of welfare states illustrates clearly the problems of using regime theory linked to the development of mature welfare states to predict current policy decisions (see Chapter 4 for further discussion).

In recognition of this problem, Gough and Wood's (2004) work offers suggestions on how regime theory may be extended, and their concerns with the interconnectedness of systems, both through multi-national economic activities and with flows of remittances and international aid. They thus offer a new perspective on comparative analysis and tools for those who want to pursue these lines of enquiry. Yet still, their analysis does not extend to China or India or most of the Islamic world. All the analysis in this section leaves no unequivocal case for a new regime type outside the Esping-Andersen model, despite a more widely argued additional world embracing Southern Europe with perhaps parts of South East Asia and Latin America. Beyond this it may be questioned whether other efforts to stretch the use of regime modelling go too far, merely noting vestiges of the welfare approaches characteristic of Western Europe, or simply their absence.

Using regime theory today

While the roots of regime theory lie in a concern to delineate differences in the politics of welfare, modern usages focus much more on the extent to which it is possible to characterize as opposed to explain social policy systems, with the implication that the issues about explanatory power are now more concerned with explaining responses to new developments rather than origins. The original concern with the politics of welfare remains significant nevertheless. The extent to which particular welfare arrangements have political support from coalitions that protect them has been explored (Pierson, 1994, 2001) and related approaches that stress the importance of institutional pathways, in shaping change where welfare states have come under attack (Taylor-Gooby, 2001, 2002; and further discussion of this approach in Chapter 4). These ideas have had particular resonance since the late 2010s when both established and emerging state commitments to welfare have never been more fragile.

Since much of the contemporary controversy about welfare policies concerns the applicability of strongly market-oriented approaches, there may be a case for a simpler regime categorization system. It is often easier to draw a line between the liberal systems and the rest, than between the social democratic and the conservative regimes. The advocates of the social democratic approach are in many respects marginalized in the post-2008 world, and although the dissemination of models of social policy is occurring, the battle lines are in effect between the liberal and the conservative approaches.

This alternative way of considering social policy systems has much in common with Hall and Soskice's (2001) classification of varieties of capitalism. They distinguish between 'liberal market economies' and 'coordinated market economies', where they argue (2001, p. 8) that in the former,

> firms coordinate their activities primarily via hierarchies and competitive market arrangements. … Market relationships are characterized by the arm's-length exchange of goods or services in a context of competition and formal contracting. In response to the price signals generated by such markets, the actors adjust their willingness to supply and demand goods or services, often on the basis of the marginal calculations stressed by neoclassical economics.

In the 'coordinated market economies', by contrast,

> firms depend more heavily on non-market relationships to coordinate their endeavours with other actors and to construct their core competencies. These non-market modes of coordination generally entail more extensive relational or incomplete contracting, network monitoring based on the exchange of private information inside networks, and more reliance on collaborative, as opposed to competitive, relationships to build the competencies of the firm … economies are more often the result of strategic interaction among firms and other actors.

In these latter countries, the state is crucially a more active partner, linking with a range of interest groups (in the way described in Esping-Andersen's categorization of the conservative regime).

In an analysis which examines both theoretically and empirically the varieties of capitalism and the typologies of the welfare regime approach, Schröder (2009) concludes that countries nest within a scheme of difference that becomes more complex as more factors are included in comparison. Thus, rather than competing to provide a single explanation of difference between countries, the range of typologies established by different authors offers a more 'fine-grained' picture of variation among states that diverge on the key axis of difference – the liberal economic model or its absence (see Schmidt, 2009, for example, who writes of 'state influenced market economies'). As in the elaborations of specifications of Esping-Andersen's conservative regime, the 'non-liberal' countries in the Mediterranean and Asian regions are regularly found to be different from continental Europe. An analysis by Lallement (2011) sees this difference as important for understanding the responses to the 2008 economic crisis, where being 'liberal' has been shown to have significant purchase on both the form and extent of policy reform. In a similar vein, Hay and Wincott's (2012) post-crisis assessment of European countries also finds that beyond the liberal/non-liberal division, what emerges are clusters of similar countries rather than 'worlds' with hard boundaries. More importantly for social policy, however, is their argument that whether countries compete in the global market on the basis of 'cost' (cheap labour, cheap exports and so on) or 'quality' (high-level skills, high-end manufacturing) determines their welfare commitment.

What Hay and Wincott's (2012) work reveals for advanced European economies (which also has resonance for the rest of the world) is that although convergence towards a liberal economic model is neither evident nor certain, within the operation of global capitalism the space for national idiosyncrasies of welfare arrangement is perceived by governments to be far more limited than it was in the period following the Second World War.

Some of the limitations of the welfare regime approach in dealing with social policy developments not located in advanced economies have already been explored. But it is also a feature of contemporary social policy making, particularly relevant for countries with economies that are developing and/or emerging, that key areas of regulation traditionally associated with the emergence of social provisions such as trade and labour are increasingly bound by agreements and legal frameworks that operate at the global, or at least international level. This is most obvious and well documented in relation to the European Union, but other IGOs such as the World Bank, IMF, ILO and World Trade Organization play an increasingly important role in shaping the parameters of social policy, particularly in countries where the political-administrative architecture is less established or unstable. Chapter 4 recognizes these issues as a challenge that needs to be resolved in building on regime-related explanations of the development of welfare arrangements.

Conclusion

This chapter started by noting diversity as summarized by comparative expenditure statistics, and went on to show that early efforts at comparative generalization gave rather more attention to common trends than to diversity. The theoretical work that really marks the shift away from that approach is Esping-Andersen's stress upon the idea of different regimes, which has been examined in the context of the ideas of some of his main critics. Esping-Andersen's original development of regime theory continues to represent the dominant approach to social policy comparison. To dissent from the view that there are in various senses 'families' of social policy systems can only imply a wish to either stress the uniqueness of systems or to confine study to limited comparisons of specific aspects of social policy. Nevertheless, the application of regime theory remains much weaker where countries lie outside the standard frameworks of comparison, but where social policy is practised, highlighting the need to think beyond the 'worlds of welfare' and better account for worlds of social policy. Identification of this issue also links with another problem about the extent to which the central tenets of regime theory rest upon analysis of income security policies (or, more recently, employment policy). This is given attention in subsequent chapters on specific policy domains and is followed up in detail particularly in the chapter on health policy. It does seem anomalous that despite the enormous importance of health care within social policy the work specifying regimes gives it minimal attention. This is true, above all, in Esping-Andersen's own work (where health care does not even appear in the index of his original three worlds work). It can only be said that, such has been the influence of the regime approach, it has fed into questions about the use of typologization in all the policy fields explored in this book.

On the other hand, it is still appropriate to challenge with the question: why typologize? If the academic study of social policy necessarily has an inherent social purpose then typologizing for its own sake with no wider significance would have little point. It is important therefore not to lose sight of Esping-Andersen's argument that regime theory is designed to highlight the dynamics of social policy systems past, present and future. This provides a clear rationale not to depart too radically from a judiciously theorized model, or to ensure that if departure is deemed necessary there are good reasons based on the identification of an alternative dynamic, rather than simple observations that some systems are different. The arguments setting out the limits of Esping-Andersen's model are important in themselves for comparative analysis inasmuch as they highlight different processes in the ever-changing world of social policy. In this respect a fallible but well-theorized taxonomy is useful precisely because it highlights the complex nature of differences between societies. But to what extent does it, in the end, help to explain policy choices? This topic forms the starting point for Chapter 4.

4

Policy processes

Introduction

Writing when pressures towards welfare retrenchment were growing, Esping-Andersen observed that 'a theory that seeks to explain welfare-state growth should also be able to understand its retrenchment and decline' (1990, p. 32), and stressed the extent to which the coalitions that contributed to its growth also protect the welfare state from decline. This is a theme taken up in his later work, and echoed by many of those following his approach. Gamble has since indicated the 'irreversibility' of the welfare state, since the variety of welfare regimes all belong to the same transformation of capitalism where the welfare state 'has become embedded in both the politics and the political economy of all the Western economies' (Gamble, 2016, pp. 28–9).

The trouble is that there are qualifications that need to be made to this generalization. First, it only applies to the advanced capitalist states, and even within them there are grounds for rejecting the view that all should be called 'welfare states'. Second, a problem which is particularly evident in Esping-Andersen's approach, and which Gamble implicitly endorses, is that the notion of distinguishing regimes implies that some will be stronger than others. In other words, regime theory as originally developed primarily offers an explanation of differences in the growth of social policy in a specific number of states. It does not offer much in predictive terms either for the explanation of retrenchment or for events in states very different to Esping-Andersen's original sample. Furthermore, in its emphasis on patterns it avoids the determinism of the theories it replaced, by an emphasis on the economic, political and cultural factors that have influenced the diverse policies it identifies. That leaves unresolved many questions about how these influences work.

Arts and Gelissen's (2002) observation quoted in Chapter 3 about typologization as a 'means to an end' is relevant. To predict a policy outcome because a nation belongs to a 'type' is only helpful if one can go on to suggest hypotheses that derive from that statement. In the analysis of policy processes there are two approaches that conform relatively easily to expectations that hypotheses may emerge in this way. One of these embeds the explanation of policy very firmly in the power structure. The other gives attention to institutional continuities, but both approaches have had to consider the circumstances in which change will occur. This introduces questions of 'ideas' and 'choices', pertinent wherever there are grounds for doubting the assumptions about the stability of regimes in Esping-Andersen's sense. The following discussion explores these issues, suggesting that the use of regime theory has to be supplemented by policy process analysis. The connection here between what may seem to be a rather poorly integrated collection of theories and concepts is that they are central to the explanation of actual policy processes, where regime theory indicates general tendencies.

The exploration of power

Questions about power – how it is distributed and structured – are fundamental to explanations of the policy process. While care needs to be taken not to oversimplify, explanations of the observed differences between social policy systems have to involve, in some measure (even if only in terms of historical legacies), interpretations of differences in power and how it is used. Controversy about the nature of power naturally centres on different interpretations of the extent to which the forms of representative democracy present in many countries in the world are able to deliver popular choice.

Propositions that people have no real choice come in various forms, from generic statements about the overriding power of elites, to Marxist assertions offering variations of the statement by Marx and Engels in the *Communist Manifesto* (1848) that 'the executive of the modern state is but a committee for managing the common affairs of the whole bourgeoisie'. Modern applications of that proposition, often coming from many who would not see themselves as Marxists, stress the dominance of economic power both nationally and globally. Hence, while pluralist theory was originally framed in opposition to that view, there are forms of this approach that accept the structuring of power and do not see it guaranteeing political equality, but do suggest that policy will be a product of interaction between competing interests (see for example Lindblom's *Politics and Markets*, 1977). Any attention to the way in which policy is actually made is likely to involve some use of a pluralist perspective. After all, if the answer to why particular decisions were taken is preordained then there is no point in exploring what happened. On the other hand, such analysis should not be naïve to power imbalances.

An alternative approach pertinent to questions about social policy development involves recognition of changes in the distribution of power over time. There may have been times, for example the period immediately after the Second World War, when there were opportunities to challenge the status quo. Conversely, it may be the case, despite the evidence of growing inequality (as explored in Chapter 2), that we are in an era when challenge to economic elites is particularly difficult. Hacker and Pierson (2010) show how successful business groups have become in dominating American politics, noting how the 'countervailing power' of trade unions identified by Galbraith (1963) has been undermined. Indeed, Crouch (2011) shows how, in the UK, big business operates now as much through inserting itself right inside the policy process as through the exercise of external pressure, and Farnsworth (2012) has shown how the resulting material benefits accrue to corporations.

Crouch (2011) adopts a neo-Marxist approach, exploring how the needs of capitalist development inhibit democratic challenge. Hill and Varone (2016, p. 133) echo this, saying:

> there is a fear of 'killing the goose that lays the golden egg'. Social democrats (note for example a classic British text by Anthony Crosland, 1956) have laid great stress on the notion that redistribution can be most easily achieved when there are increments of economic growth to distribute. They are fearful of being labelled 'tax and spend' parties. Securing economic growth has become an obsession. Moreover this obsession often pays little attention to whether some forms of growth will bring little social benefit.

In the post-2008 period, economic growth has become 'the' condition for societal rehabilitation advocated by both national governments and international organizations such as the IMF, and without which the countries most affected by the economic crisis (such as Greece) are considered at serious risk of instability. The simultaneous growth in forms of challenge to elite acceptance of the status quo – from the rise of anti-austerity movements in Greece and Spain to the UK vote to leave the EU and Donald Trump's 2016 election campaign in the US – is also occurring in countries where people see conventional politics as impotent in dealing with a changing world. However, global economic and political developments have produced changes outside the power of individual nation states. The anti-austerity parties have achieved limited success in implementing their transformative agendas, even with political power, as in Greece, and apart from a reaction against processes of globalization and particularly migration (a manifestation rather than a cause of change), the so-called 'populist' protests in the liberal economies embody little in the way of a new political programme. These issues about the use of the concept of growth as a yardstick of economic and social success are explored further in Chapter 11.

If it is the case that the opportunities for radical social policy development lie in the past, while stronger forces rather more in favour of retrenchment and greater austerity characterize the present, then the notion, implicit in regime theory, that it is the developments of the past that determine present orientations in social policy is significant. Some historical accounts of welfare state development have stressed the way in which capitalism has multiplied social problems to the extent that corrective action by the state has become necessary. This is salient in versions of Marxist theory, particularly O'Connor's theory of a legitimacy crisis (1973). A less explicitly Marxist perspective is offered in Polanyi's (1944) analysis of welfare state development as a countermovement against the development of capitalism.

While there are important points here about the role of economic change as a trigger for social policy change, there is no need to let these assume a new form of determinism. First, because to do so could imply a curious position in which forms of choice applied in the past, but no longer do so. Second, because such a position seems to universalize a judgement that should surely still vary in its application, in terms not just of time but also of places. Third, because such a perspective underestimates the wide range of ways in which change may come about. Hence, the next section considers theoretical perspectives that explore the relationship between institutional stability and change.

Theoretical approaches to continuity and change

There is now a substantial body of theory about the policy process stressing the impact of institutions (Steinmo et al., 1992; Hall and Taylor, 1996; Streeck and Thelen, 2005; Pierson, 2005). These are seen as sources of continuity. In many modern formulations of the importance of institutions they are seen as much more than formal organizational arrangements (constitutions, laws, parliaments, civil services) but also as dominant ideologies, taken-for-granted assumptions about the policy process. In this sense, Hall (1986, p. 19) writes of 'the formal rules, compliance procedures, and standard operating practices that structure the relationship between individuals in various units of the policy and the economy'.

Hence, one of the reasons that generalizations about differences between nations, as in regime theory, may seem to hold true, lies in the stability of the institutional systems in which earlier policies were created. Lijphart's (1999) important work in this area addresses formal decision-making arrangements, and suggests that alternative approaches to democracy affect the responsiveness of political systems. He highlights distinctions between 'first past the post' electoral systems (as in the UK and the US) and those that provide voters with more alternatives (as in the Netherlands and Sweden). Lijphart goes on to describe the latter as 'consensual democracies', which are likely to be more effective and implicitly more responsive. Concretely, he argues that consensus democracies are 'kindlier, gentler democracies in the sense that their welfare policies with regard to unemployment, disability, illness and old age permit people to maintain decent living standards independent of pure market forces' (Lijphart, 1999, p. 294). This rather bold generalization has been challenged in academic writing (for example Lewin et al., 2008), and in more recent political shifts in many of the 'gentler democracies' where anti-immigration, far-right politicians have gained political power (in Sweden, the Netherlands and Finland, for example). However, theoretically it continues to point towards an approach grounded in institutional analysis that may complement regime theory. This has relevance for understanding, for example, the difficulties the UK political system has faced in handling the decision to leave the European Union, which has exposed divisions that cut across party lines.

Another approach, with perhaps an institutional theory that gives more attention to their malleability over time, involves recognizing the way in which past policies form precedents for present ones. This can particularly be seen in the way pension systems establish long-run expectations (see Bonoli and Shinkawa, 2005), a topic explored further in Chapter 5. But it is given a more general form in the notion of 'paradigms', taking a concept from the history of science (Kuhn, 1970) used to characterize dominant ideologies which then restrict the terms of discourse about policy options – see Hall's analysis (1986, 1993) of assumptions about how to manage the economy.

To complement these efforts to identify sources of stability in the policy process, other analyses have sought to develop approaches that emphasize *equilibrium* but acknowledge that it can sometimes be *punctuated*. Baumgartner and his colleagues, using the two terms highlighted in the previous sentence, observe 'the tendency of political systems to drift incrementally most of the time, only to be roused to major action when collective attention became galvanised around an issue' (Baumgartner et al., 2006, p. 962; see also Baumgartner and Jones, 1993). Notably, systems are portrayed here as 'drifting incrementally', and not simply stable. Drift implies some notion of consistent direction while its punctuation implies a change of direction. Change may be both fundamental and slow. Building on work by Streeck and Thelen (2005) and Pollitt and Bouckaert (2009, p. 18) introduces a geological analogy in this respect, seeing policy change as often a slow process in the way the action of water on limestone can be contrasted with the impact of earthquakes.

Theories of change, in the context of stability, need reinforcing through consideration of the factors that stimulate change. Such factors may come from outside the policy system and may be events that render existing policies inadequate – wars changing the shape of relationships between nations provide the most obviously fundamental *shocks* of this kind. In the field of environmental policy, natural disasters stand out as 'focussing events' (Birkland, 1998). Indeed, climate change has emerged as an entirely new policy agenda issue (see Chapter 11). Perhaps there is also a need to note that scandals forcing reconsiderations of social policy, such as deaths that might have been avoided with better policies, may be seen in the same terms (Butler and Drakeford, 2003; for the example of austerity as an economic policy with fatal effects, see Stuckler and Basu, 2013).

It is pertinent here to consider the impact of demographic change on some of the main areas of social policy, particularly pensions, health care and social care. The crucial development has been the combination of falling death rates and falling birth rates. It has been particularly dramatic where social change has been very fast, such as in East Asia. There have been very big changes in the level of demand from ageing populations: is this simply 'drift' or rather more dramatic change? The three policy areas highlighted here have different implications for policy delivery systems. In the case of pensions, longevity has pushed up costs and provided challenges to old assumptions about retirement, interacting with economics-driven changes in labour markets. In the case of health care, advances in medicine also contribute to changing demands upon the system. In the case of social care, family life has experienced changes alongside the demographic changes, altering the roles of extended families. Looking at these developments from the point of view of regime theory, are these changes just to be seen as shared issues while the regimes remain distinct (see Taylor-Gooby, 2002), or are they having bigger transformative effects in some places than in others?

While demographic change is a typical example of 'exogenously' engendered change, some theories also stress 'endogenously' induced changes. The notion of 'paradigm shift' explicitly highlights the ideological influences involved in shaping change. Hall (1986, 1993) pioneered the use of this approach in an exploration of the replacement of Keynesian approaches to economic policy in favour of monetarist ones. A related approach to the explanation of change involves a stress on the role of ideas. Béland (2005, 2007) (drawing on the work of Blyth, 2002) suggests that ideas have an impact upon political decisions in three ways:

- 'as "cognitive locks" that help reproduce existing institutions and policies over time' (as in Hall's policy paradigms perspective);
- 'as policy blueprints that provide political actors with a model for reform';
- as 'powerful ideological weapons' that allow actors to challenge existing policies (Béland, 2007, p. 125).

The first of those notions is important for the explanation of stability, the second and third suggest that ideas may play an important role in the generation of change. Ideas about social insurance, for example, emerge in various forms in international debates about responses to demographic change. As discussed further in Chapters 9 and 10 on health and social care, the use of a social insurance approach to health care seems to have made it easier, in some countries, to contain pressures upon costs and even to extend the same approach into social care. Beyond that, however, it is difficult to explain how ideas vary and change. Similar to much of the work discussed here – notably the key notions of punctuated equilibrium and of paradigm change – it is easier to note that these phenomena have occurred than to predict that they will occur. Hall's very influential and well-documented analysis of the paradigm shift in economic policy still leaves puzzles about the way neoliberal ideas were able to penetrate so deeply into the ideational structures around not only economic policy but also social policy.

Very often the interaction between exogenous factors and endogenous ones is important. This can be seen particularly in Bovens and 't Hart's (1996) analysis of 'policy fiascos' where the incapacity of institutions to cope with specific occurrences exposes their inadequacy and then leads to policy change. Often, as Pollitt and Bouckaert's identification of slow change suggests, external factors may not manifest themselves as sources of urgent change. Rather, particularly in the case of many social and economic influences, they may be seen as gradually stimulating policy reappraisal. It may be, taking our cue from discussion of changes in market systems (see Pierson, 2000), that the problem-solving capacity of established institutions decays over time, or their activities generate the emergence of new political interest groups which demand change. In that sense pressures for change may come from within policy systems. But then it all depends on what is meant by 'system' as changes in one policy area (such as social security or health care) may then provoke a need for change in another policy area (such as social care or housing).

Furthermore, the UK's 'Brexit' negotiations again provide a good example of the destabilizing effects that single policy decisions (ostensibly within one country) can have beyond the country in which they are taken. This reminds us of the extent to which powerful exogenous challenges arise wherever countries are exposed to global influences. While the turmoil around contemporary examples may make them hard to interpret, historical examples of movements of people because of wars, famines and national upheavals can be seen to have given considerable shape to, for example, social housing policies in Hong Kong, Singapore and Eastern Europe.

However, the important point in this discussion is that in various ways it is being argued that the phenomena that sustain policies (even regimes) are not necessarily stable. As noted earlier, with reference to explanations of the origins of welfare states, there have been influential theories of long-run historical change, within which policy change explanations were likely to be located. Ideas about, on the one hand, new problems to be solved and, on the other, crises to be resolved are still acutely relevant, though not necessarily explored in the broad terms of these theories.

It may be, of course, that what we observe most of the time is *equilibrium*, particularly if we follow the logic of the 'action of water on limestone' analogy suggesting that fundamental change is often very slow. In this case the assumptions of stability identified in regime theory are justified. But then, a focus on specific policies or specific institutions may reveal the small changes that contradict that assumption. This means, of course, that general trends may not be very good guides to the explanation of specific events. This leads us on to some approaches to the analysis of the policy process that may be more useful in this respect.

Agenda setting

The analysis of policy agenda setting offers a way to explore the punctuation of relative stability through the exploration of how changes come to be made to existing policy. The key formulation of this approach is in the work of Kingdon (2013; see also Cairney and Jones, 2016, for an evaluation). In focusing on the exceptions to incrementalism, Kingdon stresses (unlike the theorists who stress ideational change) what are almost accidental juxtapositions. Two analogies are used to describe the nature of change. The first is the idea of the 'garbage can' (Cohen et al., 1972), where 'what' accumulates beside 'what' in a garbage can is accidental. The second relates to the early stages of evolution in which chemical changes occurred from what seem to have been chance interactions in primeval sludge (John, 1998, p. 195).

Kingdon uses a simple model of three 'streams' – problems, policies and politics – to explain policy agenda setting. *Problems*, in this sense, are products of social concerns that get on to the policy agenda. Ideas about whether private issues are public problems (Gusfield, 1981) and the roles of political actors, pressure groups and the media in getting issues on, or equally keeping them off, the agenda are important. *Policies* need to be specified, and interest groups and others who think policy action is needed become engaged in 'policy advocacy', designing them and ensuring their progress on the agenda. Policies can be in conflict with each other, and there may be groups who oppose policy interventions as well as ones which support them. *Politics* needs to be seen as, in the first place, the competition between parties seeking power. Then much depends upon issues on which dominant parties want to claim 'credit' or avoid 'blame' (Weaver, 1986). Hence effective policy change is seen as a product of the coming together of these three 'streams'. Kingdon's key point is that the prospects for policy change are at their strongest when (a) there is a widely acknowledged problem to be solved, (b) there are policy prescriptions for solutions to that problem effectively promoted by policy advocates and (c) there is a political party (or parties) seeking power, or in power, who support the case for an appropriate policy initiative.

Kingdon's model was developed to explore policy making in the US. The division of powers in the US – both between the president and the two houses of Congress, and between federal and state government – makes the coming together of the streams particularly necessary, and perhaps exceptionally important. However, the model perhaps reflects a more consensual era in US politics compared to the, at the time of writing, adversarial political battles between President Trump and Congress. The model's more general use, and particularly its applicability to comparisons between nations, needs to be subject to qualifications. More unified systems may bring the three elements together more systematically through ideologies and mandates. Conversely, global policy making may manifest Kingdon's perspective in extreme forms. In the case of unified action to try to limit climate change, even the dominant problem definition is challenged by those who do not want to see the issue on the agenda, policy advocacy involves a cacophony of voices, many funded by interest groups, and domestic political agendas crowd out global concerns (see further discussion in Chapter 11, and also Giddens, 2009 and Gough, 2017). But focusing on less difficult cases than that, Deacon's work (2007, 2013) explores ways in which global policy actors may come together despite institutional complexity.

The topic of 'policy advocacy' merits further consideration. For Kingdon's model this comprises the way in which members of Congress take up particular issues and then recruit staff to further policy thinking. Regarded from a Western European perspective this activity is much more likely to be concentrated within departments of permanent civil servants. This implies a stronger follow through from policy advocacy to policy formulation. Moreover, in many areas of social policy – particularly health and education – there may be professionally qualified people engaged in this process.

Outside of advanced economies, policy choices in less powerful states are more constrained by agenda setting that is much more likely to be influenced by external state and non-state actors (see for example Stone, 2008; Sklair, 2000; Tallberg and Jönsson, 2010; Murphy and Kellow, 2013), indicating a much more 'complex multilateralism' in policy making (O'Brien et al., 2000) which is further underpinned by the operation of more fundamental competing ideological visions at the global and regional levels (Kaasch and Stubbs, 2014).

Kingdon's streams approach successfully opens up questions about the issues to be considered in relating broad models of the determinants of social policy to approaches to the explanation of specific policy changes. It is not alone in doing this, and the following sections further elaborate on even more explicit ways to explain what actually happens.

From agendas to outcomes

It may be that a focus on policy agenda setting points towards a focus on prominent and specific political events that may exaggerate policy change. In an appendix to the latest edition of his book, Kingdon explores US health policy reform as a good illustration of his approach. May (2015, p. 293) takes this analysis further in terms of the notion of 'policy regime' arguing, with respect to the reform of health policy under Obama's presidency (Obamacare), that given

> the institutional design of the health care reform and the dizzying array of formal requirements, the forces for aligning implementation efforts have been insipid. The sense of common purpose in providing affordable care has been undermined by glitches in enrolment and inconsistent actions by states, insurers and federal government. The detractors for the reform have had a stronger voice than the proponents, undermining the energy behind the effort.

In other words, complex and contested reforms may well not end up as expected. Without focusing too closely on the micro-politics of the policy process, an outline of some approaches to policy analysis that may be important for explanations of reality, and may also contribute to explanations of the differences between policies in different countries, is necessary. To do this there is a need to unpack the activity needed to translate a policy, deriving from high-level political processes, into the form in which it is experienced by the public when it is implemented. Knoepfel and Weidner (1982; see also Knoepfel et al., 2007) write thus of a substantive policy core ringed by a number of elements: 'operational', 'evaluative', 'procedural' and 'political administrative' (financial means and other resources).

A useful example in understanding this element of policy making is the extension of availability of social care to older people. This example draws loosely on practice in the UK, but is arguably more widely applicable. Such a policy requires the elaboration of a new set of formal rules about how entitlement is to be determined. Civil servants rather than politicians will draft these. The rules will often not be within the original legislative act but set out in supporting regulations and codes. There will be a need to specify who is to apply these rules, which may imply national and local administrative changes, both in operation and structure. Questions will have to be addressed about how the policy will be funded. Finally, there may well be a need to have a system to monitor what actually happens.

A particular aspect of this complexity will very often be that translating policy into action involves collaboration between different actors. The now considerable academic literature on implementation explores this issue (see Hill and Hupe, 2014). There is a need to be careful about the very varied use of the concept of implementation, to embrace everything from the realization of political goals to the detailed practice of workers at street level. It is probably helpful to distinguish policy formulation (settling the detail to be passed on to the implementers) from implementation per se. With respect to this intervening task the notion of 'instrument choice' has been developed (see particularly Howlett et al., 2009; Doern and Phidd, 1983). Using a rather simpler formulation, Hood (1986, 2007) has written of choices made between the 'tools of government'. It is not necessary to list the wide range of 'instruments' identified, but the key point is that in pursuit of policy goal choices, governments may intervene in many ways: public provision, subsidy, regulation, taxation, persuasion and so on. The history of government interventions with respect to the use of alcohol, tobacco or recreational drugs illustrates variations in choice of some instruments very well (Monaghan, 2011). Chapters 7–9 in this book, on education, health and housing, illustrate more specific variations in the use made of public provision, subsidy and regulation.

Instrument choice has been seen as influenced by the power of those whose activities the government seeks to control (Linder and Peters, 1991; Lascoumes and Le Gales, 2007). Schneider and Ingram (1997) argue that decision makers will opt for an instrument targeting a specific group according to assumptions about how this target group behaves. Target groups may be seen in terms of two dimensions: deserving versus undeserving, with strong versus weak political power. Hence, in putting these dimensions together Schneider and Ingram argue that there will be: (1) 'advantaged' groups, with a positive image and a high amount of power; (2) 'contenders', who suffer from a negative social perception, but are nevertheless powerful; (3) 'dependent' groups with a positive image but little power; and (4) 'deviant' groups that have a negative image and are powerless. The power and status of the target groups thus shapes the range of policy instruments that governments are able and willing to use and the extent to which they are persuasive or punitive, but also provides a framework through which to present and promote policies in public discourse.

There are, as noted earlier in relation to the role of big business, other actors who seek to influence the shape of policy, and this is the focus of another influential approach to the analysis of policy in action: the 'advocacy coalition framework' (for a recent exposition see Sabatier and Weible, 2014). This sees the policy process – from policy inception through to implementation – as involving an 'advocacy coalition' comprising actors from all parts of the policy system. Advocacy coalitions consist of 'actors from a variety of institutions who share a set of policy beliefs' (Sabatier, 1999, p. 9). Recent elaborations of the theory explore the likely presence of 'minority coalitions' as well as a 'dominant one', and go on to explore factors that may influence change as more dissident participants grow in power. It is argued that the theory facilitates comparisons between coalitions on different issues or in different countries, but while it generates understanding of the interactions of actors, it does so at the expense of situating them adequately within the bigger picture of structural power.

Policy transfer and policy convergence

Mention of the advocacy coalition framework as an approach bridging many aspects of the policy process leads on to the topic of policy transfer. Some scholars have suggested a case for 'policy transfer theory' as a distinct 'framework of' policy analysis (see Dolowitz and Marsh, 1996, 2000). It is evident that in the contemporary world a great deal of effort is put into policy transfer, both by national policy makers and by international organizations. But it is important to note that policy transfer comes in many forms, influenced by links between governments in the modern world of 'governance' as an international phenomenon. Hence, the word 'transfer' rather oversimplifies the issues. Gilardi (2014, pp. 187–8) suggests a need to distinguish the following:

- Policy transfer – a process by which decision makers use policy ideas from another political system to formulate their own policy.
- Policy diffusion – when a policy change adopted in a given political system is systematically conditioned by prior policy choices made in other political systems.
- Policy convergence – simply the fact that policies adopted by different political systems become similar over time.

Holzinger and Knill (2005) provide an elaboration of this, summarized in Table 4.1, which explores the many ways in which policy convergence between nations may occur. What is important about their approach is the emphasis on

Table 4.1: Sources of policy convergence

Mechanism	Stimulus
Imposition	Political demand or pressure
International harmonization	Legal obligation through international law
Regulatory competition	Competitive pressure
Transnational communication	N/A
Lesson drawing	Problem pressure
Transnational problem solving	Parallel problem pressure in a shared context like the EU
Emulation	Desire for conformity
International policy promotion	Legitimacy pressure
Independent problem solving	Parallel problem pressure

Source: Simplification of Holzinger and Knill (2005, p. 780, table 3)

the way something more than simple policy choice may be involved. Their first category stresses direct compulsion and the second, third and fifth indicate the significance of indirect pressures upon policy makers. There are several different sources of compulsion, and the forms vary from strong to weak. After international conflict, victor nations may explicitly impose policy requirements upon the vanquished, as in Germany and Japan after the Second World War. Collective agreements between nations may carry with them both explicit policy expectations and limitations upon policy-making freedom. This is the case with some aspects of EU law, though the nations required to comply are also participants in the policy-making process (Knill and Liefferink, 2007). It also applies to looser associations between nations, coming together in international organizations to deal with problems with roots lying beyond nation states (as in the case of climate change). A more complex aspect of this – as in Holzinger and Knill's emphasis on competitive pressure – is the extent to which economic interactions between nations impose, directly or indirectly, constraints upon domestic policy. Clearly this last point is particularly significant where the power relations between nations are particularly unequal.

Issues about aid bring additional considerations into play here, in which single nation states, international organizations and even private donor bodies may play a role in making support for a nation conditional upon the adoption or rejection of specific policies. The term Washington Consensus was coined towards the end of the last century to describe the processes by which international aid relationships and the policy advice given by international organizations such as the World Bank carried with them a particular neoliberal emphasis upon tight expenditure controls, minimum economic regulation and privatization (Peet, 2009). The past tense is used here, given certain assertions (Krugman, 2012) that this consensus has been challenged in the post-2008 crisis context (although see Farnsworth and Irving, 2018b). Nevertheless, national reliance on international financial support through development loans, as well as bilateral aid, still plays an external role in shaping national policies, if only in terms of what is and what is not supported (see McGoey, 2015). What Dolowitz and Marsh (1996) termed 'coercive' policy transfer, while reflecting the involuntary dimensions of policy development in many low-income and indebted countries, tends to oversimplify the underlying historical and structural balance of world power. Thus, while there are instances where specific policies may be identified as having been 'coercively transferred' through loan conditionality for example, both the operation of global policy actors and policy development in the global South are subject to much greater diversity and complexity than this strand of transfer categorization can capture. This is a theme which is present in Part II.

Conclusion

This chapter took as its starting point the need to recognize the limitations of regime theory to explain the contemporary evolution of social policy in different countries, especially those which do not belong to the group of advanced economies with mature welfare states. The question that it is reasonable to address with respect to the additional analytical tools explored in this chapter is whether they take us any further. Much of the theory explains events retrospectively. When it is applied to efforts to predict the future it is often used selectively, influenced by hopes and aspirations. Policy analysis and policy advocacy thus become intertwined.

The underlying methodological question about policy studies is whether they will evolve significantly towards a systematic body of theory, comparable to that of physics for example. Schlager (1997, p. 14) has described the subject of policy analysis as having 'mountain islands of theoretical structure … occasionally attached together by foothills of shared methods and concepts, and empirical work … surrounded by oceans of descriptive work'. The implication is that it can do better, but how much better? The alternative is to see the subject as closer to history. Historians have more or less abandoned heroic efforts to generalize about the future from the past, but they still raise questions about how we may learn from experience (see for example Macmillan, 2008). The point then is that policy studies has developed a range of concepts to help ensure that the right questions are asked. These concepts come from a variety of sources and may often be described as analogies or metaphors. Kingdon (2013, Chapter 8), for example, writes of policy windows opening and shutting, and of streams joining, and describes 'policy advocates' as surfers waiting to catch the big wave. Working systematically with ideas and concepts such as these enriches comparative, international and global perspectives in social policy studies.

The second point relates to the recent development of the role of ideas in the policy process, as discussed earlier in relation to Béland's contribution. This must be seen as a challenge to the more determinist theories. If ideas are supports for both existing policies and challenges to them, then this can (potentially at least) democratize the making of policy. But then policy advocacy is most effective if supported by an understanding of how the policy process works, and an understanding of the bases of support for existing policy in context. Pralle (2009), for example, uses agenda-setting theory to indicate strategies for advancing a policy agenda in the case of policies to combat climate change.

Particularly important aspects of the debate that regime theory provoked among social policy analysts do indeed concern Esping-Andersen's justification quoted at the beginning of this chapter that theories of change need to be able to explain both expansion and decline. The 'industry' that his work stimulated – on change, country and policy exceptions, the pathways of middle- and low-income country social regimes and so on – seeks to address this aim. Where supplemented by the ideas and theories discussed in this chapter, positive channels of enquiry can be opened up that take regime theory further from the original functionalist theory it challenged, but this is only possible where regimes are recognized as national snapshots in an ever-changing world of social policy, rather than impervious and enduring characterizations.

Part II

POLICY DOMAINS

5

Income security

Introduction

Income security policy is collective action to protect individuals against income deficiencies. It is often alternatively called 'social security' and is sometimes described as 'social protection', though this concept tends to embrace more than simply income security. An American term – 'welfare' – has increasingly entered into English-language discussions of this topic, but this tends to blur important distinctions between different approaches to the provision of income security inasmuch as it is a term particularly linked to last resort means-tested support, and consequently also often involves a pejorative usage. Collective action to provide income security may be taken by a variety of social actors, including employers, charities and voluntary organizations. In some circumstances it may even be appropriate to identify the extended family as playing this role, particularly in countries where capacity for public funding is more limited, state administrative architecture is still emerging and employment remains largely informal. However, when analyzing income security systems in advanced economies, these are systems in which the state has a dominant role.

Income security entitlements may thus be seen as an addition to measures an individual may take to protect her or himself. An important element of context here is philosophical assumptions about the extent to which collective and/or state responsibilities exist. The variations around these can be highlighted by the contrasts offered in the recent history of Chinese income security policies. In urban China, after the establishment of a socialist society by Mao Zedong in the 1940s, the expectation was that publicly owned enterprises would provide an 'iron rice bowl' (Leung, 1994): support from the cradle to the grave regardless of work capacity. More recently, considerable effort has been put into the development of collective contributory insurance schemes to replace the iron rice bowl. Where this is absent, particularly in rural areas, income support is seen to be based on the 'three nos' principle, where it is applied only to people who are 'without family ... unable to work and ... lacking sources of income – the three nos' (Leung and Xu, 2015, p. 99).

This contrast highlights two themes that run through comparisons with respect to income security: variations in assumptions about (a) family support roles and (b) connections with employment. Viewed historically, it is arguable that more comprehensive income security policies have arisen out of the initial replacement of societal assumptions that there was no collective, let alone state, responsibility for this issue, through poor relief based upon three nos assumptions, to modern policies with more complicated assumptions about family roles and links to paid employment. Moreover, when comparing nations today, as the discussion of the applicability of regime theory to the global South in Chapter 3 suggests, there needs to be a clear recognition of the welfare mix, which considers outcomes involving the interactions of the public sector, the private sector and households which affect the 'well-being or ill-being of groups of people' (Gough and Wood, 2004, p. 26).

State measures contributing to income security may include both tax-supported contingent entitlements and contributory social insurance benefits, as well as means-tested assistance benefits (with benefits in cash or in kind) and compulsory savings arrangements (for example, the 'provident funds' in Singapore and Malaysia). In addition to these measures in which the state has a direct interest, there is also a state role in legislating obligations upon employers (such as statutory sick and maternity pay), the arrangements by which individuals can litigate for compensation for life events such as accidents or divorce and the regulation of private provisions, particularly pensions. A further element of state involvement is found in the ways in which contributions to income security from family members may be required in law and practice.

To these may be added subsidies provided through assistance for individuals to accumulate assets (such as subsidies for house purchases, see Chapter 8) and the provision of benefits by way of the tax system (for example, with respect to private pension contributions). What can be described as 'fiscal welfare', or allowances received through the tax system, can include variations in tax paid according to individual needs and circumstances, and 'tax credits' involving the adding back of amounts to people without tax obligations. With respect to these the line between taking away and giving is blurred. For logical completeness, and because these schemes are gradually being piloted in some countries (India, Canada and Finland for example), it is important to also recognize tax-supported measures that guarantee a minimum income for all without any recourse to means testing. Although subject to continued debate, these basic income or citizens' income schemes have emerged as new items on social protection agendas, and are significant in the context of a transformed employment landscape and attempts to address gender inequalities in social security.

The dominance of income security within social policy

Income security systems play a dominant role in national social policy systems, and particularly in state systems. Figure 5.1 demonstrates this by comparing data on public social expenditure in OECD countries with the figures for income security transfers. It shows income security expenditure at over, often well over, 40 per cent of social expenditure in all the listed countries apart from Mexico.

Of course, hidden within those aggregate figures are wide variations in the support given to various groups. What is crucial is the very high impact of pension expenditure on income security expenditure in some countries. There

Income security

Figure 5.1: Income security expenditure in the context of general social expenditure in OECD countries, 2016

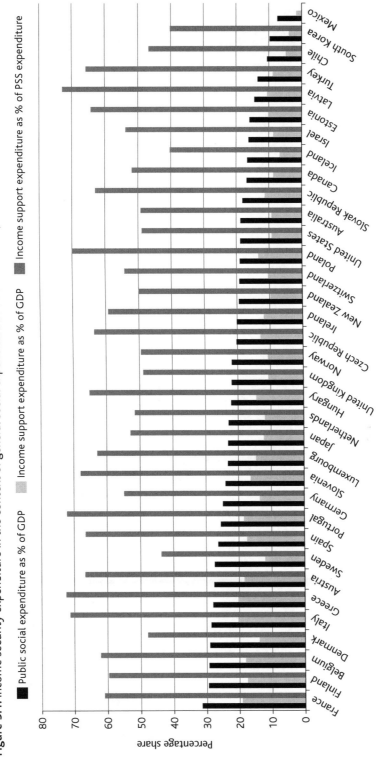

■ Public social expenditure as % of GDP   ▨ Income support expenditure as % of GDP   ▨ Income support expenditure as % of PSS expenditure

Note: Public social expenditure is defined here as the OECD defines it (see notes to OECD, 2018a, table 2.1), excluding education. If education expenditure were included the figures would be around 4–5 per cent higher.

Source: OECD (2018a) Public Expenditure Database

are considerable variations, partly explained by demographic variations since some countries are comparatively elderly (25 per cent of Japan's population is over 65, compared to 18 per cent in the European Union). But the variation also reflects differences in the political choices that have been made about where to focus social policy effort. Among many of the countries where social policy expenditure is relatively low there is a relatively high concentration of that expenditure on income support for pensioners (note, in Figure 5.2 for example, Southern and Eastern European countries). The following discussion will focus on the three main elements of income support which form the basis of distributive decisions regarding what security will be offered to whom and how: social insurance, non-contributory cash transfers and means testing.

Social insurance

In many respects the crucial turning point in the development of social policy in Europe was the invention of systems of social insurance in Germany in the 1880s (Mommsen, 1981). Since that time, systems where entitlement to benefits depends upon previous contributions have become widespread in many of the more sophisticated income support systems in advanced welfare states (see Clasen, 1997). Many countries have schemes for state pensions, protection for widows, sickness benefits and unemployment benefits developed along social insurance lines. Some countries add to these maternity benefits and benefits to provide for parental absence from work. However, the umbrella term 'social insurance' covers a multitude of possibilities. Some remain close to the commercial insurance ideas upon which social insurance was originally based, and in some cases involve private, but non-profit, organizations in the system.

Commercial insurance requires methods to ensure that the insured contribute adequate amounts matched in various ways to the likelihood that claims will be made. A consequence of this may be the rejection of some potential customers on the grounds that they will be 'bad risks'. Social insurance departs from this actuarial discipline by pooling risks much more radically across social groups, recognizing that this may mean that 'good risks' may subsidize 'bad risks' to a degree that would simply deter the former from purchasing a commercial insurance. The compulsory nature of inclusion in *social* insurance schemes deals with this problem. At the same time the state underwriting of social insurance is expected to eliminate the other commercial problem that too many bad risks may render a scheme insolvent. In fact, in many social insurance schemes the risk pooling is taken further, not merely by the acceptance of redistribution between contributors, but also by requirements for contributions from employers, and by the deliberate building of state contributions into schemes.

One of the attractions of social insurance to its founders in the nineteenth century (alongside the notion that if workers invested in their own income protection they would be less likely to support revolutionary movements) was that a system involving contributor funding could be set up with little or no impact upon general taxation. However, funding depends upon a capacity to achieve a balance between income and expenditure. While state-led social insurance is more relaxed on this than a private company could be, success in predicting demand in the long run remains a necessary feature of funding. The funding of social insurance is easier to manage with respect to the short-scenario benefits – injury benefit, sickness benefit, maternity benefit and unemployment benefits – than with pensions, where a view has to be taken about an accumulation process lasting many years into the future. However, even the short–run social insurance schemes set up in Europe early in the twentieth century were threatened by economic instability in the 1920s and 1930s. Rates of unemployment at this time were much higher than predicted when the social insurance schemes were set up, but inflation also posed problems for the adjustment of contributions and benefits over time, and undermined efforts to accumulate funds.

Funding also has a more ambiguous character in social rather than private insurance inasmuch as social insurance systems are *political creations* and require decisions on the strictness of funding assumptions. As far as it is possible to accumulate a fund (essential if funding of pensions is to be taken seriously), questions arise about what to do with it. If the money is to be invested in the private sector, then it may be seen as a form of backdoor nationalization (see Blackburn, 2002, pp. 74–6). If invested outside the country, then international business complications will arise. On the other hand, if it is just retained in the public sector it is available to be raided by governments for other objectives. However, in many respects the notion of an uninvested 'fund' makes little sense, becoming merely a public accounting fiction. It is in this sense that – in a context of economic turmoil during the twentieth century – a great deal of social insurance has come to assume a 'pay-as-you-go' character, where governments try to maintain a short-term balance but may have to subsidize from taxation in the long run. The particular implications of this for pensions policy are discussed later.

The distinctions between social insurance and private insurance suggest that the former can assume a 'solidaristic' form in which social protection is shared, and redistribution towards the less advantaged is possible. But these assumptions should not be taken for granted. In some cases there are separate social insurance schemes for different groups of workers (for example, in Taiwan there are separate schemes for soldiers, public servants and teachers alongside the general scheme for other workers). And even when there is a shared scheme across occupational groups, the use of the insurance principle implies differentiation where what is taken out may be required to be a reflection of what has been paid in.

It is important to recognize that the notion of social insurance originates from measures to protect labour market participants following a 'male breadwinner' model. An examination of the origins of social insurance in the UK, particularly highlighted in discussions in the Beveridge Report (Beveridge, 1942), shows how it was designed to protect male labour market participants, with women and children securing support only as their 'dependants' rather than as individuals. Thus, historically, social insurance has provided partial coverage, and the pooling of social risks does not guarantee redistribution. While solidarity may well equate with egalitarianism it does not necessarily do so, and the form of distribution being attempted – between individuals, between generations or across individual lifetimes (see Hills, 1993, pp. 15–21) – is important. The levels at which the minimum benefit is set and the extent to which the egalitarianism of a social insurance scheme is offset by incentives to the better off to make separate provision also affect the distributive impact (see Korpi and Palme, 1998). Social insurance schemes with graduated contributions but flat rate benefits will be highly redistributive, while a scheme with both graduated contributions and graduated benefits may well only achieve a comparable rate of income replacement across the income groups. Real-world country cases can be very complex mixes, but it is possible with reference to these issues, and to the strictness with which insurance contributions conditions are enforced, to compare schemes in terms of the extent to which they embrace principles of solidarity, covering all risks, and redistributing resources from those at low risk of dependence to those at high risk.

These issues are rendered all the more important if work is not available to all who want it, or is available in informal, part-time or temporary forms, or if caring responsibilities reduce labour market participation. Social insurance has at its heart the notion of the containment of its costs within the group most vulnerable to unemployment, sickness and disability. While many actual social insurance schemes widen the insured group and allow for cross-subsidy from the less vulnerable to the more vulnerable, there remain many senses in which equalization is limited. Furthermore, particularly in the treatment of unemployment, the concerns about the reinforcement of labour market participation embodied in poor relief have been carried forward into insurance schemes. In the industrialized countries these issues have emerged as sources of problems, as support schemes resting upon assumptions of full-time employment in a secure contract with an employer are seen to have decreasing applicability. Various forms of female labour market participation have offered particular challenges to schemes designed for the male working class. But so have changes in the nature of the labour market in which casual, part-time and insecure employment are widespread.

The ILO (2017b, p. 1) reports that unemployment increased by 3.4 per cent to 201 million people in 2017, a rate of 5.8 per cent which 'is not expected to drop anytime soon'. If, overall, the volume of employment on offer is declining, the problem of constrained redistribution through social insurance will intensify. By the same token it must be emphasized that the labour market characteristics of much of the global South, including emerging economies, do not offer simple 'seed beds' for the importation of social insurance approaches to the alleviation of poverty. This issue is rendered more acute given that the 1.4 billion workers in 'vulnerable employment' (which is always informal) in 2017 are largely found outside the advanced economies. The number of such workers is estimated to increase annually by 11 million people (ILO, 2017a), and this group provides a clear example of those for whom social insurance is an unworkable policy choice. Issues about job security are discussed further in Chapter 6. The traditional social insurance model is based upon an expectation of continuous labour market participation, and this model of employment is being increasingly eroded for all workers.

In summing up this section it is worthwhile going back to the points made about policy stability made in Chapter 4. Social insurance is very much a survivor, its survival assisted by the way the contributory principle creates expectations. It is alive in its country of origin, Germany, despite the fact that Germany has experienced three policy earthquakes: runaway inflation in the 1920s, Nazism in the 1930s and 1940s and division followed by reunification after 1945. Perhaps the word 'despite' misleads – it may be that offering the prospect of a return to normality was why it survived. In the German case it is also pertinent that there are links between social insurance as a source of cash benefits and as a source of health and (more recently) social care. Elsewhere, many of its links have grown very weak, except in relation to retirement pensions.

Non-contributory cash transfers

The simplest approach to the provision of income maintenance involves guaranteeing payments if specific demographic, social or health status criteria are fulfilled, without reference to contribution conditions or means tests. An example is where the only criteria for payment of a pension may be age, and claimants merely have to prove that they are above a qualifying age. Systems of this kind have emerged out of the extension of contributory schemes to the point where past benefit records are disregarded in the interests of the inclusion of everyone. Pension schemes in Norway and Sweden provide guaranteed minima in this sense (Pedersen and Kuhnle, 2017). Another rather less straightforward kind of benefit in this category is income replacement based on proof of disability. However, as Bolderson and Mabbett (1991) indicate, rules may restrict entitlement by reference either to the 'cause' of the disability (such as injuries sustained in combat or in an accident at work) or to the demonstrable consequences of it. Such entitlements are often judged through medicalized ability tests that are used to discriminate between claimants according to a set of rules which define levels of disability.

In all these cases complete universalism is partly undermined by rules which confine the benefits to specific groups and, in all cases, to citizens of the country concerned. In many countries, therefore, migrant workers may contribute through taxes but be denied support. Given that the movement of people is one of the defining features of contemporary policy debate, this remains supremely challenging for the 'real states of well-being' (as noted by Gough and Wood, 2004, mentioned earlier).

Means testing

The provision of income maintenance through schemes involving tests of means has a long history in many societies. At a simple glance this approach seems to satisfy the requirements of both a desire for equality and a commitment to efficiency. Equality, because means testing is generally designed to concentrate help upon those in greatest need. Efficiency, because such targeting is designed to keep expenditure to a minimum. But a deeper examination of means testing reveals many problems, which may undermine these two goals.

Firstly, because means tests necessarily have an income point at which the test is applied, they can be viewed as very unfair to those whose self-provided incomes are marginally above the level they guarantee. In this sense, for those of working age, a means test may represent a disincentive to accept employment with a low rate of pay. Since governments are keen to ensure that even the lowest-paid jobs are filled within their wider economic strategies, the policy solution has tended to be the use of a taper that enables means-tested support to be gradually reduced above the guaranteed income level. However, perceptions of the fairness of entitlement will then depend upon the rate at which this tapering off effect occurs. If it is rapid it will effectively be a draconian tax on lower earnings. This is the phenomenon of the 'poverty trap', which has the effect of holding substantial numbers of households at income levels only a little above the level guaranteed to those not in paid employment. Second, means-testing systems are also likely to assess more than individual resources and consider individual applications in ways which take into account the needs and resources of other family and/or household members without recognizing inequalities of income within households.

The final problem with means tests arises from the general implications of disincentive effects, the nature of family obligations and the morality of administrative surveillance. The process of obtaining and retaining means-tested assistance will be experienced as degrading and stigmatizing to applicants. This may be regarded, by governments and by those not in need of help, as a desirable feature of means-tested income maintenance: deterring claims to assistance, keeping costs down and discouraging behaviours at odds with a belief in self-help. Disincentive effects, however, also undermine the efficiency of means testing. Together with the complexity of the rules relating to benefit determination, such systems lead to situations in which large numbers of people entitled to help do not claim it. Walker quotes studies of take-up showing rates around two-thirds with respect to means-tested benefits in the UK and the US, and well below half for social assistance in Germany (2005, p. 194).

In many countries there are contributory benefits to meet contingencies, accompanied by means-tested 'safety net schemes' for people not protected by those benefits. While safety nets may be seen as necessary to meet temporary or structural deficiencies in contributory schemes, or to assist people whose circumstances prevent them benefiting fully from contributory schemes, there is a tendency for them to also be seen as the appropriate form of support for those deemed less 'deserving' among groups unable to secure support through the labour market. This dualism of contributory benefits underpinned by means-tested benefits is widespread. Inconsistencies may develop in an income maintenance system as a whole, as a result of the operation of very different principles for the determination of benefits which are side by side. This particularly arises if the income guaranteed by a means test is similar to that provided by contributory benefits, and it creates situations where there will be many people who, despite the fact that they have entitlements to contributory benefits, find that means tests determine their final income. This is an effect that erodes support for the contributory principle. The UK is a country where these issues have gained prominence, while the systems in other countries have avoided this problem through ensuring a wider gap between contributory and means-tested benefits, either through the generosity of the former (the Nordic countries) or the meanness of the latter (the US).

In the 1990s, Eardley et al. (1995) conducted a major comparative study of means tests (see also Gough et al., 1997), which suggested that 'the careful study of means-tested benefits ... muddles, but ultimately enriches prior comparative models of welfare systems' (1995, p. 171). A taxonomy of types of social assistance systems developed from the study is set out in Table 5.1.

More recent commentary broadly reinforces the picture provided by Table 5.1, but notes the extent to which economic developments have expanded means testing (Bahle et al., 2010). As the original study was limited to OECD countries

Table 5.1: Taxonomy of social assistance systems

Type of system	Characteristics	Country examples
Selective welfare systems	All benefits are means tested	Australia and New Zealand
The public assistance state	'An extensive set of means-tested benefits, arranged in a hierarchy of acceptability and stigma'	United States
Welfare states with integrated safety nets		Britain, Canada, Ireland and Germany
Dual social assistance	Various categorical assistance schemes	France and Benelux countries
Rudimentary assistance	Some national categorical schemes and otherwise local discretionary relief	Southern Europe and Turkey
Residual social assistance	Social assistance marginalized by the presence of comprehensive social insurance	Nordic countries
Highly decentralized assistance with local discretion	'Elements of both the Nordic and Southern European models'	Austria, Switzerland

Source: Based on Eardley et al. (1995, pp. 168–71)

it is important to recognize that there is a category missing, prevalent in much of the global South, which may be described as: basic and often highly decentralized assistance in a context where there is no other state social security (authors' categorization, but see Barrientos and Hulme, 2008 and Leisering and Barrientos, 2013 for discussions of this theme).

The complexity of means testing has led to a search for approaches that are simpler. In advanced economies with mature systems of fiscal administration, various forms of tax credit systems have been introduced: in the US, Canada, Ireland, New Zealand, Denmark, Finland, Austria, Belgium, France and the Netherlands (Bahle et al., 2010). The provision of benefits through the tax system has the additional merit that it does not merely offset tax liabilities, but may involve payment to people whose incomes are too low to reach the tax threshold. While this may be administratively simpler, it remains a form of means testing, since it is based on level of income. It also retains many of the problems with means testing since the taper effect is present. The transition between benefit status and tax status as income changes is complex, and is complicated further because income fluctuations are particularly prevalent among those on low incomes, requiring regular reviews and consequent delays in adjustments with significant temporary impacts on the financial well-being of recipients. As with other means-tested benefits, fine tuning to take into account family responsibilities, rent payments and other exceptional liabilities also adds to the complexity. In the UK, the development of a (comparatively) universal tax credit scheme has proven to be a source of controversy, and contrary to its goal of simplifying core elements of the social security system, has created more gaps and failures to meet needs than existed prior to its introduction (Millar and Bennett, 2017).

Concerns about the increasing complexity of means testing, and its role in compensating for low or insecure earnings, has led to heightened interest in basic income as an alternative approach to social transfers. At its simplest, the idea is that the state should transfer a regular sum to all citizens (or all those of working age), offsetting the regressive effects of this through tax (and the withdrawal of generic tax concessions). With such payments in place most means-tested benefits would become unnecessary, although possible exceptions such as housing allowances, where big variations between people with respect to the incidence of costs, may require retention. An OECD analysis of this idea suggests the following:

> A growing interest in simple, reliable and accessible income support can be linked to major economic trends and to social concerns associated with them, including growing inequality, the rise of atypical forms of employment, also associated with the digital transformation, the risk of job losses due to automation, as well as imbalances between work, family and leisure. (OECD, 2017c, p. 1)

Basic income has gained support among economists (for example Atkinson, 2015), as well as campaigning organizations, and offers a challenge to perspectives on income security that privilege work as the primary source of income. A basic income transfer could have effects upon labour market participation both in terms of the extent to which it might encourage non-participation on the one hand and flexible participation on the other. There are also questions about its impact, in the absence of other controls, upon exploitative forms of employment, and its wider impact on other welfare services, since many on the political Right also advocate such cash transfer systems alongside the removal of state obligations for health care and other provisions. There are various basic income experiments being conducted across Europe (De Wispelaere and Haagh, 2019), but any aspiration to effect a national shift into this sort of income support system faces considerable problems. The OECD (2017c, p. 5) offers an important observation that while the basic income idea is very simple, 'existing social benefits are not', so that 'replacing them with a universal flat rate benefit produces complex patterns of gains and losses'. Thus, while it is possible to argue for a modest basic income scheme, largely funded from the existing benefits and tax allowances, this may be a poor instrument for the alleviation of poverty, leaving many worse off and a need for some means-tested benefits to remain in place. On the other hand, to achieve an effective alternative approach to poverty relief by this route would place heavy new demands on taxation. Inevitably, the OECD assessment of the basic income idea concerns the implications for OECD countries where complex income security measures are already in place. It offers no discussion of the idea's potential as an egalitarian approach to the disbursal of new resources in countries where there are limited existing benefits and attempts to raise income may be more welcome.

In the global South, another form of means-tested benefit, conditional cash transfers (CCTs), has developed in response to the problem of widespread poverty and inadequate structures for the operation of contributory insurance systems. These forms of social security payment have gained momentum since the 1990s, in Latin America particularly, but also in countries across all world regions – over fifty countries in all. CCTs combine the provision of categorical guaranteed cash payments to those below national poverty thresholds, with built-in conditionality related to welfare behaviours such as the school attendance of recipients' children and attendance at health clinics. As a relatively new addition to the suite of income protection measures they represent a hybrid of social policies which, although expected to address income, health and educational needs, have explicit economic rather than social goals, in that they aim to optimize economic growth through improving human capital and labour market productivity. Standing (2008) argues that the operation (and deficiencies) of CCTs provides evidence to support the case for a more authentic form of basic income, while LoVuolo (2012, p. 12) assesses the capacity for CCT schemes in Brazil and Argentina and concludes that 'the affinity between the CCT programmes and the BI [basic income] scheme is weak'. The feasibility of adoption of more 'authentic' versions of basic income depends upon political acceptance of a big shift in the distribution of resources. Added to this, potential pitfalls in implementation could include the 'modality of payment' (De Wispelaere and Stirton, 2012). Financialization, in the sense of the embedding of individual monetary exchanges within the financial services market, is an established feature of benefit payments in advanced economies where recipients are required to have bank accounts into which transfers are made (lacking a bank account in these countries can attract a 'poverty premium' of extra costs associated with cash payments). However, financial exclusion is a much wider problem in many countries in the global South and creates a significant practical obstacle to the diffusion of basic income, and the achievement of income security more generally.

Regardless of the practical barriers to implementation, the key issue is that while CCTs are targeted only to those regarded as deserving (through categorical selection and behavioural conditionality), basic income is underpinned by a principle of the deservingness of all, a principle which remains highly contested within the politics of social protection. The question of deservingness is fundamental to the design of income security systems, and the element where this is least contestable is in provision for retirement.

Comparing pension systems

The combination of the dominance of pension expenditure within public income security expenditure, with nevertheless considerable variations between countries (as shown in Figure 5.2), was explored briefly earlier. Alongside demographic reasons, efforts to minimize the public contribution to pensions play an important part in any explanation of this variation, and have become more acute since the 2008 financial crisis.

In all free societies individuals are at liberty to make their own pension arrangements through the private market. Where the state does engage, there is a key question regarding the extent to which it should take responsibility for the whole pension for any individual, or only for bringing individual pension income to a specific minimum level. An influential report by the World Bank (1994) describes pension systems in terms of three 'pillars' (see Table 5.2), and argues that the state should only be directly responsible for the first pillar in any pension scheme, that is, to secure a basic minimum for its retired citizens. States should then take an indirect regulatory responsibility for a second private pillar and accept that beyond these, the third pillar should be entirely a private matter.

To understand the arguments about the appropriate respective roles of private and public provision in this area it is necessary to explore the alternatives on the policy agenda. The standard form of a purely private pension involves an agreement between a contributing individual and a pension provider that is no more than an undertaking to safeguard and invest savings and repay them in some form after retirement or attainment of a specific age. What the individual 'gets out' is then a product of what was 'put in' plus whatever interest is earned on the investment.

Income security

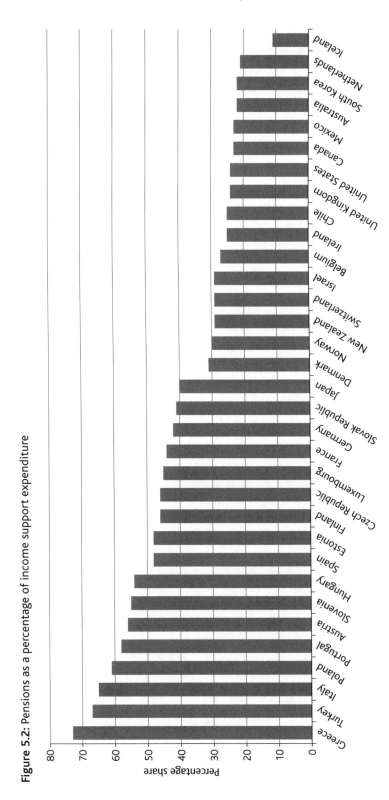

Figure 5.2: Pensions as a percentage of income support expenditure

Source: OECD (2017g)

Table 5.2: The World Bank Report's Pension Pillars

	First Pillar	Second Pillar	Third Pillar
	Mandatory publicly managed pillar	Mandatory privately managed pillar	Voluntary pillar
Objectives	Redistribution and co-insurance	Savings and co-insurance	Savings plus co-insurance
Focus	Means-tested or minimum flat rate	Personal or occupational savings plan	Personal or occupational savings plan
Financing	Tax-financed	Regulated and fully funded	Fully funded

Source: Adapted from World Bank (1994, p. 15, figure 3)

Where employers are involved in the provision of private pensions they may modify this 'defined contributions' principle by making advance commitments about what individuals may take out on retirement, offering instead 'defined benefits'. To offer defined benefits is to take a risk that ultimately payout obligations will exceed the resources of the fund. Within the world of private pensions, defined benefit schemes are largely confined to large and strong enterprises. In the contemporary capitalist world of rapid organizational change and increasingly embedded financialization of organizations, commitments to pay out defined benefits are regarded by even the strongest corporations as unacceptably risky despite the advantages they bring in terms of workforce security and consequent productivity gains.

When we turn to public pensions it is important to note that, while in discussions about overall state provision, 'public' means hypothetically available to all (subject to whatever contribution or means–testing rules are applied), the state may provide special guaranteed pensions for its own employees as alternatives to, or in addition to, general state pensions. Many of these pensions predate general public pensions, where states made commitments to their employees (particularly soldiers and officials of the central state) long before they considered legislating to protect others.

It is in the area of state-guaranteed pension provision that many of the examples of contribution-based and -funded defined benefit schemes are found. For general forms of public pensions, governments have to make a series of choices about how they will operate (bearing in mind the concepts that are applied to private arrangements). These are set out in Figure 5.3.

Alongside the World Bank's analysis (1994), there have been various attempts to develop ways of comparing pension scheme choices (Bonoli and Shinkawa, 2005; Meyer et al., 2007; Hinrichs and Lynch, 2010). There are four major variants. First, defined benefit schemes that provide high replacement rates from contributions, which are nevertheless not funded (these are widely described as 'pay-as-you-go' schemes). These schemes have been characteristic of some of the continental European countries. Second, defined benefit schemes that provide modest replacement rates in a context where there is encouragement of private

Figure 5.3: Public pension choices

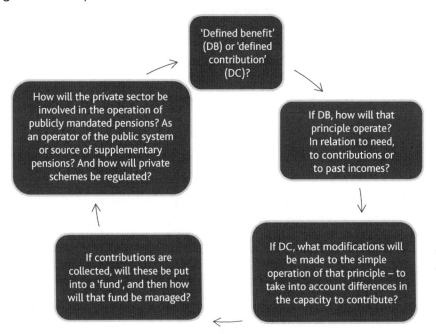

provision. The two prime examples of this are the social insurance schemes in the US and the UK, and in practice they are also pay as you go. Third, defined benefit schemes without contributions, and with availability regulated by means tests. The best example of this kind of scheme can be found in Australia. Fourth, defined contribution schemes in which the state has developed a funding system. The main examples of this are the 'provident funds' of Singapore and Malaysia.

Since the early 2000s, there have been substantial efforts to develop second pillars that have privatized elements. As was noted in the general discussion of social insurance, the funding question is central because of the long-run nature of a pension arrangement (with contributions covering a period of over forty years and payments covering another twenty or more). Similarly, it is notable, in the twentieth century, that notions of funding have been replaced in practice by pay as you go, so that balancing income and outgoings in the short run have taken the place of long-run preoccupations. This obviously makes sense for the short-term benefits, but the older social insurance pension schemes have tended to, de facto, acquire the same treatment. Efforts to avoid this policy problem (see OECD, 2017c, noted earlier) have been fuelled by a political preference for pension policies as public–private partnerships. This is manifest in funding schemes that involve the investment of pension contributions. Such developments operate with individualistic and market-based solutions that make citizens rather than the state responsible for retirement planning.

The OECD's *Pensions Outlook 2016* describes the changing pensions landscape as one in which 'assets backed pension arrangements' are increasing in importance

(OECD, 2016c; see also Sorsa, 2016 for an exploration of the complexities involved in these types of pensions). This approach has long been a feature of policy design in Latin America, but has two major flaws. One is that as the returns from work are falling due to lower pay and less continuous employment, self-provision is becoming more difficult. The other is that there are good reasons to doubt the long-run security of investments. This is partly a problem of predicting the future, but there are also complex macroeconomic issues summarized by Barr (2001, p. 4) when he argues that 'individuals must exchange current production for a claim on future production', hence 'both funded and pay-as-you-go plans are claims on future output, and they are of no use to retirees if the country is not producing enough goods and services to meet those claims' (see Hill, 2007, Chapter 7 for a fuller discussion of this issue).

Given the combination of variations between schemes, and in the individual circumstances of pension claimants, comparing pension funds is therefore a Herculean task, even within one country. Furthermore, any patterns identified would likely only apply to similar cohorts of new pensions claimants, and so disregard the extent to which the crucial questions concern not just what pension systems offer currently, but what they will offer in the future. Predicting the pension prospects of a new entrant to the labour force requires assumptions about their long-run employment prospects, but also potential changes to pension schemes across their working life (see Meyer et al., 2007 for an exercise attempting this task). This highlights the two, potentially competing, concerns in pension system change: the needs of people already old enough to retire and those of future generations of retired people. From an electoral point of view the first concern will be the most pressing. When the pioneer nations set up their pension schemes, the size of the older population was small and their life expectancy was low. Their needs implied limited demand on the public budget, easily funded by relatively low contributions from the younger workers required to join pension schemes. By contrast, pension reform in advanced economies today takes place in the context of large and growing retired populations. The shape of the working age to retirement age population ratio is therefore a key political question in states where pension systems are currently in earlier stages of development.

There is a substantial literature about the changing balance between age groups, particularly in Europe and some East Asian countries (for a review see McDaniel and Zimmer, 2016). Pensions provision is a primary concern, but rising demands related to health and social care are also policy challenges. The expression 'demographic time bomb' is sensationally applied to predictions that in due course the ratio of people beyond specifically defined pension ages relative to the working population is increasing to a crisis point. The 'dependency ratio' describes the population over 64 relative to the total population aged between 15 and 64 (or variations on that formula), and World Bank figures indicate a world ratio of 13.3[1] in 2017, varying between 27 in high-income and 6 in low-income countries. These figures suggests a potential challenge to the sustainability of pensions, but their accuracy is limited. Although longevity is increasing in many countries, rates of life expectancy can change quite rapidly and birth rates are far from predictable (for an alternative assessment of demographic trends in East Asia, see Gietel-Basten et al., 2015).

In policy terms, there are several ideas on the agenda which aim to address the challenge of an ageing population. To reduce the number of people claiming pensions one response has been to raise the age at which pension entitlement arises. Some countries, such as South Korea, have attempted the more long-run solution of an increasing birth rate. In Europe, inward migration has been advanced as a solution, but objective debate is largely confounded by political concerns and popular support for limiting immigration. All of these policy responses are fundamentally linked to the availability of work, however, something that cannot be deduced from demographic predictions. Together with this and the unpredictability of demographic change it is perhaps surprising that so much policy attention is given to efforts to achieve robust pension schemes that will survive until the quite distant future.

Comparative analysis of income security systems today: an overview

While overall national income security systems are complex and diverse it is possible to identify three broad groups, as set out in Box 5.1.

Box 5.1. Distinguishing between national income security systems

- Systems which still emphasize *self and family provision*, together with the role of employment; largely confining the state role, where it has capacity, to means-tested benefits.
- Systems in which *contributory social insurance* is dominant, making income maintenance entitlements heavily dependent upon what the individual has been able to pay in.
- Systems which combine the social insurance principle with a strong emphasis on *social solidarity*, so that there is redistribution between those easily able to contribute and those less well placed.

In advanced economies, this categorization broadly corresponds with the liberal, conservative and social democratic welfare regimes identified by Esping-Andersen (1990). It was noted in Chapter 3 that the modelling of welfare regimes has been heavily dependent on the use of data related to income security systems. Taking this fact together with the evidence on the way income security dominates social policy expenditure in most societies, it is not surprising that this equation of welfare regimes with income security systems occurs.

However, systems within actual countries are more mixed than the regime approach implies and, as noted in other chapters, the regime approach is not analytically well equipped to incorporate either advanced systems that exhibit hybridity in the operationalization of the three models, or emerging systems where social security is less driven by formal employment and focused instead on achieving a diversity of welfare goals. Many societies combine secure and high levels of entitlements for some groups (state employees, soldiers, men, long-term full-time employees, long-established citizens) with weak and largely means-tested provisions for others (women, casual and part-time workers, recent immigrants). Related to this division, it is also the case that some contingencies are much better provided for than others. Income deficiency because of old age, childhood and long-term sickness and disability tends to be given more attention than that arising because of unemployment, family breakdown and short-term sickness.

But what picture emerges if we move out of the world of the established welfare states? The so-called 'transition economies' in East and Central Europe mostly now feature in OECD data. Accounts of their evolution suggest a conflict of ideas between collectivist institutions maintained despite the fall of Communism, the pre-communist political underpinnings in each country, the social insurance models promoted by the core members of the European Union and the neoliberal ideas promoted in the 'transition' to capitalism by international organizations such as the IMF and World Bank, which saw privatization as the main road to development (Golinowska et al., 2009; Cook in Castles et al., 2010). Subsequent post-2008 austerity has perhaps strengthened the last named influence. Russia and its former satellites which have not joined the EU have seen the collapse of older collectivist policies with little appearing in their place. Reviewing 'post-Communist welfare capitalism', Cerami and Stubbs (2011) argue that alongside institutional inheritances, the recent history of these countries provides manifest evidence of the importance of 'political agency' in influencing policy trajectories. Castles and Obinger (2008), in an analysis that aims to update regime theory, observe a 'post-Communist cluster' of nations but also note deviations on the part of the Baltic nations and the Czech Republic.

The group of nations given most attention in accounts of the impact of development upon social welfare are the countries of East Asia. In relation to income support there is a division between those that have adopted forms of social insurance (Japan, South Korea, Taiwan and to some extent China) and those that have largely made use of means-tested benefits (Hong Kong and Singapore). There are hints of the influence of continental European ideas in the first group and the UK colonial legacy in the second. In India, Kapur and Nangia (2015) argue that in contrast to European welfare states (including the UK), social protection has developed without the clear establishment of public goods. As a result, 'India has taken the Latin American route rather than the East Asian path' (2015, p. 86) with little attention to the improvement of welfare. Latin America is the only other world region where income maintenance is systematically provided, but as the place of Mexico as the lowest spender in Figures 5.1 attests, there are structured limits to the expansion of income security measures in the contemporary world economic order. More detailed accounts of developments in Latin America suggest a mixture of restricted efforts to develop social insurance challenged by economic difficulties, and pressure to apply market approaches, particularly for pensions (Huber and Bogliaccini, 2010). Barrientos (2004) uses the notion of a 'liberal–informal welfare regime' to characterize this region.

It is argued by Bonoli (2005) and Taylor-Gooby (2004, 2013) that divisions within income support policies stem from a categorization of social needs expressed, for example, in the Beveridge Report (Beveridge, 1942), that the role of the state was to provide social policies supporting a system of full employment by male wage earners, exceptionally broken by ill health or unemployment and ultimately (but briefly, given the life expectancy at the time) by retirement. Hence changes to industrialized societies have generated a politics of 'new social risks'. These new risks in reconciling work and family life, changing family forms including lone parenthood, caring responsibilities, lack of marketable skills and the less than full-time character of employment (Bonoli, 2013, pp. 16–17) all pose widespread challenges to social policy, beyond income support systems. This 'new social needs' emphasis is echoed in the discussion of a 'social investment' agenda. It finds its roots in Esping-Andersen's edited volume *Why We Need a New Welfare State* (2002). It is a theme taken further by Hemerijck (2015), writing about social investment as 'The quiet paradigm revolution'. Hemerijck's approach seems to provide a combination of attempting to generalize this development with its advocacy. It can be seen as offering ideas about the capacity of the European social policy model, as to some extent idealized in regime theory, to adapt to a harsher economic climate, although adaptation is arguably required more of the citizen than of the economy. Aspects of this idea, and its focus on human capital, are revisited in Chapters 6, 7 and 10 on employment, education and social care.

In different contexts and forms, these risks are also relatable to the not-so-new risks faced by individuals and households in the global South, where work informality, family support obligations and lack of access to education also mean that the Beveridge model and its cousins are equally ill-fitting, especially because environmental risk is an added source of insecurity. As noted in Chapter 3, these changes in, or wider recognition of, risk are part of wider social and economic change which presents challenges to previous understandings of welfare state development and its divergent paths into distinctive 'worlds'.

The contrast drawn between 'old' and 'new' social needs is particularly significant with respect to gendered income security. Many of the 'old' systems were built around a model of male breadwinners with women and children as their 'dependents'. Direct provision for dependents was only included within schemes where those 'breadwinners' were absent. Related to this approach were assumptions that benefits were to be calculated with reference to the needs of households rather than the individuals within them. The alternative, long advocated from a feminist perspective but nowadays necessitated by new forms of family arrangements, is to see both entitlements and resources in terms of the incomes of individuals. Changes in this respect have emerged in social insurance systems but not necessarily in the operation of most means tests. Children further complicate the equations; where child benefits partly deal with this there remain problems about to whom those benefits are paid and why, and also about the extent to which the work of caring for children is recognized as a contingency for benefit purposes. A comparative focus on these last points can be found in work which studies differences between countries in the overall package of child support (for example, Bradshaw and Richardson, 2009).

Conclusion

Writing on comparative public policy in the last century, Heidenheimer et al. (1990, p. 265) concluded their chapter on income maintenance policy with the observation that 'no country has tried entirely to replace market based determinations of purchasing power. Common policy tools in social insurance and means-tested social assistance are used, but in different combinations and with different emphases.' However, the issues about the choice of policy tools need to be seen in relation to concerns about policy outcomes, driven by variations in commitment to tackling poverty and reducing income inequalities.

There is a risk that preoccupation with systems loses sight of the underlying questions about policy output, and the effectiveness of redistributive measures. Much depends here on the detail of benefit systems: who qualifies and how income and assets are taken into account. Hence, the main concern of this chapter has been consideration of the possible policy tools in a way that may seem paradoxical – means testing, which seems to conform to the Marxian slogan 'to each according to their needs', has tended to be advocated by the political Right, while the extension of social insurance has particularly been advocated by the Left. The source of this paradox lies in the fact that while means tests may seem to offer the most efficient way of addressing poverty, their effects are socially divisive. Contrastingly, social insurance offers a more solidaristic approach to income security and represents the 'paradox of redistribution' (Korpi and Palme, 1998), where greater income security for higher earners achieves better redistributive outcomes than targeted measures, and commands universal support, because all are potential beneficiaries.

The argument for social insurance linked to labour market participation was never particularly strong in nations without near full employment. Since the last quarter of the twentieth century, economic, social and demographic changes have engendered difficulties in sustaining social insurance even in its European heartland. The advocates of social insurance have been forced to think again about the model it offers. Some have reluctantly accepted policy shifts that move social assistance back into a central role in income security, but have sought to reinforce solidarity through the protection of rights to support. Others, such as those who have made the case for basic income, are trying to establish new ways of establishing a universalist core in this area of policy. To explore these concerns, further attention needs to be given to the issues of work and employment, which are the focus of Chapter 6.

6

Work and employment

Introduction

The title of this chapter uses the terms 'work' and 'employment' with the aim of avoiding the implication that those who are not in formal paid employment are not working. This is important for both a historical perspective on the way modern labour markets emerged from earlier models of the organization of work and for a geographical perspective that recognizes that there are many workers around the world whose activities are not identified within formal definitions of employment. The distinction also highlights the limitations of modern economic analysis focused on markets, treating labour as a 'commodity'. These contextual issues are explored before going on to discuss available data on employment in order to highlight its limitations and the impact of this on the conclusions that can be drawn from it.

Before proceeding to discussions of policy it is important to explore how complicated an issue employment is for social policy analysis, particularly because of the difficulties of drawing a line between economic and social policy. The discussion of actual policies highlights the work–welfare relationship, and further explores how earlier efforts to simply compensate 'the workless' evolved into 'active' labour market policies with a specific preoccupation with the characteristics of the supply of labour. This leads to a final section on patterns within the global labour market and the significance of migration, which from a welfare perspective is a way to share the global supply of work, but from an economic perspective is a way to circumvent national labour shortages and minimize the costs of employment.

The meaning of work in its social context

The social policy concern with work and employment needs to be seen in the context of the role and meaning of work in human social contexts. It is useful here, at risk of oversimplifying, to identify three alternative models:

1. Work as a collective activity in which people join together, sharing what needs to be done and sharing the benefits. This may further be seen, inasmuch as it extends beyond meeting basic needs, as an activity through which individuals meet their own psycho-social needs for fulfilment, social interaction, personal accomplishment and so on.

2. Work as an activity in which obligations are forced upon some people by others, in which neither the tasks nor the benefits are equally shared.
3. Work as the subject of contractual arrangements in which labour is bought and sold.

Models two and three clearly involve power relationships, but while the first model seems to suggest an equal power relationship, this does not rule out the possibility of coercive human relationships (such as those explored in group studies within social psychology laboratories). In the third model, the notion of a contract can be presented as avoiding the risk of coercion, but that assumption is vitiated by the extent to which one party (normally the employee) experiences implicit coercion because of the possibility of destitution and starvation if a contract is not accepted. On the other hand, while the second model seems explicitly coercive, it may be embedded in a social context in which duties for the weaker party are accompanied by obligations on the stronger one.

All three models have been the subject of philosophical idealization. The first has been seen as the characteristic of an idealized egalitarian past (expressed in the slogan of the 1381 English Peasants' Revolt: 'When Adam delved and Eve span, who was then the gentleman?'), but it has also inspired contemporary communitarian movements. The second has been seen as an idealized inequality, as expressed at the height of the advance of industrial capitalism in a verse of a nineteenth-century British hymn, 'All Things Bright and Beautiful': 'The rich man in his castle, the poor man at his gate, God made them, high or lowly, and ordered their estate' (Cecil Frances Alexander, 1848). The third finds various forms in the philosophy underpinning neoliberal economics, for instance: 'the democracy of the market offers the masses more than the democracy of politics' (Seldon, 1990, p. 103).

The three models should not be taken to provide an evolutionary account of work relations through the ages, as all three models can and do coexist both within and across countries. In the contemporary context, the first model is apparent not just in widely dispersed examples of small-scale communitarian movements, but also as an aspect of ad hoc collaboration between those in situations of extreme deprivation. The second appears in the context of both structural inequalities, such as those between women and men, and the continuing existence (or reinvention) of various forms of slavery, termed 'modern slavery' and including child labour. The presence of the third is apparent both in the highly regulated labour markets of advanced economies and in the emergence of global labour regulation, although the international legal framework underpinning this is at present very limited. What is important to recognize are the ways in which, as already noted, power inequalities dictate so-called contractual arrangements. The case of global labour regulation illustrates these inequalities, tilted as it is firmly in favour of powerful business interests, to the disadvantage of millions of workers around the world.

These models have been identified here because of the extent to which social policy involves interventions that may mitigate or reinforce their operation.

Behind each of them there lies a work obligation, although based on different ideas regarding to whom the obligation pertains and whether it is enforced through mutual responsibility, necessity or law. In fact, all three notions currently operate as sources of societal pressure and unrest where obligations are not met. Since the financial crisis in 2008, the obligations of those who had hitherto successfully exploited others have come under greater scrutiny, raising important questions about the circumstances in which the expectation of work is waived. For example, under what circumstances do societies accept there are people to whom the work obligation does not apply? And what form and extent of activity meets this obligation? The simplest kinds of policies about work (or lack of it) involve the identification of categories of people whose support can be implicitly, if not explicitly, provided without an obligation to work. Historically this has included, for example, the very young, the very old and those in poor health. More recent developments involve provisions in relation to motherhood, acceptance of disability affecting the capacity to participate in the labour market, a widening of expectations of childhood dependency to embrace education and training and the emergence of the notion of retirement as a 'chosen' rather than forced option. In addition, as discussed in Chapter 5, provisions such as CCTs have also evolved, which create indirect obligations, mostly for parents, to ensure that their children will become part of the productive workforce in the future.

More controversial are extensions of these assumptions where the work obligation may be waived not because of the characteristics of individuals but because of the lack of work. In public policy this tends to be framed in terms of the formal expectation of work: as employment. Comparative statistics tend to reflect a view of employment dominated by assumptions drawn from labour economics in capitalist markets with a clear 'formal' view of what employment means, and therefore an explicit identification of the incidence of *un*employment with some (conceptually and statistically problematic) identification of the need to exclude from this equation those 'excused' from labour market participation.

Labour as a commodity

Standing (2011, 2014), in an important analysis of contemporary developments, writes of the emergence of the 'precariat': arguing that the global market system requires most workers to be flexible and insecure. Relevant as the concept of a precariat class may be, it rests upon a contemporary analysis somewhat limited in perspective in space and time. Over much of the world workers have long belonged to the precariat, unprotected by law or status, and women's patterns of labour market participation have also evolved largely according to this precarious model. On the other hand, among the early industrializing nations (in Western Europe and North America) the process of transition from feudalism to capitalism involved first the development of a market ideology, which certainly aimed to create a precariat, and then a 'counter movement' (Polanyi, 1944) which aimed at a compromise between capital and labour.

The emergent capitalist marketplace treated employment as a matter of an individual contract between capital and labour, indifferent to any inequality of bargaining power. Classical economic theory then treats free marketplace interactions as the guarantor of economic efficiency. In this sense labour is simply a factor of production, like raw materials, capital and land. While some of the classical economists expressed some qualms about the implications of this for the driving down of wage levels, notions of rights affecting employment were absent from the discourse. Many writers on the Poor Laws have explored how this perspective led to a very strict approach to relief for workless people. Polanyi thus quotes the justification used as follows: 'No assessment of wages, no relief for the able-bodied unemployed, but no minimum wages either, nor a safeguarding of the right to live. Labor should be dealt with as that which it was, a commodity that must find its price in the market' (Polanyi, 1944, pp. 117–18).

The point here is that there was a sequence of developments, starting in the middle of the nineteenth century, extending beyond issues about poor relief to shape the relationship between capital and labour. These may be seen as a combination of humanitarian concerns and political pressure, involving emergent trade unions and the development of representative democracy. A model of the relationship between the state and the labour market was developed, involving policies which regulated the world of work. This relationship developed further in the 1930s when massive increases in unemployment in the advanced economies at this time led to further challenges to assumptions that governments should not interfere with the 'natural' working of the labour market. These challenges were further sustained by the requirements of economic management during the Second World War.

In the decades following that war, difficulties in governmental management of the economy led to challenges, especially from the late 1970s, from those who reasserted the classical view that labour markets should operate with the minimum of government intervention. A return to economic liberalism from the 1980s has contributed to undermining the case for protecting workers, at the same time as the global character of the economy makes this increasingly a supranational rather than a national issue.

But what developed in the twentieth century was essentially a policy debate *within* nation states. Many of those states were colonial powers accepting (from the middle of the nineteenth century onwards) that the most direct forms of slavery were no longer legitimate, but still allowing licence to entrepreneurs to operate with no regard to rights among colonized subjects. Indeed, one institution that developed after the end of slavery was indentured labour in which employment rights remained negligible. In the Caribbean, for example, workers were imported, effectively as commodities, from India and China through business deals which left them without rights outside their countries of origin. The modern forms of indentured labour include what is euphemistically called 'guest worker' status, where workers are recruited from poorer countries without their families, and with none of the rights with respect to social protection accorded to full citizens. Since this practice has become more regulated, resort to modern slavery has occurred, where practices range from highly exploitative employment relations to explicitly criminal activities such as human trafficking.

Since the First World War, international institutions have developed that aim to stabilize and regulate the global economy. The ILO, in particular, came into existence in recognition that peace and social justice are inseparable,[1] but also with economic drivers including the desire to level the playing field of international competition through a convergence of labour standards. In many ways the qualitative and quantitative problems of employment were little changed on the 100th birthday of the ILO in 2019, as tensions remain in the relationship between employment policies within nations and policies which attempt to address their global context.

Comparative international data on employment and unemployment

Modern comparative international data inevitably present a picture of employment and unemployment reflecting an approach to the meaning of 'work' which sees it as formal contractual employment in a market context. The implication of the discussion so far is that this will provide an incomplete picture, varying from nation to nation because of differences in the formality of the modes of provision, and expectations about the extent to which productive activity takes an organized form. Reflecting this, two different measures of employment are used in official statistics: labour force participation rates and unemployment rates. Both make assumptions about the potential labour force, using a relatively arbitrary definition of this as comprising people between the ages of 15 and 64. The arbitrariness of this definition is located in its increasingly unrealistic assumptions about the ages at which people will begin and end their working lives.

Comparing labour force participation (employment to population ratios) tends to raise more questions than are answered by the raw figures themselves. For the world, the total participation rate in 2017 was 59.1 per cent (71.9 per cent for men and 46.3 per cent for women) (ILO, 2017a). Looking at the figures by world region, we see highs of over 70 per cent for men in South and East Asia, Latin America and the Caribbean, and sub-Saharan Africa, and a low of 59 per cent in Europe. For women, the low is Northern Africa (18.3 per cent), with highs of over 58 per cent again in sub-Saharan Africa and East Asia.

A key problem with simply comparing labour force participation is that such statistics give no indication of the nature of the work and to whom it is available. This is a topic that has been given considerable attention in the annual ILO reports: *World Employment and Social Outlook* (see particularly the 2016 report subtitled *Transforming Jobs to End Poverty*). It is also problematic, in international comparisons, to separate out the issues about the nature of work from other factors that contribute to inequality. The ILO analyses attempt to capture some of these problems in their presentation of measures other than unemployment, for example those which link work and poverty.

Work is most often regarded in policy pronouncements as the route to avoid poverty. However, there is ample statistical and qualitative evidence to demonstrate the incidence of poverty in work, both in advanced economies (for example in the EU) and in the global South, where work is far less reliable as an indicator of income security (Lohmann and Marx, 2018). The ILO estimates show that 40.1 per cent of the working population in developing economies are in 'extreme working poverty' (workers with an income of less than \$1.90 per day) and 26.2 per cent in 'moderate working poverty' (between \$1.90 and \$3.10 per day).

Another measure is 'vulnerable employment', which is intended to capture both the lack of social protection afforded to informal (family workers) and 'own-account' workers, and their lack of capacity for collective bargaining. Currently, the ILO estimates that 42 per cent of workers globally are in 'vulnerable employment', and in low-income countries the proportion is 76 per cent (ILO, 2018), with a projected increase in numbers in 2018–19, and an overall upward trend towards this type of employment. The vulnerable employment measure has advantages in promoting a more nuanced view of the security of employment, but given the existence of, for example, 'bogus' self-employment[2] and undocumented domestic workers, there are many people who lack both 'protection' and 'voice' in their employment but who fall outside this definition. The ILO (2017b) gives a calculation that 55 per cent of the world's population, for example, is not covered by even one social benefit (around 4 billion people). In addition, the idea of vulnerable employment indicates a voluntaristic assumption that it is the type of work undertaken which has inherent vulnerability, rather than the structural conditions in which it is undertaken that *cause* it to be vulnerable.

In the advanced economies, the issue of insecure and/or intermittent employment is, although different in form, nevertheless increasingly problematic in terms of designing employment (and social security) policies that protect workers and ensure that flexibility is a condition of work that is 'for' workers rather than simply 'of' them. The various forms of employment that have been described as 'precarious', 'atypical' and 'non-standard' (paid work which is less than full time and/or based on a continuous contract) have expanded since the 1980s, and alongside the recessionary aftermath of the 2008 financial crisis and increasing automation are likely to evolve further over the coming years.

Globally, the unemployment rate in 2017 was 5.6 per cent, and according to the ILO's revised data methodologies, after a rise from 2016 the projected rate will be stable to 2019, although the number of unemployed will rise by 1.3 million people. However, this figure masks massive variations between countries, and the way that unemployment is defined in statistics, such as those used by the ILO, is problematic in many ways. The ILO unemployment rate is calculated by expressing the number of unemployed persons as a percentage of the total number of persons in the labour force, which itself is calculated as the sum of the number of persons employed and the number of persons unemployed (see Box 6.1).

Box 6.1: ILO definition of unemployment

The unemployed comprise all persons of working age who were:

- Without work during the reference period, i.e. were not in paid employment or self-employment.
- Currently available for work, i.e. were available for paid employment or self-employment during the reference period.
- Seeking work, i.e. had taken specific steps in a specified recent period to seek paid employment or self-employment.

Official definitions such as that of the ILO are problematic partly because a clear distinction between being in work and out of it is difficult to determine given some of the issues already identified in relation to employment. In addition, although unemployment data might provide a general indication of economic health at world, regional, national or subnational level, and can also indicate differences in rates between women and men, ethnic groups and so on, it cannot capture the more pressing concerns for social policy. These concerns are located more in the challenges of maintaining incomes, regulating working conditions and improving life chances for those whose un/employment experience is simultaneously unpredictable and insecure *and* enduringly so.

Measuring underemployment, or employment that is not full time or continuous, has been of statistical interest to organizations such as the OECD and the European Union since the 1980s and involves the collection of data on 'discouraged' workers, 'marginally attached' workers and 'involuntary' part-time workers and other supplementary measures designed to account for underemployment and its origins. However, these measurements are also inadequate, particularly in relation to gender divisions, since women's incidence of part-time work is both greater than men's and not easily divisible into voluntary and involuntary categories due to the wider gendered division of labour which channels women into part-time work. According to OECD statistics (OECD, 2017e) 16.7 per cent of employment is part-time in the OECD as a whole, and over two-thirds of part-time workers are women.

As already noted, difficulties in the definition of unemployment and its distinction from employment highlight the profoundly problematic terrain of policy making in relation to work. At the macro level, concerns lie in the generation and management of economic conditions in which jobs can be created and sustained, while at the meso and micro levels social policy has to deliver conditions of work that are protective, fair and contribute to human flourishing. The following section considers how policy has emerged to address these different concerns.

Employment policy as social policy

Taking a cue from the ILO evidence on unemployment, underemployment and poor work conditions to explore the policies needed to address these social ills, it is clear that complications, contradictions and controversies remain in the consideration of the way in which policies may be formulated. First, do the remedies for unemployment lie with social or with economic policies? As noted in Chapter 1, a narrow perspective on the scope of social policy is ill-fitted to the contemporary context of global welfare, and similarly the drawing of a line between social and economic policy is also unfruitful for a search for policy solutions. As observed above, around the middle of the twentieth century it became recognized that social policies to protect those affected by widespread unemployment were inadequate if attention was not also given to problems in the capitalist mode of production. It has also been noted that there was a subsequent reaction against that view. While the conflict between these positions can be treated as an ideological controversy, the fallout has been a world in which the management of the economy has come to occupy a central place in political debate, making economic and social policy issues impossible to separate.

Employment policy cannot simply be reduced to managing the number of jobs – it also has to address questions of job quality. This is a central issue in ILO publications, where it is clear that work inequalities cannot be expressed simply in employment and unemployment statistics without regard to work security and the rewards for work participation. With respect to the advanced economies, this theme is given a specific comparative emphasis in the worlds of welfare theory discussed in Chapter 3, and is a key element of public and policy discourse, particularly in the European Union. In global terms these issues introduce concerns about the relationship between quantity and quality in the provision of jobs, and the fundamental question is whether these can be addressed together or whether there will always be a conflict between them.

Third, the incidence of unemployment varies markedly from country to country and some countries have close to full employment. The notion of 'full' employment is debatable given that in 2017 even in countries with over 80 per cent of the 25–54 age group in employment and less than 5 per cent unemployment overall (Czech Republic, Germany, Iceland, Japan and Norway), there is lower labour market participation in the 55–64 group, and beyond that there has been little examination of rates of labour market participation by the increasingly healthy over 65s.[3] However, once countries have achieved these high levels of labour market participation there are various strategies open to policy makers: efforts could be made, for example through training, to bring into the labour force the missing 20 per cent or so, particularly when they have low skills or poor health, or on the other hand to remedy skills shortages in the labour supply. Some unemployment is temporary and might be tolerated as the existence of movement in and out of work provides for labour force flexibility. More negatively, labour discipline may be seen to depend upon there being a 'reserve army of labour'. Countries may also use the global supply of labour as a means to manage the labour market. Since there are substantial differences between countries in the rewards of work, the global movement of workers is a potential equalizing force. However, national altruism is limited in this respect and economic migration may rather be seen, by governments and employers, as a simple way to deal with specific or temporary labour shortages rather than as a contribution to global equality.

Work and welfare

As mentioned earlier, in policy terms work is widely regarded as the 'best route out of poverty'. Indeed, if expressed in a more resolute form, such as 'governments should treat the pursuit of well paid work for all as among their highest priorities', it would meet with little dissent. The more everyday political questions that follow are, in terms of economics, how best to pursue work for all and, in terms of 'social policy', what should be done to protect those for whom that ideal cannot be realized. As discussed in Chapter 6, the nineteenth-century liberal approach to this question was to expect a free labour market to deliver the answers to the first of those questions, but to leave the protection of the labour market's casualties to a minimalist relief system (less eligibility), offering help in conditions that minimized disincentives to labour market participation. Towards the end of that century a variation of self-help emerged, related to the second question, in which (perhaps with state support) individuals insured themselves against unemployment, which seemed to offer a simple social policy to reinforce the market without the coercion associated with the Poor Law.

Winston Churchill, in his days as a social reformer in the UK, argued in 1909 for the introduction of unemployment insurance in terms of its simple qualifying rules: 'I do not like mixing up moralities and mathematics' (quoted in Fulbrook, 1978, pp. 137–8). But early reformers were unable, in practice, to leave the problem to 'mathematics'. Private insurance uses the concept of 'moral hazard' to describe situations in which the insured person can manipulate the system for their own benefit (see Barr, 2001, pp. 21–4), and the designers of unemployment insurance schemes included rules to prevent payment if unemployment could be deemed to be self-inflicted. At the time, this raised a range of questions about the relationships between individuals and the labour market around the conditions of dismissal, work refusal in the absence of decent wages, or on the basis of skills and preferences and so on (see Fulbrook, 1978, for a discussion of many of these issues).

This development in employment–social policy discourse indicates that the relationship between work and welfare raises concerns beyond the relationship between work and cash benefits. The conditions of dismissal and right to refuse job offers highlight the fact that they must be seen in the context of wider questions about the extent to which governments should regulate employment. In nineteenth–century Europe this issue first emerged in concerns about the safety of the work environment, with a particular focus on the protection of women and children. But this opened up into much wider concerns about all the terms under which work opportunities were offered.

A related development concerned the role of the state in relation to injuries and diseases caused by work. Flora and Alber (1984, p. 51) describe 'the introduction of accident insurance or workmen's compensation … [as] the least radical break with liberalism since it could be rationalized by redefining the old idea of liability for individually caused damages'. They go on to report the widespread development of compulsory insurance schemes in Western Europe. However, that rather simplifies a complex subject since the remedies possible run from individual litigation, through the possibility of criminal prosecution, to insurance schemes, and much depends upon the extent to which there are government enforcement agencies. Moreover, issues about 'cause' and 'fault' arise in many cases, and there are wide variations in the acceptance of responsibility for unhealthy or unsafe work conditions. These problems endure within advanced economies, but in a global perspective are writ large in the safety failings in many industries and workplaces in the global South. Fatal accidents through negligence, lack of safety of manufacturing premises and inadequate occupational equipment have been widely reported in India, Bangladesh and Qatar for example, but accountability and future responsibility for prevention is invisibly woven into the intricacies of global value chains, and the social compromises that low-income countries are compelled to make in the face of economic pressures and the power of international investors.

The reformist concern to protect people *from* work is now twinned with rights *to* work, particularly women's rights, but also with action against other forms of discrimination. At the same time the conditions under which work is provided have come under scrutiny, including the extent to which the state (or global institutions) should play a role in regulating the employment contract. A core element of this is the regulation of wages, and in particular legislation to guarantee a minimum wage. In the UK minimum wages have been prescribed for certain trades from as far back as 1909, but the adoption of a universal minimum wage did not occur until 1998. ILO conventions in this regard date back to 1928, and were adopted by many countries; but conventions do not equate to legally enforceable guarantees. The ILO (2014) reports renewed interest in minimum wage policies in the 2000s, with eleven new countries having ratified Convention No. 131 which obliges countries to 'establish a system of minimum wages' since 2000, taking the total to fifty-two. Signatory countries are represented across the world regions, but obstacles remain in terms of coverage of informal and migrant workers, minimum wage levels, exceptions and enforcement mechanisms.

Parental leave is another example of a right for employees available in some countries and circumstances. Here again the issue of any rights to withdraw from work need to be considered in relation to the availability of pay or benefits when exercising this right. There is also an important issue about the fact that work situations need to be organized so that it is truly a parental option, not just a maternal one. Parental leave is also an example of the emergence of pressures originating from a variety of welfare, equality and economic arguments that question the ways in which work can be balanced against life. While policies for a work–life balance are predominantly located in advanced economies, the struggles to reconcile economic imperatives with human obligations are not, and present no less a challenge in countries where care–employment relationships are managed through the precarity of informal work and migration patterns discussed in this chapter.

Standing's (2011) posited emergence of the precariat suggests a neoliberal fightback against many of the developments in labour rights which take the form of reductions in job security (see also Streeck, 2014; Waite et al., 2015): zero-hours contracts, temporary and part-time work and labour-only forms of self-employment (or 'self exploitation'). This fightback drew upon and reinforced a discourse about labour flexibility. Wheelock (1999, pp. 79–80) has characterized country responses to the demand for labour flexibility as a contrast between a 'high road' and a 'low road'. The low road means that 'Global competition and the structural shift to services puts downward pressure on the wages of the unskilled, wages which are already at the lowest end of the market', while the high road relies on the functional flexibility of the highly skilled in emerging industries such as biotechnology and petrochemicals. Considering the implications for welfare states, Hay and Wincott (2012) similarly argue that the extent to which countries compete on 'cost' or 'quality' is a key determinant of the 'competitive-corrosiveness' of welfare spending. The former group includes countries in Eastern and Central Europe, Mediterranean countries and, arguably, the UK, but the choice of 'road' taken has important implications too for welfare state building in the global South.

The shift to 'active' labour market policies

Since the 1990s, substantial policy-making energy has been devoted to shifting employment policy from measures that are considered to be 'passive' (that is, compensating through transfers the costs of not having a job) to a more explicit focus on 'activation' (that is, maximizing labour market re-entry and participation). This active labour market policy (ALMP) includes measures such as employment training and publicly subsidized employment, as well as direct job creation and enterprise start-up incentives for both self-employed individuals and companies. ALMP also includes what are termed 'intermediary services' – the provision of information and support services intended to enhance the employability of their users and match their skills with available job vacancies.

In the global South, ALMP is most obviously operationalized in public works programmes such as the Mahatma Ghandi National Rural Employment Guarantee Scheme in India, which according to official figures for 2016–17 has provided employment for nearly 13 million households – around half of the number of households which have 'demanded' employment.[4] In the North, activation has been most characterized by a more punitive range of job-seeking conditionalities attached to the receipt of income support measures. This form of conditionality is grounded on the assumption that in the changing world of work, labour supply rather than labour demand is the problem, and therefore adaptive behaviours by employees are required more than those by employers.

At state comparison level, it has been suggested that the social democratic countries of Northern Europe have been more easily able to meet the need for labour market adaptation in the face of economic change than liberal or conservative-corporatist models, because their labour market policies were already characterized by weak labour market regulation in terms of numerical flexibility of workers combined with strong social protection (see for example Esping-Andersen, 1999; Huo et al., 2008; Iversen and Stephens, 2008). This notion was captured in the term 'flexicurity', which although originating in the Dutch context, was argued to apply to the Swedish, and particularly Danish labour markets through the 1990s/2000s, and also features in the advocacy of social investment strategies (as discussed in Chapter 5). The picture was rather more blurred than this in the 2010s, however, as it appears that while ALMP remained a key feature of policy discussion among IGOs such as the OECD and ILO, austerity meant that actual spending on these measures has been declining in many countries where it was a key element of employment policy (see Hastings and Heyes, 2018).

Scrutiny of the most recent OECD (2018b) data on labour market policy suggests that, seen in the context of all public employment expenditure on labour market policies (including benefits), ALMP spending is very low. The overall OECD expenditure, as a percentage of GDP, is 1.27 per cent: 0.53 per cent on active policies, 0.74 per cent on passive ones. Bear in mind that the OECD figure for public social expenditure as a whole is about 21 per cent of GDP. Table 6.1 shows the countries on which data are available (note the absence of the UK), contrasting expenditure on active and on passive measures.

Table 6.1 shows a Western European dominance in terms of overall levels of labour market expenditure, and a rough 'correlation' between higher and lower spending commitments on the two measures. The particular Nordic dominance here reinforces these observations. Norway and Hungary stand out as low spenders on active measures but high on passive measures. The presence of France, particularly high on both dimensions, alongside the Nordic countries can be seen alongside the higher unemployment level in that country. A difficulty of interpreting high levels of passive expenditure is that a sophisticated analysis requires taking into account not just unemployment levels but also the extent of (a) coverage of the unemployed population and (b) benefit levels. Many of the lower spenders on passive measures have unemployment benefit schemes that provide both limited coverage and low income replacement rates. Exploring the political and welfare regime context, Vlandas (2013) identifies important aspects of divergence linked to the different elements within ALMP (employment incentives, rehabilitation measures and training) which compete with other party political desires with respect to responses to unemployment, notably direct job

Table 6.1: Labour market expenditure as percentage of GDP

		Passive measures				
		<0.24	0.25–0.49	0.50–0.74	0.75–0.99	>1
Active measures	<0.49	Chile Estonia Japan Latvia Slovakia US	Czech Republic South Korea Lithuania New Zealand Poland	Norway	Hungary	
	0.50–0.99	Australia Canada Israel Slovenia		Germany Luxembourg Portugal Switzerland		Sweden
	1–1.49			Austria Belgium Ireland Italy		Denmark
	>1.50			Netherlands Spain		Finland France

Source: OECD (2017e, statistical annex, table R)

creation, and in countries such as Sweden the capacity to absorb unemployed workers into the public sector. Thus, high levels of active expenditure also mask differences in aims and the philosophies which underpin them.

The global labour market

A key challenge for contemporary employment policy is that although, for the majority of people undertaking and seeking work, the labour market is local, the patterns of demand and supply of labour are driven by a global market. Thus, as alluded to earlier, national decisions regarding the kind of economy desired – high skill, high wage for example – are taken in the wider context of where governments see their countries' competitive advantages as being placed. These industrial and employment strategies (or sometimes the lack of them) influence the types of economic investment that governments are willing to make and their regional location, and this clearly has an impact on both the numeric availability and quality of jobs and the extent to which local skills match these jobs. Where there are gaps in labour markets due to skills shortages, or where the level of remuneration or job security does not match the needs of those seeking work, then governments will tend to enable the use of migrant labour to take up the labour market slack.

The importing and exporting of labour are important drivers in the movement of people and in so-called economic migration (rather than movements driven by conflict or political or social factors). In practice, distinctions between economic migrants and refugees are both imprecise and usually politically motivated based on historical 'immigration regimes' (Castles and Miller, 2003). In the current climate, where conflicts have given rise to significant and sustained humanitarian crises, divisions are also part of a wider policy drive to harden borders. Migration patterns are far more complex than a simple division between those voluntarily seeking work and those who are not. It is both fluid (as people both emigrate and return) and includes those whose work falls into the equally imprecise categories of, for example, domestic labour.

A comprehensive discussion of the issues about migration would go far beyond the concerns of a chapter on work and employment. On the other hand, a discussion that simply focused on those who explicitly move to seek work in another country would provide an inadequate consideration of all the issues about work, in both the importing and the exporting countries. Goldin et al. (2011) distinguish between economic, social and refugee migrants. Clearly their 'economic' category links most closely to work and employment, but it needs to be recognized that their 'social' category may include people who, in practice, join the labour force and in any case are likely to be involved in unremunerated work within households. Their refugee category will also include large numbers of people who will seek work once their status is accepted, as in the future may their children.

The movement of people is difficult to count accurately and, in particular, on account of government controls, emigration figures are likely to be more reliable that immigration ones, though both are likely to be complicated by control evasion. However, the UN's *Population Facts* (2017) reports 258 million international migrants in 2017 (3.4 per cent of the world's population). About 10 per cent of international migrants are refugees and asylum seekers. The United Nations Refugee Agency estimated in 2017 that there are 65.6 million 'forcibly displaced persons' worldwide. Their distribution between regions is 30 per cent in Africa, 26 per cent in the Middle East and North Africa, 17 per cent in Europe, 16 per cent in the Americas and 11 per cent in Asia and the Pacific. In terms of concentration of refugees, there are 2.9 million refugees in Turkey, 1.4 million in Pakistan, 1 million in Lebanon and close to a million in each of Iran and Uganda; 55 per cent of all refugees originate from just three countries: South Sudan, Afghanistan and Syria. Clearly, prospects of work in countries with high concentrations of refugees depend largely on refugees being able to move elsewhere.

The ILO (2015) provides details from a global survey of migrant workers which estimates that there are 150.3 million migrant workers in the world, about 4.4 per cent of all workers. Almost half (48.5 per cent) of migrant workers are concentrated in two broad subregions, North America and Northern, Southern and Western Europe. But there is also a considerable number, relative to the working population, in the Arab states. Table 6.2 provides further details, highlighting two particular (and obviously overlapping) groups: domestic workers and women. Over the last two decades, exploration of the operation of global care chains, as delineated by Hochschild (2000), has improved our understanding of the ways in which the separation of work and care has become even more blurred when viewed through a transnational lens (see also Yeates, 2004, 2012). In this

Table 6.2: Distribution of migrant workers by world sub-region, 2015

	Migrant workers as % of all workers	Domestic workers as % of all migrant workers	Women as % of total migrant workers
Northern Africa	1.1	9.0	25
Sub-Saharan Africa	2.0	7.3	41
Latin America and Caribbean	1.5	17.2	44
North America	20.2	1.7	47
Northern, Southern and Western Europe	16.4	6.2	49
Eastern Europe	9.2	0.6	55
Central and West Asia	10.0	3.6	57
Arab States	35.6	17.9	15
East Asia	0.6	20.4	54
South East Asia	3.5	19.0	44
South Asia	1.3	5.0	43

Source: ILO (2015, table 2.9)

case, we see migrant journeys by unpaid carers from low-income countries to take on the roles of paid carers in rich countries, with consequences for family care needs in their countries of origin (see also Chapter 10). These patterns have important implications for the global gendered division of labour as well as for opportunities for 'decent work', which is a policy goal now directly linked to the SDGs established in 2016.

The approach to 'decent work' developed within the ILO is that this concept can form a basis for the reform of global labour practices, through enabling collective action for workers and formal dialogue among social partners (the state, employers and trades unions). In its transition to a global objective in the SDGs, Goal 8 states the wider aim is to achieve 'full and productive employment, and decent work, for all women and men by 2030' (https://sustainabledevelopment.un.org). One issue with this objective is that it relies on some of the assumptions questioned in earlier sections: the understanding of work as employment, employment as the best route out of poverty and job creation as the ultimate challenge for goal achievement.

This understanding of work and strategies to generate quality jobs emphasizes improvements in employment regulation and the international governance of labour rights, as well as production processes, trading relationships and local economies. While these policy areas are all essential to the improvement of employment conditions and individual livelihoods, there is also a need to better recognize both the operation of gender disadvantage and the increasingly transnational character of employment. Policy continues to rely on assumptions concerning economic behaviour that are disconnected from the complexity of working lives in the contemporary global labour market, and work practices that continue to reflect the globally unequal distribution of resources and opportunities and power between North and South.

Finally, it is important to look at the issues surrounding migration from the perspectives of the 'sending nations', where both positives and negatives can be found. The obvious positive lies in the earning opportunities for those who migrate, but there are also important questions about the extent to which incomes accrue back to the country of origin. Gough and Wood's (2004) regime analysis (see Chapter 3) takes into account the extent to which welfare in many societies depends upon contributions from family members living and working elsewhere in the world. Figure 6.1 shows how important remittances are for many countries, where they represent a considerable share of national GDP.

Figure 6.1: Countries with migrant remittances inflows of 10 per cent or more of GDP (US$ millions), 2018

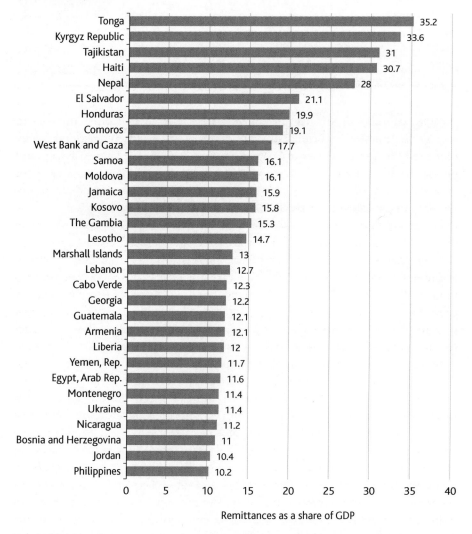

Remittances as a share of GDP

Source: World Bank Migration and Remittances Data, http://www.worldbank.org/en/topic/migration remittancesdiasporaissues/brief/migration-remittances-data

Inasmuch as transnational working is regarded as a temporary phenomenon, benefits may flow back when migrants return, particularly when they bring not just cash assets but also the knowledge and skills they have acquired elsewhere. It may also be noted that retirement to the country of origin may be an important source of benefits. Collier (2013), however, notes a potential contradiction here that the better the deal secured by a migrant worker, in terms of going beyond the status of temporary worker to become a full citizen of the country of destination, the more unlikely it is that benefits flow back to the country of origin.

Conclusion

This chapter has dealt with three interrelated aspects of work and employment that complicate the examination of specific policies. First, there is a complicated relationship between work and employment influenced by key issues about the nature of work and power in societies. While work is essential for human welfare it does not necessarily arise in contexts in which there are formal employment arrangements (relationships between an employer and employee). A great deal of work occurs within family and communal human relationships in which providing and nurturing occurs on a reciprocal basis, but without any formal contract or specific financial arrangement. Where, moreover, it is formalized, such work may occur in a context of inequality and duress, including many situations (even today) where the term slavery may be applicable. Inequalities with respect to gender, ethnicity and national origin may be in evidence. Employment relationships involving a free labour market and perhaps regulated by governments belong largely to the modern world in the global North. And even within that world much work is undertaken under duress and with minimal social protection.

Second, issues about work and employment, and particularly the latter, have an important influence on the configuration of social policy as a whole. It is generally the case that other social policies are underwritten by employment, inasmuch as their funding depends upon work. There are some peculiar exceptions to that statement, including societies where there is a large source of income with respect to which the work input is minimal (the big oil-producing states of the Gulf and Brunei, and some tiny states with large gambling industries such as Monaco and Macao). But in fact, these exceptions merely highlight the fact that provision for non-workers depends upon the controllers of an income stream. In other words, welfare depends upon those who generate and control the resources that pay for it, and linked to this, the dominant view that as far as possible people should provide for their own welfare. This view is expressed, as observed in this chapter, in the idea that work is the best form of welfare. And it is reflected in many social policies where insurance elements are present: the expectation that individuals protect themselves in the good times against future bad times. Of course, the questions about solidarity between the more and less fortunate run through all social policy analysis, but the point here is that it is employment that is seen a providing the vital bridging concept. Accordingly, those who cannot work, and those for whom work does not imply employment, are problematic for these kinds of policy models.

This leads directly to the final point, that policy issues about work and employment often cannot be addressed by individual nation states inasmuch as they have to be addressed with the supranational or indeed global context in which they arise. In many ways the ideal of the welfare state is a product of European nations in the nineteenth century (and particularly just after the Second World War), where notions of solidarity across the population depended upon comparatively full employment, facilitating the acceptance of exchanges of resources where there was a relatively even balance between need and capacity to pay. In the mid-twentieth century, British discourse about the welfare state was dominated by not only the ideas of William Beveridge on social insurance but also John Maynard Keynes, who argued that the roots of unemployment lay in a lack of effective demand by industry, a problem that could be tackled by government policies to stimulate demand (Keynes, 1936). Together they could be seen as pointing towards a vision of the future in which progress would depend upon the coordination of work and welfare. That vision has been subject to sustained challenge, undermined by economic change but also by the widespread rejection of a view of the role of government that gave priority to economic management on behalf of citizens.

In many parts of this book the limitations to that vision have been noted, in particular its assumptions about gender and family roles. Here the emphasis is rather on the idea that it was a vision (in the North) of solidaristic exchanges, and thus remedial policies, that could be contained within single unitary states. But even at its time of peak validity that vision posed questions for nations that were not able to operate as closed economies (as was true of the larger countries) or did not control economic resources in demand outside their boundaries. More seriously, it also required a recognition that the advantaged nations of the North operated in a post-imperial world in which there were many disadvantaged ones in the South. In analyzing these topics today, there is a need to recognize, as this chapter has, that any aspiration to provide employment policies for the whole world has to face up to the presence of an enormous pool of unemployment worldwide, together with considerable subemployment and unremunerated work. At the same time, the economic advantages of the North are slowly dissipating, so that even the most fortunate nations face social problems that are rooted in difficulties in sustaining a work-based welfare state. While it has been possible elsewhere in this book to write of policy agendas – in relation to health, social care, education and housing in particular – that are to a large extent contained within nation states, this is not the case for work and employment.

7

Education

Introduction

Education is a topic that is sometimes examined as an aspect of 'social policy' and sometimes disregarded or given separate treatment in both academic scholarship and data collection: education is not defined as social policy in OECD statistical compilations, for example. There is a substantial specialized comparative education literature within which connections to the wider social policy literature are relatively absent, and similarly, education for development debates are also often marginal to the concerns of studies of global social policy. Within the education studies literature, there is a large body of small-scale comparisons, but international organizations such as the OECD have an interest in commissioning research and assembling international databases that has increased since the 1980s.

Aside from its purpose as a means to general human enrichment, the interest of ostensibly economic organizations in comparing education systems and their outcomes reflects the role of education in the accumulation of 'human capital', and its use in the competitive strategies of nation states within the global economy. The national context of education policy and provision may therefore be indicative of both political progress – and how governments respond to the challenges of popular demands for knowledge and the widening of opportunities – and economic progress, and the ways in which politics reconciles these demands in educational investment arrangements. Since the 1980s, along with the expansion of global markets, policy attention to the economic purpose of education policy has largely suffocated debate about its purpose in advancing social progress, and thus the discussion of the shape of national educational provisions is closely allied to national economic growth strategies. Before proceeding further with the exploration of the relationship between education and social policy, some illustration of the contemporary patterns of education expenditure highlight how countries differ in their overall investment decisions.

National expenditure on education

Figure 7.1 shows both a snapshot of the level of national spending on education and also the proportion of this spending which is drawn from private and public sources. Although there is a mixed economy of education provision in all countries there are clearly some countries where the balance is far more in favour of the state than the private sector (the Nordic countries for example), in comparison to countries where private spending is more significant. The latter is the case

Figure 7.1: Public and private expenditure on primary, secondary and post-secondary, non-tertiary education as a percentage of GDP in OECD countries, 2015

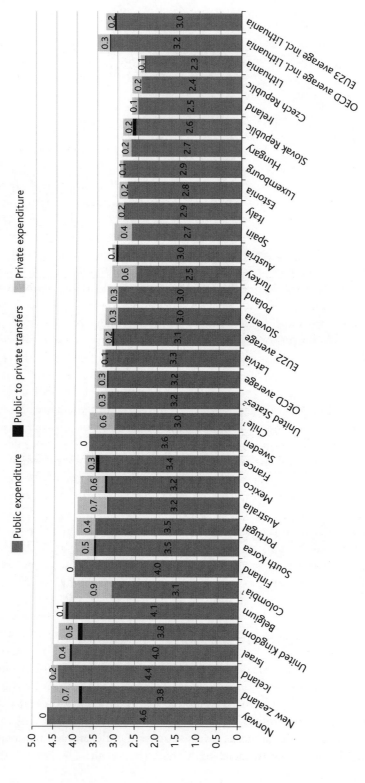

Notes: [1] Year of reference 2016; [2] Net student loans rather than gross, underestimates public transfers.

Source: OECD (2018c, graph C2.2); total expenditure on educational institutions as a percentage of GDP by source of funds (2015), cited in public, private and international sources, by level of education, in Financial Resources Invested In Education, OECD, https://doi.org/10.1787/eag-2018-graph137-en

in the liberal Anglophone OECD countries as well as South Korea, Japan and several Latin American countries.

Table 7.1 sets out some recent expenditure figures (for varied dates from 2013 to 2017) from selected countries beyond the OECD, in order of highest to lowest in terms of spending. There are no recent figures for China, Nigeria or Saudi Arabia for example, and the figure for Malawi is an estimate. As noted in previous chapters, it is difficult to situate expenditures as proportions of GDP in relation to countries where low GDP and low public expenditure are generally characteristic. The proportion of GDP figure in itself can only give a relative indication of the importance of education spending since GDP changes year on year, and it is always necessary to be reminded that the level of spending tells us neither how the funds are distributed nor what outcomes are achieved.

Table 7.1: Education expenditure as a percentage of GDP, selected countries

Country	Education expenditure as % of GDP	Year
Brazil	6.25	2015
South Africa	6.13	2017
Vietnam	5.65	2013
Argentina	5.57	2016
Jamaica	5.27	2017
Turkey	4.29	2015
Malawi	4.03	2017
India	3.84	2013
Russia	3.82	2015
Iran	3.79	2017
Indonesia	3.58	2015
Hong Kong SAR	3.31	2017
Mali	3.09	2016
Sri Lanka	2.81	2017

Source: UNESCO Institute for Statistics http://data.uis.unesco.org/

Education and social policy

Wilensky (1975) argued against the study of education policies as belonging within social policy analysis due to an apparent absence of a direct influence on social equality. Busemeyer and Nicolai (2010) reject that view on the grounds that the indirect influence of education may be considerable. Their position is well established in sociologically informed class analysis as well as in contemporary policy debates on social mobility. This disagreement points us towards a range of explanations: seeing education and other aspects of social policy as complementary; seeing the forces that drive them both as separate but interacting; and seeing them as alternative approaches to social goals.

The case for the first of those views rests upon evidence that the same political forces that drove the development of other social policies also drove the growth of educational provision. Relevant here is the place of education alongside other social policies in political arguments. In terms of outcomes, the evidence for such a perspective lies in the relatively strong relationship between education spending and other social spending. Busemeyer and Nicolai (2010) demonstrate this using OECD data from 2005, and Figure 7.2 provides more recent data to support that position. Rough correlations of this kind only provide limited indications, however. Busemeyer and Nicolai (2010) note that several countries (Germany, Greece, Japan, Spain and Italy) appear to spend less on education than indicated by their general spending, while the opposite applies in the US, Switzerland and New Zealand. Furthermore, the Nordic nations stand out as exceptionally high spenders on education. But this also tends to support the second of the views suggested above. What we may be looking at here are general tendencies among the richer nations, while other factors such as population size and the demographic profile of any nation are likely to influence the level of spending for particular age groups. Further analysis needs to explore the drivers of expenditure in each case, a point we return to later in two ways: one which rests on efforts to apply regime theory to education, the other using historical analysis to examine the relationship between education and society.

The third view, of education and other social policy (particularly social security) as alternative avenues to similar goals, is more contentious. It is expressed in general terms by Hega and Hokenmaier (2002, p. 145), who argue that scholars such as Heclo (1985) and Castles (1989) have indicated that there is a 'trade-off' between public investment in education and the expansion of other social programmes. They claim that state support for public education programmes and social protection programmes should be considered as alternative welfare state policies, and that welfare regimes are distinguishable by the extent to which 'budgetary preference' is given to either social protection systems and income guarantees or public education systems as a means to improve social mobility. What is important to stress here is the extent to which education has been seen as an alternative road to social equalization. It can be seen as a feature of ideological positions that reject direct efforts to redistribute resources, in favour of the enhancement of social mobility through education. Busemeyer and Nicolai (2010, p. 496) refer to the notion of the 'social investment state' (see the discussion in Chapter 5), which regards this as a feature of 'a new conception of social rights in which participation in labour markets is the prime motivation and goal'.

Efforts to either apply regime theory in Esping-Andersen's original form or develop a new kind of regime theory for education that attends to developments in a wider range of countries, have to grapple with ways of addressing these contrasting perspectives. To do this, questions must be answered about how the historical development of education may be explained. But if a regime theory is to be applied then there must also be recognition of the extent to which the political explanation that lies at its heart needs to be modified with reference

Figure 7.2: Education expenditure and social expenditure as a percentage of GDP, 2015 or latest available

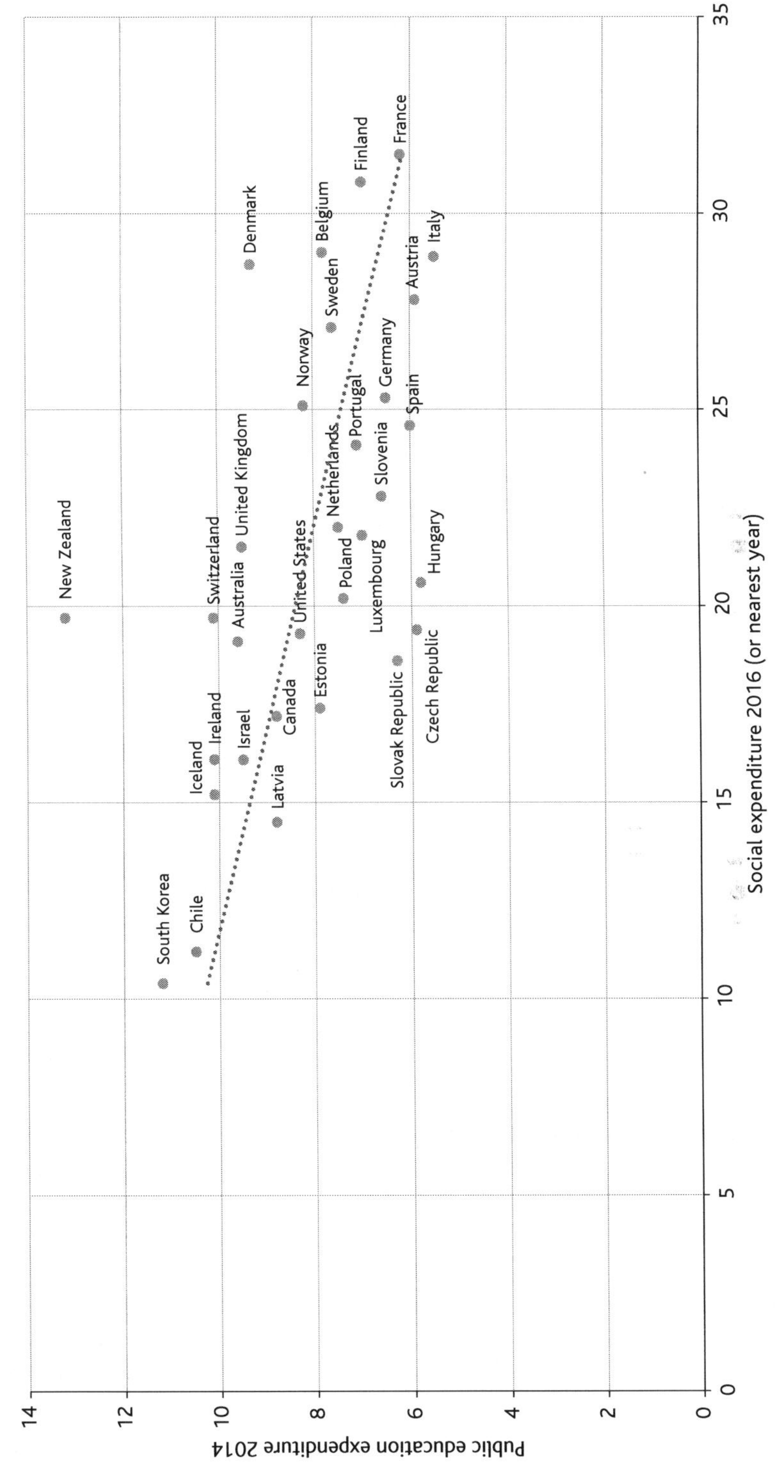

Source: OECD (2017a)

to, on the one hand, the requirements of capitalism as explored in 'varieties of capitalism' theory, but on the other hand, the impact of cultural forces and particularly the role of religion. On the sociological dimensions, regime theory is much less robustly developed. The next section thus explores some key elements of the relationship between education and society.

Education and society

The state's role in education in all industrialized societies is obvious and significant, but it is also important to see the variety of ways the family, the market and the community are involved in education. While there is a great deal of formal and institutionalized activity in the field of education, it is also the case that in many respects, individuals educate themselves. Once literacy is achieved, most often in childhood, the personal capacity to secure knowledge is hugely expanded. Before the arrival of universal formal education in many societies, people were often self-educated, and colloquial reference to the knowledge and wisdom acquired through participation in everyday life is often used as a means to valorize personal experience. Whether education is acquired within or outside formal institutions, the success of individual flourishing remains likely to partly depend upon the support of families and friends, and the role of these 'teachers' (in the broadest sense) in socialization has been identified as a core element of human need (Doyal and Gough, 1991).

The evidence from the expenditure data quoted in Figure 7.1 shows that the private sector has some role in education in all OECD countries, and clearly education is something that may be purchased, but there is also a range of ways in which publicly provided education systems are supported by private expenditures. The costs of education extend beyond the provision of teachers and buildings to, for example, books, writing materials and technology (for example, computers and laboratory equipment), as well as travel and maintenance costs such as food and accommodation. There are many situations in which all or part of these costs are met by parents or students. Where state expenditure is limited, education systems depend heavily on these additional private inputs, but even in the systems with the highest levels of state funding there is scope for private expenditures by individuals to enhance the resources available to them. Finally, participation in education can also generate opportunity costs, where it limits participation in other activities, most significantly employment. Families often have to forgo the earnings of children and young people to enable them to secure education.

There are other social institutions between the family and state (Archer, 1979). A particularly salient institution in the development of education in many societies has been organized religion. Religious bodies have an interest in education as a means to inculcate a set of beliefs, and organized religion has been often a rival to the state for control over education systems. The development of nation states in Europe and conflicts over religion went hand in hand as part of the same story. The identification with, or protection of, particular religious beliefs played a key part in state formation, and similarly during the colonial period religious missions shaped the education institutions of many countries in the global South. Religion continues to influence educational provision in much of the world, often in conflict with the drivers of secularization.

Two separate, and sometimes conflicting, themes dominate explanations of the emergence of public educational provisions. One of these concerns what will be called 'citizenship', while the other concerns economic interests. It has already been established that individuals have an interest in securing education. It gives them access to a range of ideas, symbols and beliefs which may be loosely described as 'culture', and so opens up possibilities for religious and political participation. In this sense education may be seen as being historically transformed from the preserve of aristocratic and religious elites to a public good that is more widely shared. Opening the system up in this way was therefore among the demands of democratizing movements in Europe in particular. The specific interaction between the role of democratization in bringing demands for mass education, and the extent to which demands for democracy follow upon the expansion of education, is complex, and has become even more so in the context of development in the global South.

It is, however, possible to identify reasons why elites and states promoted education before democratization, and religion is of key significance here too. Where a state's claim to rule over a territory was based upon the assertion that there was a single religious community, it was in the state's interest to promote that religion and ensure its dominance. Alternatively, where there are religious divisions, as historically in the Netherlands and currently in countries such as Nigeria, compromise arrangements are likely to be sought eventually. But the establishment of nation states depended on other aspects of culture as well as religion: language in particular was important. Also important were things like the acceptance of a common currency, common ways of measuring and common conventional and legal practices to deal with matters of dispute. Education could play an important part in achieving a measure of unity, particularly if it began to impose a common language. Green's (1990) exploration of the role of education in state formation considers these processes, particularly in relation to Germany in the eighteenth and nineteenth centuries. In some studies of the role of education in the colonial period, and in countries where there is external domination, it has been suggested that education may play a key role in 'cultural domination' (Welch, 1993; Brock and Alexiadou, 2013).

Green's analysis goes on to show how, as the activities of states increased in complexity, so their educational needs increased. The development of an army, a civil service and a legal system had to move outward from dependence upon a narrow, educated elite, to draw in a wider range of citizens. Moreover, even the education of an elite is something that states find risky or inefficient to leave entirely in private hands. The tendency was inevitably for states to want to control elite education. Then, as will also be suggested with regard to health policy, aspirations to state control tend to generate pressures for subsidy or direct provision.

There are obviously very different concerns embedded in narrow arguments that people should be educated to read and write a common language, and to participate in basic political and legal institutions, than those which relate to the education, socialization and selection of governing elites. However, the two are connected by democratization. One key demand of democratic and radical movements has been for state interventions to open up elite education to other social groups. Another has been that the education of citizens should be a common process, in which elite and mass share, as far as possible, common educational experiences (Dewey, 1976). In the post-colonial world, the conflict of competing aims of identity assertion and state power is complicated. This is, as Brock and Alexiadou (2013, p. 28) suggest, not only because English is 'a global language of international discourse' but also because states are mostly formed with ethnically permeable borders where the privileging of one language over another has consequences far beyond education provision. To illustrate, the authors cite the example of Malaysia where the promotion of the use of Bahasa Malaysian in formal education in order to facilitate unity and control the advance of Indian and Chinese linguistic alternatives has proved problematic.

The issue of competition for scarce opportunities touches on the second theme of this section, the 'economic' arguments for education and their influence upon the state. It is not a passion for democratic participation which motivates most pressure for more state support for education, it is a belief that education provides a route to upward mobility. For human capital theorists (for example Becker, 2008; see also Blaug, 1970), this is an obvious truth. However, the demands of employers for specific or general qualifications and their selection of employees on the basis of educational qualifications should not be regarded, as suggested by this theory, as sufficient evidence in itself that the educational efforts that produced those qualifications are essential to the needs of the economy. Rather, differences in educational attainments provide simple approaches to employee selection. The key point is that educational achievement, whether intrinsically necessary or not, is often important for individuals in competition for economically advantageous positions in industrial society. This is what generates intense concern about education in democratic political systems, stimulating demands for state provisions and expenditure and fuelling the pressure for equality of opportunity in education.

Employers are also interested in ensuring that the state shoulders the main burden of the costs of education. Their interest links with the citizenship and culture issues, in that economic activity requires the use of shared linguistic and mathematical skills and the capacity to participate in a common economic community. But it implies an approach to education that is much more pragmatic than the concerns about the sharing of a complex common culture embodied in traditional approaches to elite education. It may also embody views about topics the education system *should not* cover, perhaps including those encouraging and enhancing aspirations about citizenship rights. Some analyses of educational policy have stressed the strongly capitalist-determined model of education deriving from that perspective. It is argued that employers prefer education to shape a disciplined and conformist labour force, rather than active citizens who may seek to challenge the inequalities of rewards and power implicit in the labour market contract. In the 1970s, radical analyses such as those of Bowles and Gintis (1976, p. 48) suggested that the demands of capitalism have created a narrow model for state education. More recently, this idea can be identified with the 'social investment' agenda, which makes links between educational content and the needs of capital (with country variation) much more explicit.

Marxist theory regarding the need for the state to socialize some of the costs of capital is amplified in various ways with the notion that the state has economic needs of its own. In the field of education this has taken its strongest form in emphasis upon the need for substantial educational investments in 'basic education' in low-income countries, although not necessarily via the state (Bonal, 2002). In economically advanced societies the 'development' concern involves a preoccupation with maintaining competitive advantage over other nations. Governments and commentators may then identify weaknesses in the education system, such as a lack of qualified engineers, or a lack of scientific innovation, or the dominance of a teaching philosophy that undermines the entrepreneurial spirit. While there is a need to critically assess such arguments (see Hüfner et al., 1987), this concern has had an important influence upon comparative work, encouraging a league table view of education systems in which questions are raised about whether the perceived inadequacies of economic attainments of particular nations is attributable to aspects of their education systems.

Competing models may be specified, against which an education system's performance on this issue may be evaluated:

- One ideal may be that education should not sort individuals for different occupational opportunities at all. In this sense education would be a process of socialization for citizenship in an egalitarian society. It will be apparent that this is an educational ideal that is not translated into practical policies, but it does serve as a model of aspiration for many educationalists and has influenced some educational developments, for example in curriculum content.
- An alternative egalitarian ideal is to see education as contributing to equality of opportunity in a society, and particularly as ensuring that its outcomes (which ideally lead to job opportunities) are not determined by criteria other than innate ability. There are difficulties in determining what that last expression really means given the extensive nature/nurture debate about the determination of performance in education and particularly in tests. Nevertheless, a great deal of attention has been given to efforts to arrive at educational systems which do not discriminate in terms of race, gender and social class.
- The third alternative involves the rejection of the other two. It has two alternative but closely related forms. One of these is embodied in the preoccupation with the economic function of education. It suggests that the concern about inequality hampers the efficiency of education in equipping people for the labour market. The object should be to ensure that the system

is efficient for each strata in society, educating or training them to become effective employees. The other form of this perspective is rather more content to see education as socializing individuals for their, largely predetermined, stations in life.

The exploration in this section suggests that versions of this third alternative dominate in much contemporary education policy making. This is particularly manifest when a comparative and global view of education is explored, as will be shown.

Characterizing and comparing education systems

Figure 7.1 and Table 7.1 showed how public education expenditure needs to be seen in a context in which private expenditure is often significant. Private education is not left entirely unregulated by government, as quality concerns and child protection issues prompt some controls. It should also be noted that – as in other policy areas like health and social care – there are various ways in which there are public–private mixes. In some countries there is a combination of public finance and private provision. Private providers will include religious and other voluntary groups as well as profit-making bodies.

Exploring the public–private relationship, particularly with respect to education expenditure, seems to suggest the applicability of Esping-Andersen's regime categories for the comparison of education systems. Iversen and Stephens (2008) and Jensen (2011) provide support for that contention, drawing on varieties of capitalism theory and elaborating with a notion of 'welfare production regimes' (Estevan-Abe et al., 2001). Iversen and Stephens suggest a need to consider differences between education sectors (from pre-school through primary and secondary to tertiary). Busemeyer and Nicolai (2010) add this sectoral element to the problems of comparing expenditure, but also suggest that the mixed economy of provision (state, church, private sector) and extent of decentralization also need attention. They use cluster analysis to arrive at 'three relatively robust groups of countries: Northern Europe, the Mediterranean countries, and the English-speaking countries (plus Japan)' (2010, p. 499). Their analysis does not feature the more recent OECD members, but they elaborate with three subclusters within the large Northern European group as set out in Table 7.2.

Table 7.2: Northern European divergence in models of education provision

Finland, Sweden, Norway	Germany, Austria	France, Netherlands, Belgium, Ireland
State led dominance; commitments to comprehensive education	Segmented system; strong public–private partnership with respect to vocational education	High public spending except at the tertiary level; widespread non-state (particularly religious) provision

Source: Adapted from Busemeyer and Nicolai (2010)

Busemeyer and Nicolai's analysis implicitly raises the underlying question for regime analysis relating to its ideal types which was discussed in Chapter 3: that it is only as one moves to subcategories within regimes that many of the important questions emerge. Before leaving this subject, however, it is pertinent to look briefly at efforts to apply regime analysis to, on the one hand, tertiary education and, on the other, pre-school provisions.

The quotation from Hega and Hokenmaier (2002) above raised the possibility that there is a trade-off in social policy between social security and education investment which affects regime choice. A study that does seem to offer some support for such a proposition is reported by Pechar and Andres (2011). They divide nations using Esping-Andersen's typology and suggest that there seems to be some sort of trade-off between higher education expenditure and other social expenditure – but only in a comparison between conservative and liberal regimes. In social democratic regimes, as is the case with education expenditure in general, higher education expenditure and high levels of other social expenditure coexist. However, Pechar and Andres' work also highlights crucial qualifications to the general descriptions, with regard to different kinds of tertiary education and the kinds of funding models (particularly the variations in the mix of tuition fees, loans and grants). This points us towards the need to disaggregate the sectors that make up the education policy system in order to make sense of the complexities of policy choices.

Perhaps a better place to begin to consider the world of education systems requires moving away from issues raised by regime theory to look at structural considerations: these include when education begins and ends (and what the related limits are for compulsory education), how education systems are divided along age lines and, often closely related to this, the ways in which they offer forms of specialization or stratify by ability as well as age (and how they are therefore structured according to a nation's perceived economic needs).

In most advanced economies there is comparatively little divergence in the number of years spent in primary and secondary education. The OECD reports that on average, from the age of 5 to 40, individuals in the member nations will spend seventeen years in full-time or part-time education with a range from fifteen years in Mexico to nineteen plus years in Australia and the Nordic countries (OECD, 2016a, p. 283). By contrast, UNESCO (2016) reports that there are between five and eight years of compulsory schooling in the global South compared to between nine and thirteen years in the North. In some countries, for example Mozambique, there is no compulsory schooling. The report also estimates that in the world as a whole, there were 263 million children not in school in 2014, of which about 61 million were of primary school age. Table 7.3 shows the regions where most of these children lived and gives an indication of the significant, although narrowing, gender differences.

The latter stages of educational participation are also subject to significant differences: within the OECD an average of 36 per cent of today's young people across OECD countries are expected to graduate from tertiary education at least

Table 7.3: Gaps in school enrolment by region and gender

Region	% of males out of school	% of females out of school
Sub-Saharan Africa	19.2	23.3
Oceania	8.9	14.3
Western Asia	7.8	13.7
Southern Asia	5.8	6.8
Latin America and the Caribbean	6.2	5.8
World	8.9	9.7

Source: UNESCO (2016, p. 3, table 1)

once before the age of 30 (OECD, 2016a). Figure 7.3 shows quite wide variation between countries. While the term 'graduate' is applied to all, the OECD note that on average 'in 2014, a majority of first-time tertiary graduates (72%) earned a bachelor's degree, 12% earned a master's degree and 16% earned a short-cycle tertiary diploma' (2016a, p. 316). These OECD statistics include India, Mexico, Indonesia and China but do not extend to the many low-income countries in the global South where the availability of a tertiary education is limited, and students with the means may need to travel to other countries to secure this education.

In considering the 'social' dimensions of education policy and their impact on length of time in education and the consequent positional goods acquired, an important division concerns the extent to which nations attempt to give children a common schooling regardless of ability or performance. Generally countries adopt unitary (comprehensive) systems for children up to the age of 11, with

Figure 7.3: Percentage of tertiary graduates, 2016

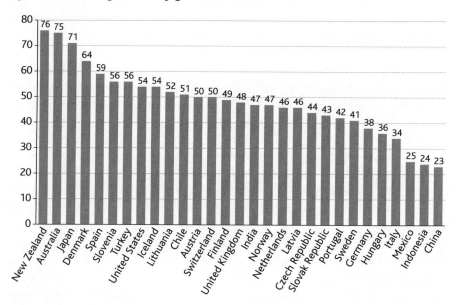

Source: OECD (2016a, chart 3.1)

some provision for children with exceptional needs. In some societies, even at this early stage performance differences affect progress between grades (Switzerland, France, Japan) and children do not automatically move through the system with their age group. After the age of 11, systems move at various speeds towards some degree of educational segregation. The rationale for this lies in the differentiation of educational needs based upon future occupational expectations and economic drivers. This brings us to issues about educational outputs, where the OECD has played an important role in the development of comparative studies through its Programme for International Student Assessment (PISA) programme, which itself is a factor in determining how states see the relationship between economic drivers, occupational or skills-focused expectations and investment in education.

Education outputs: the PISA data source

The OECD's PISA programme is now a well-established source of comparative data on education performance (Meyer and Benavot, 2013). The data from the 2015 survey, which was largely concerned with science studies, were published in December 2016 and secured substantial media attention as countries responded to its results, and their placement in the league tables. The OECD press release (OECD, 2016b) reported: 'Singapore outperforms the rest of the world in the OECD's latest PISA survey, which evaluates the quality, equity and efficiency of school systems. The top OECD countries were Japan, Estonia, Finland and Canada.'

The same press release observed that 'high levels of youth unemployment, rising inequality, a significant gender gap, and an urgent need to boost inclusive growth in many countries, mean more must be done to ensure every child has the best education possible' if Goal 4 of the SDGs (achieving inclusive and equitable high-quality education and promoting lifelong learning opportunities for all) was to be met by 2030. However, there is continuing debate about the usefulness of Goal 4 of the SDGs itself in measuring progress in education (Unterhalter, 2019), and PISA is also subject to considerable critique in terms of its use as a tool in the transnational governance of national education systems (Grek, 2009).

In a review of the global-national testing frameworks and their impact on educational freedom, Lingard et al. (2013) suggest that a 'global panopticism' has emerged with 'testing' as the key driver of policy change. The fact that PISA has been extended with the 'PISA for Development' (PISA-D) tests designed for low-income countries (Addey and Sellar, 2018) adds support to this view. Addey and Sellar suggest that PISA may have a role for countries in demonstrating 'cognitive' and 'normative governance' and the sharing of values and evidence for policy, and it may also enable leverage to improve educational provision in low-income countries, but in the global North it is most often used as a proxy measure of countries' competitiveness and a means to influence their educational investment decisions.

Many scholars are highly critical of the assumed functional equivalence of testing across countries which is inherent in PISA, which neglects the range of social, political, economic and cultural differences that affect educational achievement and the impact of policy. The flavour of this critique is expressed in a nutshell by a letter to *The Guardian* from an education statistics expert, Harvey Goldstein (2016), doubting that PISA results

> tell us anything useful about the relative performance of different educational systems.
>
> Each of the 70 or so countries taking part in Pisa has a unique educational curriculum, structure and method of delivery, that reflect tradition, politics and social norms, and it makes little sense to try and judge them using a common test. This is in addition to all the myriad problems associated with translating across languages and cultures; the fact that the vast majority of test questions are not released for public perusal; and the technical difficulty of making any valid comparisons over time.
>
> In addition, the notion that differing performances across nations can be ascribed to the characteristics of national education systems and associated policies is patently absurd. Educational performance is influenced by a variety of socioeconomic factors in addition to what goes on in schools, so that even if we could be satisfied that any given comparison was valid, we could not then simply ascribe it to any particular educational policy or feature.

But it is not just the methodological aspects of PISA that require critical attention; PISA also conceptualizes assumptions about the role of education in relation to the economy, linking these with a simplistic logic to policy transfer, as expressed by Morris (2015, p. 471):

(a) Country A has a high-performing economy, which is largely the result of the education system producing workers with the required skills as evidenced by international tests.
(b) Country B has the opposite features.
(c) If B adopts the critical features of the education system of A, it will improve both pupil performance and the state of the economy.

Even if the PISA data are reliable, its use in this way jumps from correlational analysis to causal explanation, taking education out of its cultural context. It can be seen as adding what Ball (1998) argues are 'performative' metrics to international educational comparisons which further embed the belief that the role of education is primarily to support economic competition between nations. Some value of the PISA dataset lies in the more dramatic contrasts between nations, which can be used to explore variation within individual countries and to indicate some of the social correlates of educational inequality, such as socio-economic status, gender, parental education, migrant status of parents and type of school. However, the place of PISA in supporting competition between nations, especially those of the global North, is more closely linked to the contemporary idea of education as a business. This theme has been given some attention in the discussions about the possibility of identifying East Asian welfare regimes, and their productivist characteristics. However, Ramesh's review of social policy in Hong Kong, Singapore, South Korea and Taiwan concludes that in these countries expenditure is particularly concentrated at the primary and secondary levels, so the 'widely held belief that … [they] place an exceptionally high emphasis on education is not confirmed by public expenditure data' (Ramesh, 2004, pp. 186–7).

Education as a global enterprise

Education as an area of policy has been a central, although sometimes ignored, aspect in processes of globalization. Ball (1990, 2008), for example, provides an early exploration of how the field of education has been established as both a commodity in transnational markets and a means to generate and maintain support for these kinds of markets, particularly through the activities of international organizations, and specifically the World Bank, which has seen education investment through a purely economic lens (Bonal, 2002). Neoliberal economic thinking promotes increasing efficiency by way of competition. This may be just a matter for policy decisions by individual governments, but globalization in this sphere means that there is a worldwide 'education services market' (Ball, 2008, p. 42). Education has become an internationally tradeable product both through the increasing transnationalization of study, notably in higher education, but also in the operation of educational services and service providers (for example in IT services, 'off-the-shelf' programmes of study and the expansion of university-allied international colleges which prepare students for access to higher education courses). How far this extends depends not just on national decision making, perhaps involving 'policy transfer' (see discussion of this in Chapter 4), but also upon the ways international trading rules oriented to 'free trade' and international organizations may promote this. Education policy itself has become globalized with the terms on which it is delivered, that is, through the market, being promoted and advanced by international actors. Part of this marketization is the international measurement, and comparison, of educational outputs exemplified by the OECD in the PISA project discussed in the previous section, but the global drive towards privatized rather than democratized education is a significant trend that runs counter to the ideas of education as a means to general human enrichment, and is even more significant where it is embedded in a development agenda.

Human capital theory has contributed to and channelled debates about the role of education in development, and the global expansion of a Western model has reinforced its function as a means to economic self-help (Brock and Alexiadou, 2013). In practice, the World Bank has contributed to spreading an individualized and privatized model of education through its programmes, which has not been conducive to the development of robust public education systems. As a consequence, educational inequalities have been reinforced (Altbach and Knight, 2007), with the better off making use of both national private education provision and the possibilities in the international market, particularly in higher education, while lack of commitment and investment in the public sector has stalled the expansion and improvement of state education. Such inequalities are then enhanced by the dominance of the English language. Brock and Alexiadou (2013) explore these difficulties in establishing a satisfactory relationship between higher education and basic education in sub-Saharan Africa, and highlight the importance of higher education in the modernizing projects of India and China, for example, but at the cost of the many left behind.

The evidence for the economic value of education tends to rest upon showing how the most educated are the most successful and how rich countries are, broadly speaking, educated countries. But correlations can mislead when translated into causal statements. The economic value of education may be conceptualized in both individual and collective terms. The individual version sees education as making a distinct contribution to the earning power of a person. The reasons why individuals may enhance their earning power through education are multiple, and may owe as much to social conventions about selection as to real increases in their value to society. Herein lies one problem about human capital theory: the real effects of investing in people (that is, allegedly enhancing human capital) may be illusory when viewed from a society wide perspective (Wolf, 2002), however much social processes make it obviously beneficial to the individuals concerned. Another is that its preoccupation is solely with the needs of the formal economy and not with the worth of such investments to society in a wider sense. This focus on the economic 'worth' of educational investment leads to the contemporary post-crisis climate where many of those who have lost their jobs are considered 'zero product marginal workers', i.e. not worthy of the employer investment required to retain them in the occupations in which they were previously employed.

As far as economic development is concerned the relationship between individual benefit and social benefit is further complicated by a point embodied in the title of a book on migration, *Exceptional People* (Goldin et al., 2011), suggesting that those who migrate are among the people most likely to make positive contributions in terms of abilities, skills and entrepreneurship. Discrimination by receiving nations in favour of the more skilled and better educated has the effect of diminishing the pool of talent within their countries of origin that may be crucial for economic progress. It also implies that countries lose the benefits that they might have expected to flow from expenditure on training and education. This issue is particularly pertinent for questions about the ways in which higher education is made available in low-income countries through national institutional investment or through scholarships for international study.

Conclusion

Education policy is a curious and difficult phenomenon to analyze because there is very broad support for it in general terms – nationalist, economic and democratic arguments all come together on this. The controversies materialize in relation to its content, its delivery and its financing. The debate about the content of education is also very confused by the extent that actual educational needs are masked by the uses made of evidence on educational achievement in the job selection process. Here, the whole picture is influenced by the characteristics of elite education. This puts educationalists, particularly those of an egalitarian disposition, in considerable difficulty. Elite education embodies fundamental cultural values – about those parts of historical, literary and philosophical heritages which should be passed down from generation to generation. Herein lies the justification for education *for its own sake* – not for economic growth or social peace or individual advancement. But this comes up against the argument that all should share an education offering benefits beyond the elites, one that then finds a particular, and potentially distorting, strength in the argument that education should be oriented towards the needs of the economy.

This tension lies at the heart of the contemporary educational controversy. Public expenditure crises, together with rising economic difficulties and attendant unemployment, lead many to demand that education expenditure – meaning of course expenditure on the education of those who use public education – should be concentrated on subjects of clear economic relevance. Those who argue for a distinctive egalitarian but not utilitarian approach face a dilemma. Egalitarianism in education has often involved a hostility to traditional education because it transmits a conservative set of cultural values. In that sense there can be some identification with the quest for greater relevance in education. These ideas are sometimes brought together in curious ways; for example a British politician of the Right, Michael Gove, argued in a speech in 2009: 'Schools should be engines of social mobility. They should enable children to overcome disadvantage and deprivation so they can fulfil their innate talents and take control of their own destiny' (quoted in Ball, 2017, pp. 21–2).

The issue here is a need to draw a distinction between the narrowly economic concept of relevance and the wider ideal that egalitarians have in mind. The latter often find themselves uncomfortably placed in education debates between the social capital school of thought and the traditionalists. Their adherence to the 'comprehensive' ideal of a shared education for democracy is under assault from those seeking to strengthen the old divided agenda, which separates a relevant 'mass' education and a traditional elite one. In the struggle of ideas here the utilitarian arguments – evaluating education policy simply in terms of its contribution to the economy – have tended to achieve dominance. This dominance arises partly because public education imposes demands on the public purse, powerful economic actors then argue the case for responses to their demands as employers, and increasingly financialized stakeholders sometimes make competing demands on the fair sharing of tax–funded positional goods.

Comparative studies of education have not engaged very successfully with the concerns of comparative social policy studies to link concerns about the efficacy of alternative models of policy with explanations of the differences between systems. Rather, they tend to highlight shared trends. In the historical analyses of educational development in Europe, aspects of nation building have been stressed, while more recently concerns about levels of economic performance have assumed dominance. That shift has tended to make a 'global' focus rather than a comparative focus important for comparative policy analysis. The concerns about inequalities within countries tend to become masked by the dominance of the view (criticized in Chapter 2 of this book) that education offers the best route to the reduction of inequality. The compelling evidence, on the other hand, of inequalities between countries seems to highlight the need for new developments in education policy. However, the combination of the power of global economic forces and the concerns of the already dominant nations to protect their economies has the effect of reinforcing the human capital perspective, as the yardstick used for policy evaluation and the public perception of education.

8

Housing

Introduction

Property 'markets' have been increasingly significant in policy debate since the 2008 global financial crisis. The notion of 'property' as an abstract factor in economic systems is in sharp contrast with its meaning in everyday life, where to most people it represents the dwelling in which they live their lives. Ideally a dwelling represents a place of security, meeting emotional and psychological needs beyond the more obvious need for 'shelter'. In reality, shelter is the best that many people are able to hope for, and for a substantial proportion of the world's population even shelter in its most basic understanding is inadequate, lacking basic sanitation and amenities and subject to high levels of insecurity. This chapter considers the variety of housing systems and problems that exist around the globe, what they share and how they differ. First, it is useful to consider why housing is often excluded from analyses of the welfare state, and whether the notion that housing is somehow different from other policy domains is helpful to or impedes understanding of worlds of social policy.

The key reason that housing has been considered difficult to assess is that, while good and secure housing can be seen as necessary to satisfy human need (Doyal and Gough, 1991), the fulfilment of that need involves the provision of a property to be used consistently over a long period of time. Such a property is often seen as an 'asset', yielding long-term gain and susceptible to profitable transfer. Those terms – 'property' and 'asset' – apply not just to the form this commonly takes of owner-occupied housing but also to state and private ownership. Furthermore, right of use with respect to the latter is also in a sense an asset, which – it is reasonable to expect – should be protected. That protection, of course, implies a trade-off between the rights of owners and the rights of property occupiers.

The discussion in this chapter will indicate that it is concerns about the latter that have had a considerable impact on housing policy. Nevertheless, there are also issues about the extent to which it is appropriate for the state to tax both the benefits accruing to owners, either continuously or when they are transferred, and the benefits that follow from occupation. As a consequence of this complexity there is, within the comparative analysis of welfare states, a diversity of models to analyze and a lack of comparable data, making it difficult to make any rigorous comparison of like with like. In addition to this, less prevalent and decreasing direct state involvement in its provision, i.e. in the construction and ownership of housing to meet general demand, has meant that where housing is incorporated into welfare states, it is more often through tax measures and social security arrangements, which make allowances and transfers with respect to the cost of housing based on means tests.

Housing is included in both Article 25 of the 1948 Declaration of Human Rights, and Article 11 of the 1966 International Covenant on Economic, Social and Cultural Rights, as an element of the 'right to a standard of living' that is adequate for health and well-being. It is mentioned more implicitly in the 2017 SDGs where Goal 11, Sustainable Cities and Communities, includes a standalone goal to 'make cities and human settlements inclusive, safe, resilient and sustainable'. However, as many commentators and activists have long pointed out, these statements do not translate into a universally realizable guarantee of shelter.

While states are more willing to make guarantees in relation to health and education, claims for housing remain politically and economically problematic. This is partly because housing is directly linked to the economy at the systemic level, as an asset, and partly because adequate housing has implications for both the provision of wider infrastructure and the deeper redistribution of wealth. Thus, while states have obligations to 'respect, protect and fulfil' rights to adequate housing (UN-Habitat, 2014), politically they may regard direct involvement in housing provision and its (re)distribution as going beyond the correction of market failures to a level of economic management inconsistent with the prevailing aim of a global free market. The following sections will consider these two elements of housing provision, since both are at the heart of contemporary housing issues.

Housing and the market

Property has always been a way to store and grow capital, but the significance of housing in the wider global economy is most readily apparent in considering the unfolding of the 2008 economic crisis. Instability in the weakly regulated subprime mortgage market in the US was the catalyst for the subsequent collapse of financial institutions around the world. Tracing the unravelling of highly complex and globally woven financial instruments, linked to the mortgage loans of low-income US households, demonstrated the significance of the housing 'market' beyond its role as a safe 'bricks and mortar' investment for individuals, or even a source for wealth investment and direct accumulation more attractive than any productive industries.

As Stiglitz (2016) points out, this situation negatively affects economies in various ways as investment is shifted from productive activities – manufacturing and services – to 'fixed assets'. Property investment directs capital away from more productive investment and, in recent times, has increased the costs of housing in rental and owner-occupier markets. This both reduces households' income available for consumption and restricts access to these markets to the better off, increasing inequality, insecurity and hardship for those unable to buy or rent.

Wider economic policy clearly has a part in creating and sustaining these conditions as governments make choices on rates of interest, and fiscal arrangements with respect to capital gains and inheritance, for example. Those with property investments also benefit from the collateral these provide and are thus able to obtain further credit in financial markets and expand their property portfolios still further. The risk of housing 'bubbles' is ever present, and again can be seen in the aftermath of the 2008 crisis as some countries such as Spain and Ireland experienced deeper and more prolonged economic crises partly due to credit-fuelled overexposure of the construction industry. While housing construction does create jobs, their security remains dependent on the highly volatile supply of credit, and as demonstrated in the post-crisis period, this sector cannot be relied upon to solve the deeper problems of deindustrialization and unemployment (Norris and Byrne, 2015).

The reformulation of housing, from shelter to its treatment as the material base of an intangible and largely uncomprehended world of financial transactions, has thus created a serious regulatory predicament for governments. This predicament is global in reach, but has yet to achieve solutions outside national boundaries, where policy attention is focused on market access. At a fundamental level, the post-crisis housing problem for governments has been appositely summarized by the former UK Prime Minister Theresa May, who stated, 'We cannot make the case for capitalism if ordinary working people have no chance of owning capital' (Party Conference Speech, 3 October 2018, Birmingham). At the policy level, however, as Aalbers' (2015) periodization of housing development indicates, wherever 'financialised accumulation' underpins the global economy, a focus on market access or the 'commodification' of housing is unlikely to solve the problems of unsustainable housing costs, and the consequent household debt, poverty and housing need that are shared by countries across the globe.

To illustrate the 'unaffordability' of housing, the measure used in the OECD Affordable Housing Database[1] indicates that in 2014, among the rich OECD countries, over half of people in the bottom quintile income group who rent privately, or own with a mortgage, spend more than 40 per cent of disposable income on housing costs in Portugal, Spain, Greece and the US. In the UK, the percentage of private renters in this 'overburdened' group is 59.2, while the figure for owners is 32.9. For those in the bottom quintile owning with a mortgage, the proportion who are overburdened is also over 50 per cent in Chile, Japan, Italy, Estonia, Mexico and France. While these countries may be dissimilar along many dimensions of social policy comparison, the unsustainable weight of housing costs at the household level is clearly a global problem.

Housing and the state

Leaving aside the global financial system, at the national, or more accurately local level, unlike education, health and social security, housing has for the most part been left to the market, linked as it is to land and property, both of which form the fundamentals of civil rights in the Western liberal model of democracy, and to land rights in other political systems. There are historical examples in the advanced economies of the development of 'social' housing alongside the expansion of particular industries. These include housing built by factory owners to house factory workers, or by philanthropists and charitable organizations to meet the needs of specific groups such as older people or ex-military, the development of 'garden cities' and in Austria and Germany the building of 'reform blocks' as dwellings for working-class residents (Hall et al., 2005). But in the wider scope of history and geography, public housing, that is housing which is owned and managed by the state, has played a minor role. The period in which public housing was at its peak was, as Aalbers (2015) indicates, the mid-twentieth century when a confluence of factors compelled states to engage in house building to meet the general need: housing (and its significance in wider public health provision) was understood as a core element of the 'welfare state', and the physical destruction incurred by European countries during the Second World War necessitated physical reconstruction as well as a route to economic and social reconstruction.

Even during this period of accepted state intervention, however, the share and importance of public housing within the overall shape of housing arrangements differed considerably across the global North. The period following the First World War was of course a precursor to the responses to housing need pursued from the 1950s to the 1970s. Added to the destruction of housing during the war was the political and public desire for slum clearance, or eradicating 'squalor' in Beveridgean terms. The level and speed of investment required for construction of high-density housing and large housing estates in the post-war period, and the limited prospects for profit from this building, implied a depth of state intervention in the housing market that has not been replicated since. This housing either passed to the control of local authorities (for example in the UK), or housing associations (for example in France), and was subject to subsidized and/or controlled rents in order to ensure that those on the lowest incomes could be housed. In contrast, social rented housing in the US for example, which accounted for only around 4.3 per cent of housing stock in 2015, has never been more than a limited and residual element of social provision, while in other European countries the figure is much higher – 34.1 per cent in the Netherlands, 26.2 per cent in Austria and 22.2 per cent in Denmark, for example. As Figure 8.1 shows, private renting as the main form of housing tenure remains the case in Germany, Switzerland and other European countries, although the interaction between the idea of social housing and tenure is less easy to discern here, since much social housing in countries such as Denmark and Sweden has historically operated on cooperative, solidaristic models of supply and ownership.

In Central and Eastern Europe, post-war ownership and control of public housing followed a much more centralized model within the broader framework of command economies (Hall et al., 2005). In countries such as Hungary, where from the 1950s until the political transformation in the 1990s, the state determined the rules of housing supply and demand (although combined with high levels of private ownership and, as Kemeny and Lowe, 1998, argue, not without an 'informal' market operating in practice), these governance frameworks have been rapidly and significantly modified by the twin pressures of privatization and financialization of property that now characterize the global accessibility of

Figure 8.1: Percentage share of households by housing tenure, 2014 or latest available

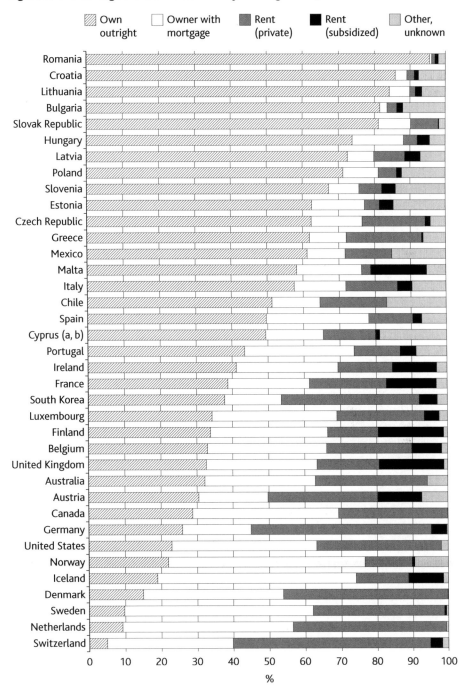

Source: OECD (2016e), Indicator HM1.3 Housing Tenures, http://www.oecd.org/social/affordable-housing-database.htm

shelter. In countries where social policy is emerging in tandem with economic development, housing development in the forms seen in twentieth-century Europe do not register on the policy menu, and instead the state's role in meeting guarantees for shelter is taking different shapes. Where public housing is part of welfare expansion plans, the financing and management of development is contracted out to bodies which are part market/part state and which are expected to find creative ways to raise finance and pay it back.

In China for example, where a particular form of state-controlled marketization has occurred since the 1990s, very little investment in public housing occurred from 1998 to 2005, while in line with most other countries, house prices increased considerably (Zhou and Ronald, 2017a). Zhou and Ronald report that 60 per cent of public housing in China is made up by subsidized owner-occupied housing, but since the 2008 crisis the central government has directed public housing development to shift towards the provision of rented property. This has taken a range of forms to meet central government objectives in the various provinces, including some very loose interpretations of what 'public rented housing' actually includes. Zhou and Ronald's (2017b) research indicates that even in a province (Chongqing) which benefits from municipal land availability, access to credit to fund construction and (between 2007 and 2012) a politically sympathetic environment, the targeted increase in public rented housing supply of 670,000 units was not achieved and the distribution of the units which were constructed was not to the benefit of those most in need.

The idea that housing the lowest income groups is a means to ensure social stability is not lost on governments in the 2020s any more than it was a century ago. Considering the case above, China possesses more financial resources than many of the countries for which this problem is more pressing. As both the Chongqing case and the earlier quote from Theresa May suggest, security of housing as an electoral tool is also more widely recognized, and so given its political, economic and social significance there is a clear conflict of interests for governments between intervention in the market with the effect of direct redistribution of assets, and ensuring that both wider political goals as well as party political goals are met. As indicated in the discussion above, the particular balance of state/private/third-sector engagement in housing in any country is subject to a number of political and economic meta-objectives, industrial development and its role in shaping patterns of urbanization (see Aalbers and Christophers, 2014, for a more detailed assessment of housing in the wider political economy). The next section will explore further some of the policy solutions which have emerged and are being developed as a means for governments to reconcile these conflicting goals.

Policy solutions: helping the market or helping people?

In reality, the state's options in relation to governing the supply and demand of housing are fairly limited. States and localities can attempt to control housing and related development through both the legal framework of land rights and redistribution of these through inheritance. States can also regulate the use and development of land in order to encourage and discourage income-generating activities (which have implications for habitation) and residential development. States can also further regulate development through legal provisions to shape the extent and form of housing development, its quality and its putative allocation with respect to intended householders. As discussed earlier, where they can directly intervene in housing markets, states do this by either becoming part of the market through raising and managing the financing of house building, becoming landlords or delegating this social landlord role through private and third-sector partnerships. Governments also manage the market through the use of rent controls, subsidies to individual householders and/or subsidies to private or third-sector providers to incentivize preferred patterns of housing supply. They may use taxation towards some of these ends, extracting a share of the benefits from land exploitation, the use of properties or sale and rent revenues.

Earlier discussion here has considered housing within the wider political economy, but in trying to make sense of the different configurations of housing systems, comparative housing studies have also featured prominently in scholarship, particularly from the early 1990s. Oxley's (1991) exposition of the 'aims and methods' of comparative housing study was critical of the descriptive nature of research at that time, arguing for a more scientific approach to comparison. Since then, cross-national studies comparing housing systems across two, three and more countries have become commonplace, contributing to both improved understanding of, among other things, dimensions of inequality, institutional drivers and the housing policy process, and practical lessons for policy emulation. In an examination of comparative approaches, Kemeny and Lowe (1998) also moved beyond what they refer to as the particularistic or 'juxtapositional' approach criticized by Oxley. They are similarly critical of 'convergence' theses which assume housing systems travel the same developmental road, and argue instead for approaches more akin to welfare regime typologization.

The particular place of housing as an asset in contemporary capitalism, combined with its national complexity and looseness of analytical categories, would seem to benefit from a 'welfare regime' approach. This might usefully be based on a continuum from those systems where asset ownership is privileged as a means to achieve individual welfare through the market, to those which have a greater commitment to collective solutions and public provision. However, as van Gent's (2010) exploratory study of the UK, the Netherlands and Spain indicates, the extent to which a *home ownership first* strategy is pursued in any given state is highly contextually dependent and variable over time. While in asset ownership models, policies to assist market entry and indirectly shape markets would be expected, even models which privilege collective solutions do not preclude the use of market actors to achieve desired outcomes. Therefore, although there is a significant relationship between housing and the welfare state, it is not one that translates easily into welfare state modelling exercises other than at the most general level of the public–private divide. Fahey and Norris attribute this difficulty to the fact that 'the policy instruments in this field are so numerous and their development over time so varied that positions in the debate are strongly influenced by the subset of policies focused on' (2010, p. 490). While Kemeny and Lowe (1998) are somewhat critical of schools of housing research which assume universal convergence according to assumed developmental trajectories, two decades after their review, global market forces seem to be far more significant drivers of development than they perhaps appeared in the late 1990s, and states' involvement in facilitating these seem far more invested. A later discussion of this theme by Lowe (2011), drawing on Schwartz and Seabrooke's (2008) work which classifies the politics of housing in terms of varieties of 'residential capitalism', tends to support the latter view.

State assistance for market participation in housing can take several forms of direct and indirect intervention in credit supply and/or subsidy on a 'help-to-buy', 'help-to-pay' or 'help-to-build' basis. In Iceland, for example, the Housing Financing Fund operates as an autonomous government institution which provides credit to both individuals and private and third-sector actors to support house building and the purchase of dwellings, as well as managing the housing market (notably with social objectives) and administering the housing benefit system. This institution reflects a whole spectrum of relationships between state, citizen and market in housing.

Subsidies for home ownership exist in many countries and often take the form of tax allowances on mortgages, but can also operate as help-to-buy schemes which are intended to assist market entry. In the UK a long history of tax relief has been supplemented in the late 2000s with schemes to facilitate a range of ownership models and aims: shared ownership schemes with social landlords, ownership of new-build homes (with the twin goal of stimulating house building) and schemes to prevent house repossession. These UK schemes have had very limited impact relative to housing need, with fewer than half a million participants in the help-to-buy elements by 2018.

Countries where there is a reliance on home ownership (at both the political and household level) as a means to secure income and meet welfare needs in the face of declining state support face a significant problem, however. The crux of this problem is that even in the countries which represent this type most closely, home ownership rates remain on a downward trend: the UK experienced the greatest decline in the EU between 2007 and 2017 (just under 10 per cent),[2] while the US and Australia have also seen declines over a similar period (Ronald et al., 2015). It is important to note here the relationship between housing and the labour market, and to point out that rising insecurity in employment, particularly in the countries mentioned, has accompanied the decrease in home ownership.

In the UK, targeted propulsion towards market participation occurred in the 1980s when the Conservative government introduced the right-to-buy policy for tenants in local authority housing. This policy can be seen as a triumph for New Right politics at the time, since it substantially altered the shape of social rights in the UK, and facilitated wider processes of individualization and residualization within the welfare state (Murie, 2014). Purchasers were subsidized and the government severely limited the extent to which the proceeds of sales could be recycled into social housing investment. The loss of municipal housing created needs which have subsequently remained unmet, particularly in the wake of the 2008 crisis. Right-to-buy sales peaked in 1982–3 (167,123 total social housing sales) and again in 1988–9 (135,701), with an accumulated total of just over 2 million dwellings sold by 2017–18[3] (this figure also includes sales through other schemes from 1991 to 1992). The proportion of households in the private rented sector increased from 2.1 million in 1996–7 to 4.7 million in 2016–17, and among contemporary private renters, the number of those in the 35–44 age group has tripled (MHCLG, 2018a). While the prospects of home ownership for this age group have dwindled, the ability to secure a home at all remains a significant problem in England. While the number of households accepted by English Local Authorities as homeless has declined since 2004, according to official figures (MHCLG, 2018b), the number of rough sleepers increased to an estimated 4,751 individuals in 2017 (just under a quarter of these in London) (MHCLG, 2018c).

Data on homelessness are notoriously difficult to compare due to the variety of classifications and measurements used cross-nationally. Among the OECD countries, high rates are recorded in liberal welfare regimes: New Zealand (0.94 per cent of the total population), Australia (0.47 per cent), Canada (0.44 per cent) and the UK (0.25 per cent), but also in the Czech Republic (0.65 per cent), Germany (0.42 per cent) and Sweden (0.36 per cent).[4] The issue of adequacy of housing is discussed in more detail later.

The unmet demand for social housing in England reflects the absolute decline in available stock discussed earlier. This decline in 'demand subsidies' is mirrored by an increase in advanced economies of 'supply subsidies', which selectively support people unable to meet housing costs in the private rented sector (and in owner-occupation) through housing allowances. State support in the form of 'help to pay' effectively travels from state to private landlord (and private owner). Comparatively, the UK is the highest spender on housing allowances among the OECD countries (1.41 per cent of GDP in 2015). France and Finland are the next highest spenders at 0.83 per cent and 0.82 per cent respectively, with New Zealand, Germany, Denmark, Sweden and the Netherlands further down the scale at between 0.45 and 0.48 per cent.[5]

The level of state support through housing allowances has been increasing in most European countries since the 1990s. This reflects not only a decline in direct provision of public housing but also a real decline in wage levels and an increase in the costs of rent, taking housing costs as a proportion of income beyond 'affordable' levels for an increasing proportion of households. Housing costs account for over 20 per cent of disposable income in fifteen out of thirty-five OECD countries with data available for 2014.[6] Housing costs are particularly high for owner-occupiers in most of the Central and Eastern European countries, France, Japan, Ireland, Malta and South Korea. Support to home owners can be in the form of help to buy and/or pay (see Figure 8.2), depending on the policy

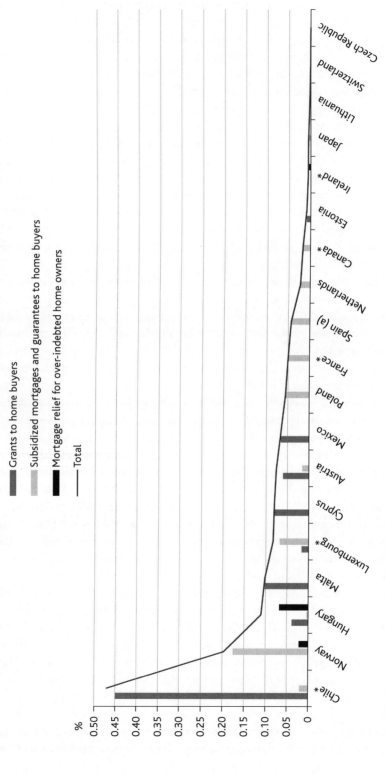

Figure 8.2: Public spending on grants and financial support to home buyers as percentage of GDP, 2015

Grants to home buyers

Subsidized mortgages and guarantees to home buyers

Mortgage relief for over-indebted home owners

—— Total

Notes: * Lower estimate due to missing data; (a) 2013.

Source: Support for Homebuyers PH2.1 http://www.oecd.org/social/affordable-housing-database.htm

aims, but housing allowances in the form of rent subsidies are proportionally more important in state spending than support for home owners in all countries.

While states struggle with their place in the housing market, their interests as regulators of housing also present a site of conflict in provision, both in practical terms because of their interests in land use and development, and in a less material way linked to the symbolism of home and identity. Self-building is an informative example of the ways in which the more abstract 'meaning' of housing, the relationship of citizen to state and the practical solutions to housing need coalesce. In terms of *enabling* market access, support for self-building is a tried and tested model of low-cost housing development in the global South, and has been considered an effective means to reconcile limited state resources with the needs of people for decent homes. The 'sites and services' approach to housing provision, where land and infrastructure are allocated to households via state mechanisms, and subsequent development into dwellings is devolved to the households, has operated since the 1970s and has regained policy interest as a model to address continued urbanization.

In the context of low-income economies, self-build has most often been a household necessity rather than an official policy solution. The incidence of 'informal settlements' is far greater than that of public housing, and in the context of the global retreat from state-centred solutions, and the role of international organizations in shaping policy in these countries, it is unsurprising that the direction of policy is towards public–private partnerships and participatory models of housing development. UN-Habitat policy manuals provide much detail on country examples where these approaches have been applied and have met goals relating to improvements in infrastructure and quality (UN-Habitat, 2011a, 2011b). In some cases (for example Namibia, Brazil and El Salvador) this has begun with changes to land tenure laws, sometimes with a view to facilitating gender equality (South Africa, Republic of South Korea). In others there has been the provision of government-backed credit facilities (Jordan, India) (UN-Habitat, 2011b).

In the global North, self-building contributes to traditional routes to home ownership in many countries and there has been increasing interest in the role of self-build both as a household economic strategy and as a political and/or ecological project (see Benson and Hamiduddin, 2017). While not generally regarded as a low-cost option for those most disadvantaged in European housing markets, self-building is promoted as lower cost (as much as 20–40 per cent lower in the UK).[7] The potential for self-building is, of course, dependent on the availability of land, and consequently countries such as the UK and the Netherlands have much lower incidence of self-build dwellings, although in the UK demand for self-build land is high (Stevens, 2017).

Housing need

Demand for housing is not just dependent on numbers of people but also on the social, political and economic context in which their lives are lived. An increasing population size does not necessarily imply increased demand for housing; for example, a higher birth rate may be combined with social factors that lead children to live with their families for longer, and an increasingly older population may be offset by other patterns of household formation. Equally, some social change may well increase the demand for housing, such as a higher divorce rate dividing one household into two (or more) or a declining co-habitation rate which implies more people wanting to live alone.

One of the key drivers of demand linked to industrialization in contemporary times as much as in the past, is the movement of people from rural areas to centres of manufacturing and commerce. The process of urbanization continues and while the rural population is expected to decline from 2021, the urban population is projected to rise from 4 billion in 2015 to 6 billion by 2041, and the world population 'projected to be 68 percent urban' by 2050 (UNDESA, 2018, p. 10). Despite these projections, and substantial rural–urban migration over the last seventy years, the majority of the populations of Africa and Asia remain in rural areas in the 2020s. Globally, low- to middle-income countries have the highest rates of urbanization, and the US aside, the numbers of those migrating to urban centres are expected to be greatest in the countries with the largest total populations (respectively China, India, Nigeria, Indonesia and Pakistan), with a rise from 28 'megacities' of over 10 million inhabitants in 2014 to 41 in 2050. This magnitude of change requires not only immediate policy responses to address current demands but also a clear vision of how increasing need will be met in the future, as well as how housing need interacts with labour market participation and social relations.

Self-build and 'slum upgrading' projects in particular, involve a range of aims beyond the production and improvement of housing in the context of urbanization, which incorporate economic desires to make use of human resources as well as social and political goals related to environmental sustainability, community building and devolved decision making. Globally the reduction in numbers of people living in urban slums is substantial (see Table 8.1), and there

Table 8.1: Proportion of urban population living in slum areas, 1990 and 2010

Major region or area	1990	2010
Developing regions	46.1	32.7
Northern Africa	34.4	13.3
Sub-Saharan Africa	70.0	61.7
Latin America and the Caribbean	33.7	23.5
Eastern Asia	43.7	28.2
Southern Asia	57.2	35.0
South-Eastern Asia	49.5	31.0
Western Asia	22.5	24.6
Oceania	24.1	24.1

Source: UN-Habitat (2015, p. 17, table 2), *World Atlas of Slum Evolution*

are countless self-build success stories, both in the global South and the global North, which have contributed to these improvements in housing. Nevertheless, the political, financial and human resources in combination with the practical requirements (for example, the supply of building materials) for these projects to achieve success are subject to a range of instabilities that increase the risk of failure. In addition to facing resourcing difficulties, low-cost housing development is most often dependent on a 'project' framework of funding and delivery, with the involvement of various private organizations, non-governmental organizations and IGOs. This model of provision lacks the security, longevity and guarantees found in state-led systems, but increasingly passes for 'policy' (see Deacon, 2013, for wider discussion of this issue). The refugee 'crisis' in the late 2010s led to even greater reliance on 'project' responses, even in countries at the heart of Europe (see for example Emmanuel, 2017, on the Greek case), and a greater role for international actors (international non-governmental organizations and IGOs, as well as private and government donors).

Refugees are by definition in housing need, and their numbers increased significantly in the 2010s in the face of escalating conflict and insecurity. This topic was addressed briefly in Chapter 6, quoting key data for 2017, and acknowledging issues about distinguishing refugees from other migrants. In 2017, Turkey hosted the highest number of refugees (3.5 million), but other than Germany, the countries with the highest numerical refugee population were all low- and middle-income countries. While the US, Australia and European countries continue to focus on the politics of refugee settlement and confront the rise of 'welfare chauvinism', which refuses social obligations to non-nationals (see for example Fenger, 2018), many of the low-income countries manage what the UNHCR terms 'protracted refugee situations', where 25,000 or more people of the same nationality reside in a country of asylum for five or more years. This situation accounts for two-thirds of the refugee population globally. The increasing significance of residence in camps as a form of refugee housing indicates the extremity of housing need. Around 36 per cent of refugees were located in camps in 2017, while the proportion of those classified as living in 'individual accommodation (private)' had declined from 67 per cent in 2015 to 61.4 per cent in 2017 (UNHCR, 2017, p. 60, table 5).

In addition to the role of the UNHCR and other IGOs and non-governmental organizations in supporting refugee housing through direct aid programmes, the role of the private sector and the market is also present in responses to the housing of refugees. In the case of Greece, meeting need has included recruiting private landlords (Emmanuel, 2017), while in other examples philanthropists and commercial companies have become involved in the design and supply of 'flat-pack' and '3D-printed' housing. While meeting emergency needs is clearly a priority for refugee populations, historically there is evidence that dwellings constructed as short-life 'emergency' housing, with less regard for quality and durability, easily become incorporated into standard housing stock – this has been the case with some of the dwellings constructed in the UK during and following the Second World War. This highlights the fact that housing is not simply a question of 'how much' but also of 'how good', and this issue is the focus of the next section.

The dimensions of adequacy and inadequacy of housing

As Malpass and Murie (1994) articulated, the universality of the housing 'question', or in the terms of this chapter housing 'adequacy', is reducible to a quantitative and a qualitative dimension. Is there enough housing to meet the needs of any given population, and is it of an acceptable standard? The previous discussion has focused on the variety of ways in which supply and demand are managed and the range of economic, social and political interests which influence policies and systems. The idea of an 'acceptable standard' of housing is equally subject to a variety of interpretations and policy responses. The United Nations Committee on Economic, Social and Cultural rights has, since the 1966 convention, specified further what 'adequacy' might mean in practice[8] and the nature of the required individual protections and entitlements. Here the elements of adequacy concern security, services and infrastructure, affordability, habitability, accessibility, location and cultural adequacy (UN-Habitat, 2014, p. 4). In the UK, an attempted definition of 'a decent home' was produced in policy guidance by the Labour government in the mid-2000s designed to regulate the quality of social housing. This guidance was focused on the absence of hazards, space, insulation, location and age of sanitation and food preparation facilities.[9] More recently, the advent and global acceptance of the SDGs in 2015 has provided a framework which, on paper at least, enables the identification of unmet need, measurable targets to address needs and a date (2030) by which signatory countries should have achieved this. Goal 11 specifically concerns cities and communities, but many of the other sixteen goals contain elements that incorporate quality of environment and housing 'adequacy' within the framework of human rights conventions.

This breadth of scope illustrates the complexity of delivering 'adequate' housing in the context of the wider processes of redistribution of material resources and individual and social opportunities that are necessary. Many of these related issues are addressed in other chapters in this book, where housing intersects with the labour market and health policy, for example. Other obstacles to 'adequacy' are inherent in wider structural inequalities such as those of gender, where women's rights to land tenure or legal protection more generally lead them to experience housing inadequacy disproportionately. Discrimination and inequality also impose disabling environments, as does unequal access to adequate housing for minority ethnic groups which intersect with class divisions. In assessing the housing agenda for the future, the core problem has been summed up by one 'task team' of international organizations, thus: 'Affordable housing is inadequate and adequate housing is unaffordable.'[10] This returns consideration of the housing problem to the deeper and more intractable issue of economic inequality, as it is only within the framework of state commitment to redistribution and the elimination of poverty within and across countries that policy measures to tackle homelessness, slum upgrading and the provision of 'decent homes' can take place.

Conclusion

This chapter has examined the particular place of 'housing' as a policy domain and a key feature of advanced capitalism. Although it is not necessarily fruitful to attempt to apply a universal logic of change to understanding the development of housing systems, there are clear patterns of historical change reflecting the economic and political acceptability of state involvement in housing as the process of industrialization and consequent urbanization have evolved.

Surveying this change across countries shows that housing systems do not, however, develop along precisely the same trajectory. In the advanced economies there is significant variation, and this does not always conform to expectations allied with the typical welfare regime models. Added to this, in the countries, particularly in the global South, where industrialization is not following the same 'logic' as in the North but is instead jumping stages and occurring in an economic context that is already dominated by the interests of the North, housing systems are also shaped by a different constellation of social needs and political pressures. Not least of these is the presence of significantly greater population numbers than found in twentieth-century Europe, including higher numbers of displaced persons than ever before. The financialization of the global economy has transformed property relations and entangled the needs and desires for a 'home' within a highly complex and global web of financial instruments.

This has, in turn, had a destabilizing effect on the mixed economy of housing, reinforcing market inequalities. It is clear that housing presents especially problematic choices for governments given an established hegemonic resistance to market interference. The housing 'problem' is not simply a question of building more homes (although this is part of the solution), but requires a breadth and depth of market intervention that states currently have little appetite or compulsion to make.

9

Health

Introduction

The maintenance of good health is fundamental for our welfare, and variations in the extent to which people enjoy good health are central to human inequality. This point is made most starkly with respect to variations in life expectancy (see Chapter 1). To die prematurely, if steps could have been made to prevent that death, is the most fundamental inequality. But when the issue is put starkly it highlights the fact that it is difficult to single out health as a 'social policy' issue from all the other policies that have an impact upon health. Although health policy is high on the public policy agenda we must not lose sight of the fact that there are many state activities that affect human health, many of which are negative in impact. Above all, there is a need to remember that nation states, long before modern welfare considerations were on the agenda, were makers of war, and that conflict continues to represent the most significant threat to health and life. Such general propositions may appear far removed from the explicit public policy health agenda today, but it is important to consider differences between nations not only with respect to the extent to which citizens enjoy specific policies to promote health but also in terms of the extent to which the broad negative influences on health and well-being are curbed.

Perhaps inevitably, passing over the most striking negative influences, an international conference at Alma-Ata (WHO, 1978) 'expressing the need for urgent action by all governments, all health and development workers, and the world community to protect and promote the health of all the people of the world',[1] continued with a sequence of affirmations starting from the following:

> health, which is a state of complete physical, mental and social wellbeing, and not merely the absence of disease or infirmity, is a fundamental human right and that the attainment of the highest possible level of health is a most important world-wide social goal whose realization requires the action of many other social and economic sectors in addition to the health sector.

The conference went on to declare that health inequalities within and between countries are unacceptable and a 'common concern to all countries', stressing the importance for health promotion of economic and social development, and asserting that 'Governments have a responsibility for the health of their people which can be fulfilled only by the provision of adequate health and social measures.' This statement was delivered within the broader context noted in this introduction.

This chapter therefore puts, up front, the key questions about inequalities in health outcomes and the central issues about health expenditure. And of course this needs to be analyzed first of all in terms of inequalities between nations. At the same time, as the challenge from scholarly work on health inequalities has shown, such an analysis must not skate over three issues: one is about the extent to which those health inequalities are influenced by factors from both within and outside health services, a second is that there are massive health inequalities within nations as well as between them, while the third is that the cultural and political contexts within which inequalities are sustained may themselves be generative of health inequalities.

These fundamental questions then lead the discussion to health policies per se, and the different ways in which public provision for health care is organized across the world. The discussion of this is prefaced by a brief examination of the use of regime theory in the analysis of health policy differences. As signalled at the end of Chapter 3, it is suggested that in the analysis of health policy differences, regime theory in itself has limited use. It does, however, point towards possibilities of developing health policy typologies. These, however, are not simple and are dominated by the conflict between the desire of states to do more to meet health care demand and the escalating costs of doing so. Those specific issues are explored in the section on financing and provision, leading to explorations of the inevitably mixed picture of efforts to enhance the established systems of the global North and develop the systems of the global South.

Health outcomes

Since good health depends upon a whole range of social, economic and environmental factors as well as direct health service provisions, there are issues to be addressed regarding the protection from risks provided by public policies beyond medicine. A model developed by Dahlgren and Whitehead (1991), which has influenced World Health Organization (WHO) work, presents concentric half-circles with genetic factors at the centre overlaid by lifestyle choices, social networks and then a wide range of policies in which health policy needs to be seen alongside all the concerns of the other policy areas discussed in this book, together with agriculture, water and sanitation. All of these are then embedded within general social, economic, environmental and cultural conditions. To guarantee and improve the health of individuals and groups, action is required not just at the individual level but also through people's living and working environments (see also Whitehead et al., 2001; Hunter, 2003; Deaton, 2002, 2013). Added to this must be the drivers of health inequalities found in the structures of social stratification, the ways in which these restrict or expand access to 'health' promoting living conditions and health services for different social groups, and the ways in which individual needs and behaviour interact with opportunities for good health.

Clearly this discussion points towards differences between nations with respect to health inequalities. Table 9.1 provides data on life expectancies, the mortality rates for under fives and the maternal mortality rate for the WHO regions in 2015.

Table 9.1: Mortality statistics for the WHO regions, 2015

WHO region	Life expectancy at birth	Under-five mortality rate (per 1,000 live births)	Maternal mortality rate (per 100,000 live births)
Africa	52	81	542
The Americas	77	15	52
South East Asia	69	43	164
Europe	77	11	16
Eastern Mediterranean	69	52	166
Western Pacific	77	14	41
Global	71	43	216

Source: WHO (2017a, p. 92)

The general life expectancy figures are, above all, reflections of the chances children have of getting through the first five years of life. Hence the variation between the regions in column two is much greater than in column one. The variation between regions is also much less than the variation between countries. In the region of Africa, the highest mortality rates for under fives are 157 in Angola, 139 in Chad and 130 in the Central African Republic, with rates over 100 also in Sierra Leone, Mali and Nigeria. The rate for Somalia (in the WHO's Eastern Mediterranean region) is 137. The inclusion within the European region of Russia and various former states of the USSR pushes up its average. Within the EU, Bulgaria has the highest rate at 10. The rate for the UK is 4. In the Americas, Canada has the lowest rate at 5; the US has a rate of 7. At the high end in the Americas are Haiti at 69, with Guyana, Bolivia and the Dominican Republic all over 30. India's infant mortality rate is 48, China's is 11. The WHO report (WHO, 2017a), from which these statistics are taken, includes a variety of other national statistics that may contribute to explanations of variation between nations. It includes environmental factors (water cleanliness and air pollution, for example), behavioural factors (smoking and alcohol consumption) and factors likely to affect the availability of health services such as government spending and numbers of health workers of various kinds. The detailed statistical tabulation does not include indices of income and wealth, but the report naturally mentions poverty and within-nation inequalities.

The key point here is that at the extremes, health differences between nations have to be seen in the context of overall levels of wealth and poverty. As Wilkinson and Pickett (2010, p. 6) have clearly shown in their analysis of health inequalities: 'Among poorer countries life expectancy increases rapidly during the early stages of economic development.' Their work highlights the gradual weakening of the statistical relationship between life expectancy and economic growth as countries become richer, but this does not mean that when countries are compared the association between income level (as expressed in terms of GDP per capita) and life expectancy, or indeed morbidity, disappears.

There are some nations which stand out as achieving significantly higher life expectancy than might be predicted from their income level. Deaton (2013, p. 35) identifies Nepal, Bangladesh, Vietnam, China, Costa Rica, Chile and Japan as countries which illustrate this anomaly. In contrast, South Africa is identified as a 'poor performer': 'a small rich country embedded in a much larger poorer country', and Russia similarly as a country where life expectancy dropped dramatically in the aftermath of communism (Deaton, 2013, p. 34). This evidence raises questions about the characteristics of individual countries and the health inequalities within them. Investigating these questions, Wilkinson and Pickett's work identifies the many ways in which health inequalities can be correlated with measurable social and economic inequalities, while Stuckler and Basu (2013) study both within- and across-country inequalities according to the 'austerity' or 'stimulus' approach adopted by states as a response to the 2008 financial crisis. Taking a similar approach, Bambra (2016) emphasizes the geographical manifestation of health inequalities within the UK. These inequalities do not occur by chance. Risks to health are variable along a number of contextual dimensions, but it is policy choices which make the difference to their reduction.

Public policy as a response to health inequalities

It was noted at the beginning of this chapter that the Alma-Ata declaration took an explicit view that health inequalities, particularly those between nations, should be government concerns. But what does this imply? The specific development of health policies is only one such response. The maintenance of good health depends upon a combination of protection from risks provided by public policies other than medicine, as well as the decisions people take for themselves. An extreme version of this position sees medicine as an almost unnecessary intrusion into health maintenance, indeed even as a source of illness ('iatrogenic disease', see Illich, 1977). A more moderate version stresses the way in which historically health improvements in societies have depended more upon environmental improvements and raised living standards than upon medical advances (McKeown, 1980). The critique of the contribution of medicine rests upon two things: one is a comparatively narrow perception of it as centred on the roles of doctors as the providers of treatments, the other is the extent to which that role has been developed for the needs of those able to pay. Advances in medical science are important, particularly in disease prevention and the control of communicable diseases. A recent case in point is the outbreak of the Ebola virus in West Africa:

> you can't stop Ebola without staff, stuff, space and systems. And these
> need to reach not only cities but also the rural areas in which most

people in West Africa still live. First, we need to stop transmission. The source of the first human cases is no longer the primary concern. Transmission is person to person, and in the absence of an effective medical system, it occurs wherever care is given: in households, clinics and hospitals, and where the dead are tended. Infection control must be strengthened in all of these places … Second, we need to avoid pitting prevention against treatment. (Farmer, 2014, p. 39)

The point here is that systems that manage health care remain vital. What particularly distinguishes the health problems of the poorest nations from those of the richer ones is the continuing incidence of transmittable diseases. Deaton (2013, p. 31, drawing on the earlier work of Preston, 1975) discusses this difference in the context of an 'epidemiological transition', where infectious disease is a significant cause of mortality, particularly child mortality, in low-income countries, but as countries increase in wealth the causes of mortality shift to chronic diseases, generally in older age. However, he also observes (Deaton, 2013, p. 152) that 'In cities like Delhi, Johannesburg, Mexico City and São Paulo, first world state-of-the-art medical facilities treat the wealthy and powerful, sometimes within sight of people whose health environment is not much better than that of seventeenth-century Europe.' In the European context, as Moran (2000, p. 139) has pointed out, it is only since the early twentieth century that both doctors and hospitals have become a force in the advancement of medicine rather than 'a positive danger to the sick'. For this development to make a universal contribution to human health, public policies are necessary in order to extend medical services beyond those able to pay for them and govern the ways in which this extension of services is delivered.

In the context of the SDGs, the WHO has cited the health workforce, and particularly those engaged in health work at the community level (rather than in acute care in hospitals for example), as the key focus for policy makers. The roles of doctors in health services can be summed up with the view that the nations of the world can be seen to be arrayed between two poles. At one pole, represented by the US and in Europe by Switzerland, there are high ratios of doctors to population, and the rewards for those doctors are high. Internal inequalities and public policies (or their absence) suggest that additional investments in medicine itself would bring limited additional social benefits. At the other pole, in much of Africa, which has the highest and increasing projected health worker shortfall for 2030 (WHO, 2016a), there are relatively few doctors: 1.4 per 10,000 population in Mali compared to twenty-six in the US in 2016,[2] for example. Many low-income countries do not have the capacity to train doctors, and also lose many of those who become trained to a demand-led drain operating from South to North. In terms of the Alma-Ata declaration's focus on primary health care as the most effective means to achieve health, the global variance in primary health workers is little different to that of doctors. Although data are limited, coverage of nurses and midwives per 1,000 population is above the 4.5 threshold of 'indicator met' for the SDGs in all

OECD countries, while the African region was 1.8 million nurses short in 2013, projected to rise to 2.8 million in 2030 (WHO, 2016a, p. 44, table A1.3).

In these circumstances the scope for health gains, with the right policies, are considerable, but currently much of the funding for those gains is non-governmental and often conditional upon business interests (Farnsworth, 2014), particularly those of big pharmaceutical companies, or the priorities of philanthropists (McGoey, 2015), which are not always linked directly to the health needs of people. Even where philanthropic ventures with respect to health development do focus on the basic problem of eradicable infectious diseases or recognized public health concerns, the resources made available (for example the Global Health Investment Fund) are not governed strictly within a framework of health goals. Rather, they seek to promote a wider range of commercial interests outwith the regions in which the health (and economic) needs are greatest. This leads on to consideration of two key themes that underpin the advancement of health: the extent of public expenditure devoted to it and the institutional arrangements in which this spending occurs.

Health inequalities and health expenditure

Among the 'poor performers' with respect to shared health improvement in advanced economies, the US is an illustrative case since it is the highest spender on health care among the OECD countries. Figure 9.1 provides data on health expenditure in these states together with a limited selection of others (OECD, 2017d). Echoing Deaton (2013), the US is a high spender but only around 50 per cent of national expenditure is public compared to around 80 per cent in most of the European nations (although it needs to be recognized that there are some difficulties with the data since the classification of health insurance varies by country). Another exception among the high spenders is Switzerland, where only 64 per cent is publicly financed. At present, only 30 per cent of health expenditure in India and 38 per cent of that in Indonesia is publicly financed. The relevance of the distinction between overall expenditure and its public component, and the complexity of the actual insurance arrangements, suggests more attention is required in analyses of the actual mode of provision; therefore, the following section examines some attempts to identify health expenditure typologies.

Health policy typologies: the usability of regime theory?

As noted at the end of Chapter 3, while regime theory seems to have had little to say about health policy, scholars of health policy have nevertheless felt they must explore what it has to offer and either try to modify it to make it applicable or try to develop new approaches to typologization that specify, in effect, health regimes. Freeman and Rothgang (2010) argue that Esping-Andersen's modelling approach is of limited use in the study of health care systems, partly because 'decommodification' does not highlight differences between the systems that

Health

Figure 9.1: Health expenditure per capita, 2016 or nearest year

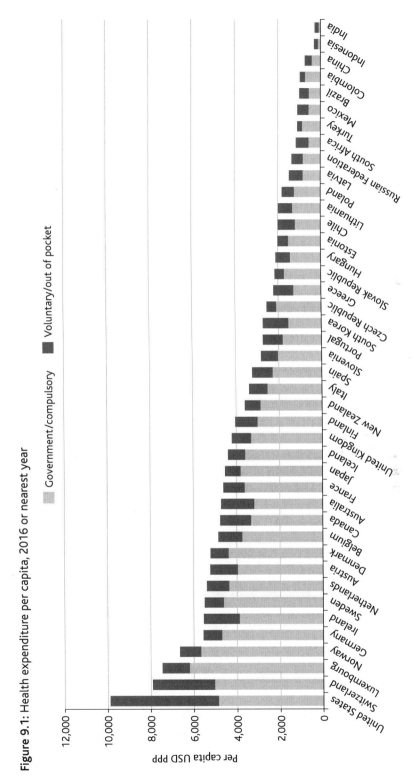

Source: OECD (2017d, pp. 133 and 137)

have developed universalism as a feature of provision, and partly because, rather than services, it was developed to account for cash transfers. They argue that 'Typologies of health care states tend to have been based on sources of financing and a dichotomy of public versus private ownership' (2010, p. 370). However, there is a danger here of characterizing decommodification too simply, confusing the idea with the way it was used by Esping-Andersen, and therefore mixing up a critique of the way regime theory has developed with questions about the concept's applicability to health services. The tendency to typologize in terms of modes of provision risks missing important questions about the extent of coverage. Esping-Andersen's basic definition of decommodification is, 'when a service is rendered as a matter of right, and when a person can maintain a livelihood without reliance on the market', and here it is perhaps rather too firmly attached to issues about income outside the labour market. When applied to health services it could arguably represent three dimensions: service as a matter of right, which is not determined by present or past labour market status and, additionally, equal treatment regardless of that status, and by implication income or wealth. It was that which led Aneurin Bevan, who played a fundamental political role in the establishment of the National Health Service in the UK, to say: 'The National Health Service and the Welfare State have come to be used as interchangeable terms. ... A free health service is pure Socialism and as such it is opposed to the hedonism of capitalist society' (1952, p. 81).

Bambra's (2005, p. 33) application of the notion of decommodification, accordingly, sees it as referring 'to the extent to which an individual's access to health care is dependent on their market position and the extent to which a country's provision of health is independent of the market'. She then explicitly 'tests' Esping-Andersen's theory by looking at health policy for the period he used in his work (the 1980s) in terms of three decommodification measures:

• The percentage of the population covered by the state health system.
• Private health expenditure as a percentage of GDP.
• Private hospital beds as a percentage of total bed stock.

Bambra's subsequent grouping of nations is rather different to Esping-Andersen's regimes. But there are problems here about using available OECD statistics to arrive at a satisfactory approach to health service decommodification. These measures obviously catch the key issue, but the problem is that most of the nations examined come out – as Figure 9.1 indicates – very high on this. The third measure used by Bambra is justified by the definition of decommodification as expenditure 'independent of the market'. But this may be challenged in terms of the question posed by a quotation about socialism by Deng Xiaoping that 'it does not matter what colour the cat is so long as it catches mice'. It is often argued that it does not matter who provides a publicly funded service, as a private organization selling health services to the government does not in itself 'commodify' the service from the patient's point of view.

While there may be reluctance in moving away from the emphasis on decommodification which is so central to regime theory, there is a need to recognize that the typologization of health policy systems tends to take a rather different form. This is particularly important if the international comparison of health policy arrangements is to have a purpose beyond identifying types in the global North. Hence, in the next section, the case for 'types' but not necessarily 'regimes' is explored.

Types but not regimes?

States may play a number of roles in relation to health care: as regulators, funders, purchasers, providers or simply in planning the systems put in place. This mix of roles will of course be found in other policy areas where services are involved (see Chapter 7 on education and Chapter 10 on social care, for example), and any specific system is likely to involve a combination of all or most of these roles. While logically there is no reason why the state cannot be involved in planning and providing without funding, in practice the three are likely to be mixed together, although the state may be only be a part funder. Typologization tends to take the form of comparing the different ways in which these roles are combined, with a particular emphasis on the distinction between tax-funded systems, social insurance systems and private insurance systems (OECD, 1987; Rothgang et al., 2005).

Moran (2000) goes further towards a conceptualization that has echoes of 'welfare regimes' and delineates alternative 'families' of 'health care states': 'command-and-control' ones with forms of direct tax funding (the Nordic countries and the UK), 'supply states' (recognizing the US as the 'overwhelmingly important' one but suggesting that Switzerland shows tendencies of belonging to this group), 'corporatist states' (Germany and others where social insurance is dominant) and insecure command–and–control states (the Southern European nations that have adopted tax funding but have difficulties sustaining an adequate comprehensive system).

However, efforts to explore differences empirically have found many examples that sit awkwardly between Moran's three (or four) main types (see for example Burau and Blank, 2006). This raises questions about the extent to which it is possible to see financing, service provision and regulatory approaches as linked by the typology. Rothgang et al. (2005, p. 191, table 1) identify the dimensions of difference as: tax funding being linked with public provision and hierarchical regulation, social insurance with more mixed provision and negotiated regulation, and private insurance with private provision and markets as the key regulatory device. But Wendt et al. (2009, p. 91) suggest the following:

> When connecting state, non-governmental and market influences
> with the dimensions of financing, service provision and regulation
> 27 combinations emerge ... three of which can be identified as ideal

types. This is the case when financing, provision and regulation are all dominated by either (a) the state, (b) non-governmental actors, or (c) the market … we argue that one dimension does not necessarily determine the other two, and that non–uniformity across dimensions can also arise: it is quite possible, for instance, for private funding to combine with public service provision and a high level of state control.

Subsequent empirical work influenced by the work of Rothgang and Wendt indicates that it is possible to delineate alternative system types, of which five are evident. Table 9.2 summarizes these findings.

Table 9.2: Five types of OECD health care systems

System type	Regulation	Financing	Provision	Cases
National health service	State	State	State	Denmark, Finland, Iceland, Norway, Sweden, Portugal, Spain, United Kingdom
National health insurance	State	State	Private	Australia, Canada, Ireland, New Zealand, Italy
Social health insurance	Social actors	Social actors	Private	Austria, Germany, Luxembourg, Switzerland
Private health system	Private	Private	Private	United States
Etatist social health insurance	State	Social actors	Private	Belgium, Estonia, France, Czech Republic, Hungary, Netherlands, Poland, Slovakia, Israel, Japan, South Korea

Source: Table developed from material in Böhm et al. (2013, p. 263)

What is different about this approach to the simple tax funding/social insurance distinction is the emphasis on variations in the state role. In 'national health insurance' cases there are combinations of tax funding and private insurance. In the 'social health insurance' cases there is relatively autonomous management of insurance funds, while in the étatist cases there is strong state regulation. This expansion of a commonly accepted three-part typology into five highlights the extent to which there are many variations in the way in which the three dimensions of regulation, finance and provisions manifest themselves in national systems. Moreover, Wendt (2014, p. 865) points out that systems are dynamic and subject to 'structural reforms' in the face of changes in demand and resourcing. In other words, while this work indicates phenomena that are likely to come together, it does not suggest hard divisions between systems. What is evident, although recognizing reliance upon a limited range of easily available statistical data, is that the three dimensions are not precisely defined. There is a need to scrutinize variations around them with respect to financing and provision.

Financing and provision

The distinctions made in the Böhm et al. (2013) model between the three kinds of funding – state, social actors and private – are far from clear-cut. To state that statutorily mandated social insurance contributions amounts to funding by 'social actors' is potentially confusing. Moreover, private funding is apparent in all systems as patients may pay all or part of their costs under certain circumstances. What the five-part typology attempts is a spotlight on differences of degree.

The delineation of the National Health Service type as tax funded may seem to be most straightforward but may involve both central and local government contributions (as in Sweden). Moreover, with growth in the cost of health care have come innovations that push towards other modes of funding; this is further discussed below.

Those points are relevant to Moran's (2000, pp. 157–8) categorization of some of the systems dependent on tax funding as '*insecure* [our emphasis] command and control states'. In his analysis, these systems were 'born in an age of austerity' and have never enjoyed the resourcing or 'administrative cultures' necessary 'to achieve the level of territorial and class equality in resource distribution achieved in the northern European command and control systems'. This assessment concerned transformations of Southern and Eastern European nations' arrangements in the 1990s, but since that time, and in a much wider range of countries with tax-funded systems, the pressures of increased demand and the consequent rationing are even more significant for service delivery in the 2020s.

In the distinction between a tax-based approach and an insurance approach, the relative autonomy of funding streams is important. This is because pressure on health expenditure is upwards, and in a context in which tax increases are largely unpopular, political decisions are required to determine how the needs of health care services will be prioritized in relation to other competing state functions. The corresponding pressure upon insurance systems comes in the form of demands for equal treatment, which will erode the autonomy of separate funds where some are afforded more services than others, leading to further state intervention.

The notion of 'social insurance' was explored in Chapter 5, but it is pertinent to say something more about its applicability to health care. The key point is that it embodies forms of social solidarity that are absent in private insurance, where commercial providers discriminate between people through variations of charges related to relative risks (and even the refusal of insurance in cases of very high risk). Private insurance, moreover, does not need to pay any attention to whether all potential customers can afford to buy policies. Historically, social insurance has tended to emerge based on the notion of contributions from employees. Its shortcomings for health provision for those not in employment has long promoted questions about how to use this model while adding in notional contributions for these people, a role that obviously falls to the state. What may then be seen running across Böhm et al.'s (2013) five types, is variation in the extent to which there have been efforts to create universal insurance systems pushing them towards at least national health insurance.

Hybrid forms of sharing between tax and insurance (as in Canada and Australia) highlight the question of whether a universal insurance contribution, in which the link between payment and entitlement is exceptionally weak, is effectively a 'tax'. Crucial here is the fact that concerns about health provision for all, lead governments to devise ways of extending coverage to (a) the families of insurance contribution payers and (b) to people with incomes too low to pay contributions. An aspect of this distinction – and perhaps another reason for describing the Australian system as an insurance-based one rather than a tax-funded one (see for example the usage in Palmer and Short, 1994) – is the role the patient is allowed to play in making an initial 'purchase' of care.

An important and growing form of cost sharing, even in tax-funded health care systems, is the expectation that patients will pay some part of the cost of their treatment (see Blank and Burau, 2004, pp. 93–6). Such payments may include charges for prescriptions, fixed charges for consultations, contributions towards dental treatment and charges for the 'hotel' costs of in-patient stays. Co-payments may also be permitted where patients are able to 'top-up' their treatment and care via payments to private providers, often as a strategy to avoid queuing (see for example Weale and Clark, 2010). There may also be situations in which government imposes reimbursement limits for services but allows practitioners to charge more. Historically, this has been a controversial aspect of the French system for example (Ambler, 1991).

These variations highlight the alternative ways in which any payer/provider split is manifest to the consumer. In unified tax-funded systems, citizens will scarcely experience the payment dimension unless there are charges for specific services (prescriptions for example), but in insurance systems they will be billed for services and then be required to seek payment or reimbursement by their insurer. Adding to the complexity, those with low incomes or absence of insurance may also need to seek state support via a means test. The ease of access and dignity to patients offered through national health care arrangements is therefore highly dependent on government efforts to make the system relatively seamless, eliminating deterrents to consumers, particularly those on low incomes.

As far as there has been a tendency for insurance systems to evolve towards the characteristics of tax-funded systems, it may now be the case that rising health demands and costs produce pressures in the opposite direction. The crucial issue here lies in different ways of dealing with this problem. In tax-funded systems, government concerns have focused on increasing resources and curbing demand upon systems, with two significant effects. One is the development of ways of charging patients and the other is the 'queuing' phenomenon, which increases the incentives for some citizens to opt for private health care. Politically, this latter effect is significant because it contributes to the more general 'middle-class flight' from public services, and consequently lessens both the political pressure for further investment in these services and their defence should governments choose to deprioritize their funding. As costs increase, the variously funded models react in different ways, however. In the simple tax-funded model, the size of the government's commitment is absolutely central. In the various insurance models, there are similar issues about the size of the direct government input. Nevertheless, political blame is more easily avoided where insurance premiums or co-payments are allowed to increase (see Weaver, 1986 on the politics of blame avoidance).

Where states have sought to develop comprehensive health insurance systems the details can be very complex, and this is partly due to a gradual evolution away from private insurance. France's compulsory national health insurance covers 99 per cent of the population but is organized into a complex network of quasi-autonomous funds (Caisses Nationales), together with friendly societies and private insurers. Germany and the Netherlands provide interesting examples of what can be described as 'partial schemes', with those on lower incomes insured compulsorily, while many on higher incomes are voluntary members. Here it is possible that choice in levels of insurance premiums, and their concomitant benefits, is offered through differentiation between types of contributors based upon occupational status or income, or provision for opt-outs from all or part of the scheme for some. This is likely, especially where private companies or organizations are partners. In such a situation the state has a role in regulating to secure a guaranteed minimum standard for all, but may also allow a wide range of possibilities for provision above that minimum, as well as the related socio-economic inequalities that are reproduced. This issue has been apparent in Germany for example, where health insurance contributions vary in the levels of charges, with the inverse effect that those with lower income and higher levels of ill health were concentrated in many of the more expensive schemes (Moran, 1994, p. 97). This unintended actuarial consequence has encouraged state moves towards creating greater uniformity, for example in South Korea where increasing demand for state intervention to reduce such inequities led to the unification of the health insurance scheme (Shin, 2003).

The US system stands out as the most privatized, both in terms of sources of expenditure and theoretical classification systems. Here too, however, there has been a slow evolution towards more comprehensive insurance coverage. Developments have included both 'Medicare', 'Medicaid' and latterly 'Obamacare'. Medicare is a federal insurance programme for those aged over 65 years, which is tax supported but to which individuals are required to pay low premiums supplemented by 'cost-sharing' charges often covered by individuals through supplementary private insurance. Medicaid is a system of health care cost subsidy for those on low incomes which is linked to the public welfare (social assistance) system and supported by federal and state taxation. The 2010 Patient Protection and Affordable Care Act (popularly known as Obamacare) was intended to address both rising costs and the high proportion of citizens unable to access health insurance due to low income and ineligibility for Medicaid.[3] The provisions of the Act only came into force in 2014 and have been subject to elements of repeal and government default from 2017 under the Trump presidency. Nevertheless, it is probably still arguable that Obamacare may have taken the US system somewhat further in the direction of étatist social health insurance.

In the efforts by the scholars mentioned earlier to distinguish modes of provision there is ambiguity about the relationship between, on the one hand, whether providers are public or private organizations, and on the other hand, about the extent to which the organizational mode gives providers autonomy to raise sources of revenue independently of the state. These two issues are difficult to disentangle, but where providers are able to offer additional services for which they charge this will inevitably build inequalities into health systems.

It is also important to recognize that hidden within the concept of 'private' provision in Table 9.2 is a variety of forms of control over provision, including that operated by charities and organizations controlled by religious groups, professionals, consumer groups and trade unions as well as private 'for profit' companies. Within these categories are differences in the extent to which there is a willingness to accept a state paymaster and/or a propensity to try to secure additional autonomous sources of funds. Historical antecedents are driving factors here and Moran's (2000) concern, discussed earlier, to identify types of states rather than modes of funding is also linked to questions he raises about how states engage with the power of the medical profession and the suppliers of 'medical technology' (embracing medicines within this).

This point returns the discussion to the relevance to provision of health care in countries where established public systems are more or less absent and formal health care is largely a private or charitable matter. A key issue in low-income countries is therefore the extent to which private provision involves effects that, de facto, commodify public health care systems. These will include the following considerations about the provider:

- The extent to which income also comes from private patients.
- Freedom to select patients.
- Rights to impose additional charges on public or insurance-supported patients.
- The extent to which business success is exposed to profit/loss considerations (a key variant here applies to those institutions with incomes from charitable sources).

The contemporary advancement of independent provider models is often justified in terms of the enhancement of choice (an argument that obviously also applies in education). In terms of decommodification that point cuts both ways. On the one hand freedom of choice may be seen as an aspect of decommodification. On the other hand the linking of choice with competition between providers undermines this, particularly where it is linked with cost considerations for consumers. However, the peculiarity of choice and competition models in relation to health care is that the investment costs of establishing new providers (at least as far as hospitals are concerned) are very high while the political costs of closing down an institution seen to be uncompetitive are also high.

Finally, it is important to return to the point made earlier in relation to the origins of different provision modes: that there is a need to give attention to issues about a powerful profession as well as powerful institutions. Doctors' support for public health care has been secured through the establishment of modes of provision which maximize their autonomy and incomes. But curbing medical domination has been an important concern of governments (and for that matter of insurance companies) in their efforts to control the rise of health costs.

Conclusion

This chapter started with a recognition of the multiplicity of factors that influence health, linking this to a recognition of enormous health inequalities both between nations and within them. A global emphasis that health improvement should be a matter of public policy tends to drive a particular emphasis upon health services, which then leads on to questions about the shape those services take. Hence, while in low-income countries public provision is minimal, often limited to controls over the spread of disease, public policy development among the richer ones has been extensive. Health inequalities persist within countries, but it is difficult to disentangle those arising from service provision inequalities and those that have other social and economic roots.

Within the nations in which extensive public provision has developed, while ideological concerns about decommodification have played a part in health policy debates, an analysis of these seems to contribute little to understanding the various ways public policies have been developed. An approach to typologization in the analysis of how health care has developed primarily concerns the distinction between tax funding and social insurance on the one hand, and the roles of private providers on the other. However, convergence on issues about how to cope with expenditure pressure, how to sustain universal coverage and how to prevent medical domination of provision is to some extent eroding these distinctions.

10

Social care

It may be asserted that, with rare exceptions, we are all both receivers of care and givers of care. This assertion points us towards some of the issues involved in identifying social care policies. First, there are many situations in which care is not seen as a public issue that calls for public policies. In this respect caring occurs in many contexts as a private concern, given and received in the context of human bonds and relationships. Second, where social care is seen as a public issue it is very often in a context in which various policies intersect, many of which may not be seen as 'social care' policies. Third, notwithstanding the ubiquitous character of care issues expressed in the opening sentence above, there are marked variations in the extent to which there is a need for care. These variations depend upon individual circumstances but are particularly affected by where people are in the life course. Consequently, following further exploration of the private and public nature of care, care at different life stages will provide the organizing framework of the discussion in this chapter.

Private issues or public concerns?

Given the universality of care as an issue, it is important to recognize that there are dimensions that may be regarded as private concerns or problems, which are significant for specific individuals but not matters for the public agenda. These may be quite specific to the individuals themselves, or they may be problems shared with others. Gusfield (1981) makes a distinction between 'social problems' and 'public problems', drawing attention to the processes that are necessary to put issues on the public agenda. The early history of social policy in Europe is full of examples of issues that were perceived as private matters, but which were then brought onto the public agenda – particularly those around family relationships and the care of children. Of course, differences of view about whether or not public intervention is appropriate remain, and these may be highlighted when comparisons are made between societies.

P68

Social care as an activity is thus something that routinely occurs within families. This connection implies a range of complexities and competing perspectives linked to understandings of 'the family' and the divisions and responsibilities within it. One such perspective involves seeing care as a family responsibility for which, normally, public support is not available. With such a view, public support only comes into play when family support cannot be secured, in cases where children have no parents or where older people have no children, for example. But this perspective may nevertheless throw up public regulatory concerns: when families are negligent or family members represent a danger to other members. There may also be questions about the definition of the family as a responsible entity: is it seen simply in terms of the nuclear family or given a wider, extended definition? Alternatively, need for social care may be interpreted in entirely individual terms. Such a stance is apparent in approaches to the care of older people, where the existence of adult children is seen as irrelevant to the determination of need. What is found in practice involves variations between these positions, with a variety of 'partnerships' or compromises between them.

In many discussions of care provision, comparisons are made in terms not so much of care policy, but of 'family policy'. For example, Thévenon (2011) uses a range of family policy indices: poverty reduction, compensation for the costs of children, fostering employment, improving gender equity and support for child development. This chapter does not frame the discussion of care this way, but it recognizes the importance of questions of the treatment of 'the family' and how family life is supported and regulated. These dimensions of care policy in a broader sense inevitably embrace consideration of income security, particularly the interaction of care leave policies, service provision and cash benefits with respect to children. In their approach to making sense of policy variations in social care as 'family policy', Lohmann and Zagel (2016) consider the extent of 'familisation' and 'defamilisation' in provision for care. That is, the extent to which the state steps in to provide support for care which enables individuals to make real choices about their engagement in care activities, and achieve 'independence from family relationships' (2016, p. 49). The literature on this topic is important because it has developed from a feminist critique of social provision, and it assists in foregrounding the essentially gendered nature of caring. However, the issues it raises about gender roles in social policy concern much more than social care policy, and this highlights the need for attention to the connections between social care policy and other social policies, which is the topic of the next section.

The relationship between social care policy and other social policies

Social care policies interact very significantly with other policies, particularly in the domains of health, income security and education. Social care is also an area of policy that stands out as one where the roles and responsibilities of the different actors – state, market and citizens – are essentially interwoven with human relationships between families, friends and communities and the ways in which these are established, tested and broken under contemporary capitalism. These 'joined-up' and 'mixed economy' characteristics deserve attention because they throw light upon crucial contemporary debates about the most appropriate ways to mix the various contributions to care and assumptions about where responsibilities lie.

Considering first the ways in which social care is threaded through other policy domains, health care and social care are particularly difficult to separate. This difficulty may be identified from an example at the heart of challenges facing management of services in many countries. If a person goes into hospital for an operation the treatment will comprise different cost elements: (1) any surgical intervention and the medical and nursing treatment of any of its consequences, (2) 'hotel' costs (bed and board) and related care inasmuch as the treatment renders that person unable to care for her/himself. Generally, following medical operations, a recuperation period is necessary when care is needed, but this is essentially 'social' rather than explicitly 'medical'. It is intrinsic to modern health policy to send people home as soon as possible after surgical interventions (ideally because it is best for the patients as well as least costly). So, an episode of health care like that described here involves both health care (meaning medical and nursing care) and social care. In the ideal world (from the patient's point of view) what is needed is a seamless package of care. In the real world there is a mix of activities involving workers with various levels of skills, and therefore different levels of costs. The whole story is then more complicated if there are different ways of receiving and paying for the different elements in the package (including of course different cost implications for the patient), and if additional social care is a lifelong need. Variations in the elements in this story lie right at the heart of many of the difficulties about the relationship between health and social care, to which this chapter will return in various places.

The relationship between education and social care involves elements that are perhaps even more mixed than the health care/social care mix in that schools (and ideally teachers) care for children at the same time as they teach them. This is particularly evident in the case of very young children, and the section 'Pre-school childcare' will explore pre-school activities that are very much a combination of care and education. It is also the case where children experience difficulties because of health problems or other learning needs that require additional systems of social support.

Perhaps more complicated still is the relationship between social care and income security, since in many cases public policies to support those in need of care, and their carers, come in the form of cash payments. Some accounts of social care activities discuss the mix of benefits and services available, to families or to people with disabilities for example (hence Castles et al., 2010 includes chapters that do this with respect to 'disability' and 'family benefits and services'). The choice in this book to devote separate chapters to income security and to social care requires recognition that there are overlapping issues.

Finally, a complicated overlap also occurs with respect to the relationship between issues about social care and those about work and employment, inasmuch as there are trade-offs of various kinds. The most straightforward of these is the extent to which care for pre-school children specifically facilitates parental (particularly female) employment. A more complicated, even potentially paradoxical, issue concerns the fact that public support for adult care provides both opportunities for carers (usually termed 'informal carers', and usually women) to move into formal employment and is a source of employment in itself for those engaged in the delivery of care in the public, private and third sectors. In the US, for example, 'home health aides' and 'personal care aides' represent the third and fourth fastest-growing occupations projected in the decade from 2016 according to the Bureau of Labor Statistics (2018). In this way, directly or indirectly, public transfers to enable people to purchase care independently, as well as private transactions, may commodify informal arrangements, and there are a range of conflicts of interest, moral dilemmas and political questions arising from this.

Variations in the need for social care

The variations in the need for social care can be seen in terms of variations in the incidence of disability and difficulties, but these tend to be recognized in terms of two periods of high need incidence, at the beginning and at the end of life. To elaborate this further, four stages in the life course will be recognized and used to structure the remainder of this chapter. These are set out in Table 10.1.

Social care policy is, as noted, an area where the mixed economy is evident. Generally, in low-income countries where public revenue-raising systems are restricted and consequently state capacity is limited, economic priorities drive

Table 10.1: Care through the stages of the life course

Between birth and entry into full-time education
Care and protection of the very young and support for their parents figure significantly. In many countries there has been a shift from seeing this issue largely as a family matter with state involvement confined to the issues of child protection and the regulation of parental behaviour, towards one of public provision of some substitute care. The analysis of the growth of this activity indicates some interactions here between care per se and both support for parental employment and early years education. Forms of support extend into parental leave policies, and the income supports related to this.
During full-time education
Aside from activities to support children outside school hours the care issues during the period children are in full-time education have three specific aspects. One of these is the continuation of the child protection concerns identified above. A second is parental leave issues mentioned in the previous section. The third is special support for children whose disabilities or learning difficulties require additional inputs into the education system than is the case for most school children. A feature of modern education policy has been the development of procedures and forms of support that will facilitate inclusion of such children in the 'mainstream' education system.

(continued)

Table 10.1: Care through the stages of the life course (continued)

Between the ending of full-time education and retirement
Inasmuch as the standard assumptions about the school years are about inclusion of all, regardless of dis/abilities, into education, so similar considerations apply after that about inclusion of all working-age adults into employment. However, at this stage social care policies need to have regard for the fact that as adults, the individuals concerned cease to be – formally speaking – 'in the care of their parents'. So we have in this category a variety of support activities (with cash payments often being salient) depending upon the incidence of particular additional needs.
After retirement
It is unfortunate that many discussions of the needs of older people treat the arrival at a formal retirement age as a crucial cut-off point, ignoring both the fact that care needs may arise before that age and the increasingly evident fact that many above that age have no need for support. Nevertheless, despite the fact that much of the need for support for older people occurs very near the end of (increasingly long) lives, it is clear that support needs increase substantially with ageing. Hence, discussions of adult social care policies (often labelled 'long-term care' policies) are dominated by concerns about care after retirement.

social policy development to focus on education, health and income security foremost, while provision for social care needs remains a distant domain for expansion. The 'balance' of provision in these countries therefore remains firmly weighted towards families, communities and voluntary organizations. However, even in more wealthy countries where the 'welfare state' is well established, the role of the state in supporting care is highly variable. Table 10.2 sets out an approach to a typology for social care for high-income countries, influenced by regime theory, particularly as examined in Esping-Andersen's (1999) rethink on family roles, developed earlier in the work of Siaroff (1994) and Ferrara (1996).

Table 10.2: A typology of systems highlighting alternative approaches to care

	Individual	Family
State	Rights to care	Support of family care efforts
Market	Purchase of care	Family on its own

Bettio and Plantenga's comparison of European 'care regimes' (2004) developed a mixture of indices of care strategies to arrive at a categorization that resembles but goes beyond that typology. They identify:

- Countries that appear to delegate all the management of care to the family (Italy, Greece and Spain) with two 'outlier' cases: Portugal, where there is high female labour market participation; and Ireland, lying between this group and the next one.
- Countries with high dependence on informal care, but where this is much more salient with respect to childcare than to care for elderly people (UK and the Netherlands).
- Countries with 'publicly facilitated, private care' (Austria and Germany).
- Countries with quite well-developed formal care strategies (Belgium and France).
- Countries with moderate to high levels of formal care (Denmark, Finland and Sweden).

However, should it be expected that the factors that influence the policies for young families are the same as those that determine responses to the need for adult long-term care? Attempts to develop a typology are surely tapping into a combination of the variation in the overall propensity to develop public social policies and alternative belief systems with respect to the role of the family, and the gender roles within it. But policies for children, which perhaps dominate Bettio and Plantenga's model, concern the role of parents, while those for adult care are more about conceptions of family obligations in general vis-à-vis those of wider society. A country where the two concerns seem to have been linked explicitly is South Korea, where the combination of a very low birth rate and rapid growth in the numbers of older people has shaped policy in a way that extends women's care obligations (specifically those of daughters-in-law) in the context of increasing female labour market participation and the consequent demand for new childcare provisions (An and Peng, 2016).

In any case, the multiplicity of factors needed to develop a comparative model operating across all social care sectors pose significant limitations. Bettio and Plantegna's (2004) model makes some very broad assumptions across a wide selection of variables and, as other comparative researchers of care have noted (Anttonen et al., 2003), the elaboration of a regime typology that makes sense across the care sectors is very difficult, particularly given the policy overlaps between care, education and social security. More useful is the body of literature that explores the gendered nature of welfare regimes – or 'gender regimes' – which has provided much greater explanatory capacity in terms of why similarly economically advanced countries differ in their approaches to care provision and who provides it (see Daly and Rake, 2003).

Therefore, although social care represents a significant area of welfare need and a distinct policy domain, its analysis is more deeply connected to fundamental human relations than a simple comparison of 'systems' allows. Nevertheless, it remains useful to consider the alternative ways in which different societies seek to meet the needs for social care, at best because this knowledge assists in evaluating what a 'good' society might be, and at worst if only to identify instances of good and bad policy in practice.

Pre-school childcare

Pre-school childcare policy can be understood as varying combinations of the following:

- Provision of care which supplements the care provided by parents, simply as assistance to reducing stress and pressures, particularly in the early years of a child's life.
- Educational activities for children that will prepare them for the compulsory education system.
- Care to facilitate labour market participation on the part of the parents.
- Child protection as a regulatory activity; a specific and generally social work-based system, which is concerned with addressing the safeguarding needs of children (it may be noted that this aspect of care extends beyond the pre-school years, and can overlap with youth justice services).

In each of the first three cases such activities may or may not be the concern of the state. They may alternatively be seen as supplements to family life that may be provided through reciprocal community and extended family networks or purchased in a private market. But then there are rather different arguments for supporting general parenting, early years education and parental employment and, consequently, rather different rationales for public subsidy of each.

In the first category – simple supplementary care – the case for state provision is likely to be seen as linked to the need for children's safeguarding and represents a tiny proportion of social spending. Such care may be provided to reduce family stress in the short term or as a preventative mechanism, or in circumstances where other informal providers – families or neighbours, for example – cannot provide it. The justification for public subsidy will be much the same as that for other parts of the child protection system.

The second category – pre-school education – tends to be justified by a view that what is provided by the regular education system does not start early enough or is inadequate in some way with reference to educational outcomes later on. Early years education and childcare has become much more significant since the 1990s and is linked to the idea of 'social investment', which has been promoted especially within the European Union and by the OECD (for example the 'Strong Starts' discourse, OECD, 2006) as a means to improve economic competitiveness in the so-called 'knowledge economy'. In this case, if the regular compulsory education system is funded by the state, then there is a strong argument for funding this form of care too. A counterargument is that it is a non-essential extra, in the same way that post-school education may be so regarded. In practice we find an official view often being taken which stands somewhere between those two positions: that it is an extra that some may purchase but that the resulting inequality requires subsidy on behalf of low-income families. This is particularly relevant where early years additional education is seen as 'compensatory', providing extra for those who may otherwise be disadvantaged in the regular education system. In official data such as those provided by the OECD, this 'care' expenditure is classified as education expenditure (see Chapter 7).

The issues about the third category are of course linked to views about the desirability of labour market participation – most significantly that of women, and among women, lone parents. Where women's employment is regarded as a matter of private choice, childcare provision will equally be regarded as a private matter, accessed by those who want and can afford it. If, on the contrary, employment is seen as every parent's right (or duty) then there will be a case for state provision of childcare. But even here provision may be left to the attention of employers rather than the state. Again, there is a middle position, which sees a need to subsidize childcare to facilitate employment where the rewards from work are low. We have, then, another example of a cost that may alternatively be absorbed by employers, employees or the state. Where the state is involved, there is an alternative to direct provision, which involves subsidy of one or both employees or employers. Where families are subsidized the expenditure may be classified as a social security expenditure or even as tax relief rather than as an indicator of state support for social care.

Figure 10.1 reproduces OECD data which attempt, for most countries, to distinguish childcare and pre-primary education expenditure from both public and private sources. This is a difficult distinction, as the discussion above suggests. There are some interesting points, however: most countries tend to report spending as 'education' and devote more resources to this. Notably Sweden, Norway and Iceland devote a greater proportion of spending overall to pre-school provision, reflecting a well-established promotion of gender equality in work and care. Conversely, there are countries where spending is generally low, such as Ireland, Japan and Turkey. This is likely to mean that expenditure is concentrated on children close to the start of compulsory education, and provision of care falls on families, and more particularly the women within them. Expenditure data, of course, do not reveal the extent to which there is a high proportion of private expenditure that is not subsidized (or only partly subsidized) by the state. This is the case in the UK, where there has been a slow growth of public expenditure, mostly concentrated upon support for children near to the start of compulsory education.

Bonoli (2013) sees the expansion of childcare provision in terms of the expansion of 'active social policy' (see the discussion of this, linked to theorizing about social investment, in Chapter 5) specifically linked to labour market policy. Hence, in his comparative study, the main explanatory variable is government efforts to stimulate employment. Alongside this he gives attention to demands for gender equality (making an assumption that these are essentially for women's increased labour market participation) and to political 'credit claiming' (particularly by governments who see few other opportunities for positive social policy making). In this analysis there is a strong emphasis on labour market participation as a core feature of modern social policy developments and rooted in an earlier analysis of 'new social risks' (Bonoli, 2005).

Social care

Figure 10.1: Expenditure on early childhood educational development and pre-primary education, 2015

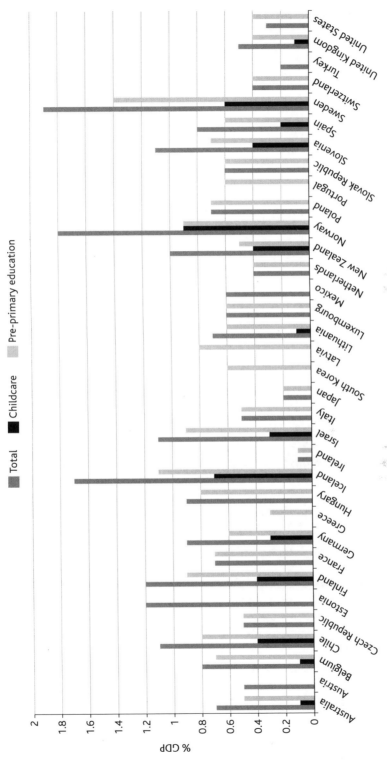

Legend: ▓ Total ■ Childcare ▒ Pre-primary education

Note: Missing data in original.

Source: OECD (2018c) Education at a Glance 2018: OECD Indicators DOI: https://doi.org/10.1787/eag-2018-15-en, table B2.3a, p. 178 https://read.oecd-ilibrary.org/education/education-at-a-glance-2018/indicator-b2-how-do-early-childhood-education-systems-differ-around-the-world_eag-2018-15-en#page17

There are, however, as Bonoli shows (2005, chapter 6), variations between the countries that have developed extensive childcare systems, both in the extent of public provision and the emphasis on pre-school education. Bonoli and Reber (2010, p. 99), attempting to develop a typology for childcare services across the OECD, reach a rather limited conclusion that: 'English-speaking liberal welfare states have relatively high coverage rates, with low public spending. Continental European countries are low on both dimensions and the Nordic countries have higher coverage, but only thanks to sizeable public investment in the field.' But they note two nations with high levels of public spending not predictable from regime theory: France and Belgium.

Thévenon's (2011) rather different family policy typology (mentioned earlier) features three regime theory groups, Nordic countries, continental European countries and Anglo-Saxon countries, but adds two other categories:

- Southern Europe bracketed with the East Asian members of the OECD characterized by lower levels of development, particularly with respect to childcare;
- Eastern European countries with very mixed packages of late development.

This reminds us that there are limitations to an account of childcare policy which concentrates upon generic formal provision, particularly if this is singled out from other public policies designed to support families. What can be observed, however, is that support for young children is seen as both 'care' policy and increasingly as 'education' policy, a development that seems to have been very much driven by labour market concerns in the context of states' desires for competitiveness in the global economy. There is thus a link with the debate about the functions of education (see Chapter 7). While on the one hand pre-school education may be seen as important for the socialization of children, policy preoccupation with early education also seems to be increasingly driven by social investment-type arguments premised on children's ultimate contribution to the workforce.

Social care from youth to old age

Over the course of establishing welfare states, provision for social care has been subject to far less policy interest than areas of state intervention which have direct relationships with the labour market or the economy more widely. Political economists of care have argued that rather than this being an oversight, it is a policy in itself in that the 'free' social reproduction provided within families benefits both the state and the economy (see for example Razavi, 2007). However, there are clearly needs for additional and specialist care that are linked to illness or physical or learning impairment that can be present throughout life or for more limited periods. As also observed above, policy responses to care issues, including those that are disability-related, may often be embedded in health, education, income security and employment policy rather than identified as the concern of what may be specifically called social care policy. Where specific services have been established with respect to disability, the direction of policy through the history of social care provision has moved, in theory if not always in practice, from an approach characterized by separation from mainstream services (and society) and disempowerment of those for whom the services were intended, towards an approach recognizing that values such as independence, individual autonomy and dignity should underpin these services. It is also based on the recognition that rather than people having 'disabilities' it is social, economic and physical environments which are more often 'disabling'. This shift in approach to care needs reflects a move away from the medicalization of care to a 'social' model. Debate continues as to where and when it is appropriate to provide additional services specific to particular needs, or to groups with similar specific needs, for example among school-age children, and often determination of these questions is linked to the resourcing and efficiency of service provision rather than achieving an ideal balance.

In the case of school-age children, the general assumption that social care is a matter for parents is again significant because it may lead to disregarding the fact that the additional financial cost of living with disability, as well as the opportunity cost to parents providing care (whose participation in employment may be constrained), has serious implications for household income and the risk of poverty. Many countries have seen charitable ventures providing support for children, and then the gradual acceptance of a state role to provide subsidies to these specialist services, either through educational settings for children with particular impairments, or through additional funding to support mainstream schools in making adaptations or providing resources to achieve greater inclusivity. Support for 'care' is also arguably identifiable in the existence of parental leave provision where cash transfers may compensate parents for lost income. However, this generally benefits parents in employment, and the policy aims are located in labour market participation rather than child welfare concerns.

Comparisons of the mixture of regulation and specific non-material support for parents in this regard are complex but, based on her review of parenting support in Europe, Daly (2015, pp. 606–7) comments:

> On the one hand the goal might be better to equip all parents for the challenges associated with parenting, to increase their confidence in the role and give them a set of resources to call on when they are experiencing difficulties. On the other hand, measures and programmes may and do seek actively to change particular parental behaviours, and in this and other ways can represent an imposition on parents by projects that are developed elsewhere and carry controlling interests.

Daly's reference to 'controlling interests' is alluding to the focus of policy on the behaviour of 'the poor' as a target group, and emphasizing individual agency as opposed to problems of material need. This approach is not new (see Piven and Cloward, 1972; and for more modern discussions Wacquant, 2009) and is regularly reinvented in projects that aim to target support.

Similarly, for people of working age, the social care of disabled people and those with temporary or lifelong additional care needs is complicated by a combination of efforts to address participatory needs, financial needs and integration into the labour market. A broad global and historical overview of policies for people in these categories suggests three patterns:

- Societies in which there is minimal public attention to the needs of such people and therefore, by implication, an expectation of normal labour market participation where possible accompanied by family support.
- Societies in which public support has been offered but often in separate (and perhaps stigmatized) institutional forms. This approach can be noted as having been developed extensively in European societies, often driven by the influence of eugenics.
- Contemporary normalization in which the second alternative is being abandoned in favour of community-based forms of support.

With respect to these alternatives a right to independent living is formally established in the 2008 UN Convention on the Rights of Persons with Disabilities. However, Mansell and Beadle-Brown (2010) provide a review of comparative evidence which suggests that the extent of the move towards community services has varied, and that institutional care remains a significant form of provision across Europe and for most low-income countries. There is a paradox here that this normalization, if not supported by adequate public services, can imply a reversion to the first of those three alternatives. This is a theme that finds echoes in the issues about care for people after their working lives.

Care beyond working life

The increasing need for social care beyond working life has moved it high up the policy agenda in many countries. It is clearly the case that in many developed societies changes are occurring in the age structure consequent upon the rapid rise in life expectancy accompanied by falling birth rates. However, it is important to recognize that policy concerns emanating from the 'dependency ratio' – the proportion of those of working age to those not of working age which is manifested in debates on pensions, for example – should not be conflated with issues arising from the relationship of ageing to care needs. Care needs generally increase with age, but being beyond working age does not necessarily imply an increased need for care. Indeed, as four decades of academic literature on the 'social construction of age' and its links to policy have shown, there has been a tendency in policy to reinforce dependency as people age. More recent research suggests that a shift in policy direction to support 'active ageing' would enable care needs to be met with greater efficiency and effectiveness and simply address

JSP p4v

many of the failings and misconceptions that underpin current systems of provision (Walker, 2018).

Hey?

The countries with the highest numbers of those aged over 80 years include China (12 million), the US (9 million), India (6 million), Japan (5 million) and Germany (3 million). Globally by 2050, it is projected that the over 80s will represent 20 per cent of the world's population, but at this point 80 per cent of the population aged over 60 will live in less-developed regions (UNDESA, 2015). These trends pose significant challenges for the global policy agenda. However, currently, as Figure 10.2 shows, in proportional terms the 'ageing population' is far more prevalent in richer countries.

Given the gaps in health care, the debilitating employment in which many people remain engaged and the levels of poverty and inequality that have been discussed in previous chapters, ageing remains an indicator of increasing need for social care. In this chapter's introductory remarks attention was drawn to the close relationship between health policy and care policy. Health care often requires specialized expertise and treatments that are costly. Not surprisingly, it is widely accepted that health problems are beyond the resources of families (and for that matter communities) and the case for public policies arises because market solutions are inadequate for many. This logic is much less evident with respect to social care, inasmuch as it can be separated from health care. The question that policy makers then have to address is: under what circumstances are the two alternatives to public provision – family help and/or the purchase of services – deemed to be inadequate? The next two sections considers the

Figure 10.2: Population aged 65+, 2017 (% of total population)

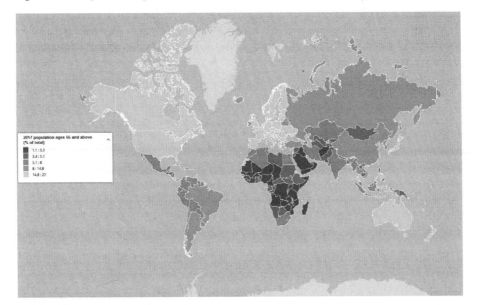

2017 population ages 65 and above
(% of total)

1.1 : 3.3
3.3 : 5.1
5.1 : 8
8 : 14.8
14.8 : 27

Source: Mapped using World Bank Data http://databank.worldbank.org/data/reports.aspx?source=2&series=SP.POP.65UP.TO.ZS&country (World Bank, 2019b)

ways in which increasing recognition of a need for public policy support for social care is emerging in the context of historical reliance on families and a more recently developed but substantial market sector. The label 'long-term care' is widely used to designate this phenomenon (OECD, 2011a), and while it is not confined to care in the last years of life it is the need for that which dominates debate.

The need for long-term care

As noted previously, it is important not to be drawn into a simplistic debate about dependency ratios, particularly in an age where geographical mobility is high, but the effect of ageing, and especially the increasing proportion of people living beyond 80, indicates that social care needs will also increase. More significant needs for social care tend to arise in the last years of life, and as medical intervention to prolong life improves, for example at the onset of terminal illness, there is an increase in chronic conditions for which there is a need for care. This is similarly the case for types of chronic illness and disease which are proportionately less frequent where life expectancy is low. Diagnoses of degenerative diseases drawn under the umbrella of dementia and associated with ageing are increasing, and not just in countries with ageing populations; the WHO reports that low- and middle-income countries accounted for 63 per cent of people with dementia in 2015. While medical research has yet to find effective treatments, intensive social care is needed for the people affected – a projected 75 million by 2050 (WHO, 2017b), which starkly illustrates the problematic health care/social care distinction noted in the introduction to this chapter.

While the need for care is increasing, however, the supply of potential carers is in question. As noted, the majority of social care takes place in families 'informally', and most often it is provided by women. Changes in the patterns of women's employment combined with greater family mobility and fluidity, and other demographic developments such as later childbearing, has created a constellation of factors that mean that old assumptions about who cares no longer reflect either the capacity or reality of contemporary families. The limits of informal care combined with the diversity and unpredictability of care needs means that there is a clear case for seeing these as phenomena that provide a justification to try to 'socialize' the responsibility through publicly shared policies.

However, what has occurred in many countries, is the opposite. Social care responsibilities have been shifted further towards informal actors in rich countries whose welfare states have eroded under post-2008 austerity measures, and a socialization of care in low-income countries has been absent from the policy agenda. In 2011 the OECD reported that 'formal long term care systems are just the tip of a largely submerged iceberg. In all countries, the major share of long term care remains "hidden", in the shape of informal – mainly family and friends – care' (OECD, 2011a, p. 38). That same report goes on to say that the size of the family care 'workforce' varies between double the formal workforce (in Denmark, for example) and more than ten times the size (in Canada, New Zealand, the US and the Netherlands). Rather surprisingly, more recent OECD data (2017b) also put the Netherlands as the highest proportional spender on public care, at 3.7 per cent of GDP (see Figure 10.3). Comparative data on long-term care spending is limited by the various distinctions between 'health' and 'social' care, and data on private spending on long-term care are even less reliable, but the OECD estimates that private expenditure in countries with the highest proportion of private funding represents around 30 per cent of spending on long-term care in Switzerland, Germany and the UK.

Another complication for any efforts to look comparatively at long-term care is that it is institutional care that is particularly expensive. OECD (2017b, p. 215, figure 11.25) data for 2015 indicate that the public cost of home care only exceeds that of institutional care in Germany, Austria, Denmark, Finland and Poland. Since it is, of course, care within the home where the enormous informal effort is present, an interesting comparative problem is revealed that cannot be adequately examined from the available data. Given the public preference for home care, a nation that is a high performer in terms of public expenditure may not necessarily be seen as doing well, if its expenditure is primarily on institutional care, in terms of either public expectations or public benefit per unit of expenditure.

Figure 10.3: Long-term care expenditure (health and social components) by government and compulsory insurance schemes, as a share of GDP, 2015 or nearest year

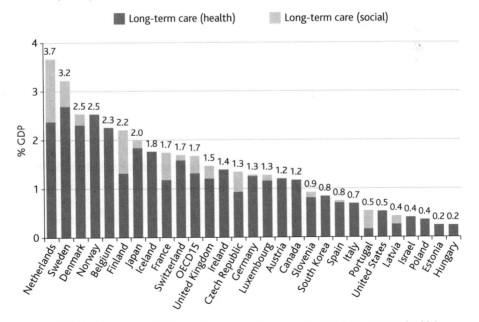

Source: OECD Health Statistics 2017. https://www.oecd-ilibrary.org/social-issues-migration-health/health-at-a-glance-2017/long-term-care-expenditure_health_glance-2017-81-en

Approaches to the provision of public long-term care

To compare nations with respect to long-term care, attention needs to be given not only to the extent to which the state is prepared to pay but also to issues about how care is provided. Since, as already noted at some length, the public care element is in many respects an add-on to care by families and communities or care privately purchased, it is not surprising to find that access to it is rationed in various ways. But comparisons need to look not just at the ways in which rationing is done but also how care is then provided. Various forms of partnership exist, not just between the state and the private, third and informal sectors but also between different public institutions themselves – social care and health care actors operate at both central and local government level and exhibit different forms of separation/integration.

The OECD (2011b, pp. 215–22) identifies three broad country clusters:

- Universal coverage within a single programme.
- Mixed systems.
- Means-tested safety net schemes.

The universal coverage category is furthered divided into:

- Tax-based models.
- Public long-term care insurance models.
- Personal care through the health system.

It may be tempting, from the OECD data, to point up examples that seem to fit the regime theory approach: relative generosity in the Nordic countries, emphasis on means tests in England (though not Scotland) and the US and care insurance in Germany, the Netherlands and Japan. However, overall the variation escapes simplistic typologization. A classification including the more or less meaningless label 'mixed systems' signals a high level of imprecision – means tests and cost-sharing provisions are evident in even the most comprehensive state systems. The OECD category of 'universal coverage' is additionally subject to various cost-sharing arrangements and exclusions with respect to individuals with high levels of income and/or assets. Given that care systems, particularly in Europe, are under public and policy scrutiny, and are likely to undergo considerable change in the 2020s, it is important to examine, in action, some examples of the key variations of so-called 'universal coverage'.

Norway, Sweden, Denmark, Finland and Scotland have tax-funded long-term care services, all with substantial local government involvement in delivery. But in all these cases there are provisions for cost sharing, particularly with board and lodging costs in care, operated with tests taking income into account. Belgium stands out as an example of long-term care funded through the health system, and Italy may be noted as having a more limited system also linked to tax-funded health care. In cases where there is tax-funded health care some forms of nursing care may be directly accessed without means testing or cost sharing. This is the case in England. Of course what is at stake here for the quality and extent of care is exactly how the health/social care boundary is drawn.

The Netherlands, Germany, Japan, South Korea and Luxembourg have long-term care insurance schemes. The Netherlands was the pioneer in 1968 with a complex scheme linked to private insurance companies, with Germany following in 1995. The South Korean scheme is the most recent, implemented in 2008. There are certain limitations on amounts of care support available, and thus forms of cost sharing (but without means tests). In all these countries there is also health insurance, and care insurance may be seen as a logical development from this. Indeed, the development in the Netherlands was closely linked to ambiguities in its health insurance system (Schut and van den Berg, 2011), which again highlights the significance of the way the health/social care boundary has been drawn. It may also be noted that where care insurance exists the provision of direct payments to those in need of care provides a way of managing the boundary between public and private care.

The OECD (2011b) cites the US and England as having means-tested safety net schemes. In the case of the US this is through the strictly means- and asset-tested Medicaid. There have been efforts to reform the English system since that date but, in 2019, that statement is still broadly correct. The English (indeed UK) situation is, however, complicated by the existence of non-means-tested benefits for severely disabled people. These, however, are set at levels well below the cost of residential care, and not linked to the full costs of domiciliary care.

Categorizing approaches does not capture the dimensions of care support that flow through cash payments. In various countries some support to social care may be provided with 'direct payments' in cash, for example benefits to working-age adults with respect to disability. Cash transfers for care support beyond working age is not a widely favoured policy solution since it is complicated by issues about the choice of and payment of carers. Glasby and Littlechild (2016, p. 64) note programmes that allow for direct payments or 'personal budgets', in certain circumstances, in Austria, Germany, Italy (though it is not in their table), Luxembourg, Sweden, the Netherlands, Norway and the US as well as the UK. They observe variations in the flexibility of the systems with respect to controls over the way money is used, noting the development in Germany, Italy and Austria of 'an unregulated grey labour market ... largely staffed by immigrant female workers' (they cite here Da Roit and Le Bilan, 2010). This highlights a further element of the global political economy of care in that the contemporary demand for and supply of services takes place in an international market where social divisions of gender, class and race can be reinforced and remade. These issues in relation to migration, primarily that of women, have been explored in the literature on 'global care chains' (see for example Misra et al., 2006).

Comparing care systems is difficult inasmuch as the most important form of rationing involves an assessment of need, in the physical not financial sense.

Government decisions to limit investment in social care lead on to rationing decisions which may draw ever stricter lines around entitlement, requiring ever more complicated tests of need. In the case of social care need, the complexities of the human condition, such as emotional and physical capacity and its dynamic nature, indicate that 'testing' will be fraught with injustice and ill-judgement. Clearly universal cash transfers directly related to quantifiable costs such as public transport are far less challenging to administer and are therefore more favourable policy solutions (see Humphries, 2013, p. 20).

In considering different approaches, it may be noted that universal tax-provided benefits or social insurance benefits help to secure entitlements to support, which cannot easily be varied by governments as they respond to their own fiscal pressures. This is particularly important inasmuch as formal care occurs in the context of massive informal care. But further strands woven into the care tapestry are those of the market and market relationships. Care as an activity has been subject to gradual marketization and more intense financialization since the 1980s, but prior to examining these in more detail it is necessary to first consider the place of market relationships in care relationships.

The idea of 'personal budgets' as a solution to meeting financial and practical care needs while also promoting human dignity provides a compelling case for widespread policy uptake, but there are counterarguments that go beyond the view that governments lack trust in citizens to spend wisely or with integrity. Policy makers' caution in permitting the use of direct payments to pay relatives to care for each other reflects not just a fear of fraudulent claims, or the assumption that families or networks are available, but also that human relationships have essential obligations: that some people *should* care for other people because of what they mean to those people, by birth, partnership or other intimate relationship, or even, in some countries, with reference to even weaker ties such as neighbourhood or other forms of social network. It is somewhat ironic that in an age where states are often more than willing to cede responsibilities to the market, in the case of care this anomaly remains.

Clearly, states do benefit considerably from informal care: in a recent report for Alzheimer's Disease International (Wimo et al., 2018), drawing on a range of international data, the researchers estimate that globally, informal care for dementia alone equates to over 41 million full-time workers' annual working time (2,000 hours), at a cost of around US$330 billion. But other than the economic incentive to leave caring to close relatives there is also the principle that caring is a 'labour of love', and while it may still be characterized by unequal gender relations (see Finch and Groves, 1983) and personal sacrifice, the givers and receivers of care may also reject the notion of bringing a cash payment into their relationship. Marketizing intimate care work in this way risks reducing meaningful human interaction to a stark transaction, but also brings with it the power imbalances between funder and service provider. To overcome these reservations, the 'universal caregiver' model of citizenship first proposed by Nancy Fraser (1997) has served as a source for moving forward regarding the debate on financial support for care (but as yet, not policy), towards a framework that reconciles the humanity of caring, but also its economic costs.

While the role of the market in the private sphere of intimate caring relationships has yet to be resolved, the role of the market within the public sphere of service provision has been firmly established as the 'care industry'. The problem for this industry, however, is that while the demand is high, the ability to pay is limited. Therefore, although from the 1980s both governments and international organizations advising low-income countries have supported the entry of private providers into areas of provision such as residential and institutional care, as well as domiciliary services, much of this provision was funded through contracts with public departments. Since the financial crisis in 2008 public spending on social care has increased across the OECD countries (OECD, 2017b), but in systems where spending is balanced towards discretionary provision rather than non-discretionary (as in the insurance-related arrangements discussed earlier) it remains fiscally constrained, making for an unstable market.

The UK provides a test case for the application of fiscal austerity measures and their impact on marketized care services. Spending by local authorities on social care services fell by 8.4 per cent in real terms between 2009 and 2017 (IFS, 2017), and as a result the domiciliary (home) care market has been described as 'on the brink of failure' in a report prepared jointly by a local authority think-tank and a large private care provider (LGiU and Mears, 2017). The report cites survey data indicating that 62 per cent of local authorities have experienced residential home closures and 57 per cent have had contracts handed back by providers. Further data indicated that councils have received 23,000 safeguarding alerts in relation to allegations of neglect and abuse. Despite the low pay associated with care work, and the entry of hedge funds looking to find places to park investments after 2008, private providers are finding care services unprofitable in the UK. A report commissioned by the BBC programme *Panorama* (Opus Restructuring LLP and Company Watch, 2017) based on business data, reported that 27 per cent of domiciliary care providers were at risk of insolvency in 2017, with 294 'zombie' companies sharing a combined negative net equity of £38 million. Many of these providers are small companies, often operating on a franchise model under the brand of a larger provider. This snapshot of the fragile care market in the UK exposes the risks of the mixed economy of welfare, but as the report details, the 'human costs' in unmet needs are far greater.

Arguably, the care market is fundamentally flawed, not simply because pricing care is morally suspect, or because of market monopsony, but because by its nature it is (or should be) impervious to the drivers of efficiency – it is unpredictable and not reducible to units of activity. It is also flawed because in the interests of outcomes it requires heavy regulation and its quality depends on boutique not mass production. Meeting long-term care needs requires conditions of stability, continuity and reliability, but the entry of hedge fund investors has rendered the market even more unstable since it is now further embedded in the global financial markets.

Conclusion

This chapter has attempted to cover considerable ground in the analysis of care as a policy domain. Unlike health or education, social care 'policy' is poorly defined. This is not necessarily problematic since it is not logical or beneficial to attempt a separation of the mechanics of care from its essential role in socialization, education and good health. The policy challenges lie in ensuring that the distribution of the taking and giving of care is equitable, and in determining how far the state should intervene in the private sphere to achieve this. It is possible to establish models of difference and similarity along some of the dimensions of success and failure in addressing these inequities (along gender lines for example). However, internationally, welfare arrangements for social care vary too greatly and along too many dimensions to lend themselves to regime type analysis. For these reasons, combined with the expansion of care needs driven by changes in work, demography and epidemiological knowledge, advancement in the analysis of care in an international and global context is of particular significance for social policy study.

11

Environment

Introduction

Environmental policy is a large and diverse field which has hitherto held a marginal position in relation to social policy. Huby (1998), an early pioneer in attempts to bring the environment into social policy, presents a classification of the range of problems caused by human activity which potentially lead to policy responses. She details these in terms of the problems caused by the use of *natural resources*, such as physical degeneration of the landscape, land subsidence, flooding and soil degeneration; the problems caused by the generation of *wastes*, such as water, land and air pollution – together with a variety of connected issues to encompass less direct effects such as acid deposition and the atmospheric effects associated with climate change; and *habitat disruption* and the consequent loss of biodiversity.

There are, of course, other environmental problems requiring policy responses that are the result of natural events rather than being caused by human activity, such as earth movements and volcanoes, which widens the range of issues that bring the 'environment' into the study of social policy. Such a point is also made in Cahill's argument for recognizing 'policy dependencies' (1994, p. 2), and in later work (2010) in his identification of the importance of issues like travel in exacerbating existing welfare inequalities and also in creating new ones. Although geographers have traditionally considered the ways in which 'place and space' affects our well-being, environmental concerns go beyond questions of location and are clearly part of the remit of social policy analysis in the contemporary world. The case for concern about the megacities that have grown up around the world, as often in poor countries as in rich ones, is not just about their associated levels of pollution, but about travelling within them, access to public space and amenities, leisure space and the countryside, and the extent to which social inequalities are created and reinforced. These points help to contextualize a more specific emphasis in environmental policy on the problems of pollution (and the significance of this issue from the local to global level). Pollution is an important focus both as a subject given increasing attention in comparative studies and as a truly 'global' problem (that is, one which crosses borders) on the global social policy agenda.

Within a more general approach to the consideration of the environment in social policy, this chapter starts with two topics that are important for much social policy analysis, but which are particularly relevant here: economic growth and its measurement, and the concern with 'externalities'. As noted in Chapter 2, dominant economic orthodoxy assumes that growth is the solution to problems of social disadvantage, and in the post–2008 crisis world the quest for a return to economic growth has driven both economic and social policy. The 'externalities' of this approach to policy are arguably more widely present in the effects of austerity (see Farnsworth and Irving, 2015), but here they are considered in their more traditional conceptualization, as the indirect consequences of economic activity. The final part of this chapter examines comparative studies of environmental policy and the ways in which environmental issues are linked with social harm, and provides an extended discussion of climate change. This offers cues for a discussion of 'environmental policy as social policy', and the chapter ends with some concluding comments on the development of this idea.

Growth and GDP: the dominance of a production perspective

The concept of the GDP is one that has been used in comparisons between nations in several chapters in this book. But there are limitations to GDP as a measurement because of the way in which its use contributes to an emphasis on economic activities without reference to their consequences or costs. Natural resource depletion and the production of waste (and therefore pollution) are among these costs. GDP is a monetary measure of the market value of all final goods and services produced over a period of time, usually one year. It was developed in the late 1930s by the economist Simon Kuznets, to try to measure change in the economy across a specified period. Pilling (2018), in an examination of its strengths and weaknesses, refers to it as 'Kuznets' Monster', noting its inventor's misgivings and the way it has been simplified in discourse about economic policy. But GDP remains the widely used standard measure of national economic development and, by implication, growth in well-being across a society. An economic recession is defined accordingly in terms of the absence of an increase in GDP across a defined period.

The OECD, a routine user of the GDP measure, in a paper making a case for it being 'satisfactory' nevertheless recognizes that 'It measures growth, but not destruction, and it ignores values like social cohesion and the environment' (OECD, 2004/5, p. 1). For social policy analysis, GDP is therefore rendered highly problematic, and this is in addition to problems identified in the inclusion of highly unequally distributed goods and services in measuring GDP (see Chapter 2), and its gendered recognition of what counts as 'production'. The GDP measure has consequently become the subject of various academic critiques (see in particular Stiglitz et al., 2009). Even its contribution to economics is questioned in *The Economist* (2016), where it is noted that GDP is 'increasingly a poor measure of prosperity. It is not even a reliable gauge of production … it is a relic of a period dominated by manufacturing' (see also Coyle, 2011). Although much work has been done to try to capture economic activity involving services, including public services, difficulties remain. Measuring GDP depends very much on being able to identify cash transactions, thereby ignoring unremunerated services, and thus of course within-household transfers. The digital age has further confounded these kinds of measurements of economic growth since benefits now emerge without cash transactions, for example through digital content sharing.

Aside from these issues, the concern here is with the extent to which there are costs from economic activity that go unrecognized. Here pollution looms large, together with all the injurious effects of economic activity (Jackson, 2009, p. 179). Ironically, a disaster may produce an increase in GDP as far as it leads to 'productive' activities to make good the losses incurred. The alternative to the use of GDP would seem to be a measure that is able to weigh benefits of economic activities against costs, but it would be difficult to assemble an approach to this that could effectively challenge the GDP discourse, in which politicians and the media cite figures that even advocates of the use of GDP accept as subject to a wide margin of error. All of these problems may be seen as pragmatic objections to the use of GDP, but there is a more fundamental moral issue too. Raworth (2017) argues that GDP, as the indicator of economic health, has become a political obsession tied to the notion that the need for growth is politically unquestionable. She goes on to commend the challenge offered in the *Limits to Growth* report (Meadows et al., 1972) and in particular Donella Meadows' observations in a lecture (1999) that 'Growth is one of the stupidest purposes invented by any culture, … growth for what, and why, and for whom, and who pays the cost, and how long can it last, and what's the cost to the planet, and how much is enough?'

However, the limits to growth argument has always been more easily applied to advanced economies than to those where there are high levels of poverty and unemployment. An alternative is the idea of 'sustainable development', a concept first popularized in the renowned Brundtland Report (World Commission on Environment and Development, 1987), which has most recently become global policy in the form of the SDGs. As Cahill suggests (2002, p. 7), sustainable development 'involves taking a global perspective' and 'should mean the countries of the northern hemisphere taking fewer resources and living with fewer consumer goods'. The SDGs express such a perspective in terms of quantifiable goals to compete with GDP measures, but provide less of a challenge to the 'problem' of 'low growth' that has dominated much discussion of the economies of the rich countries since the 2008 recession. Concern about limiting 'externalities' rather than preventing growth is thus particularly applicable to sustainable development.

Externalities and collective action problems

The notion of externalities, the indirect consequences of economic activity, is a concept derived from welfare economics which may be used about much social policy. It is seen as providing a justification for state interventions and is particularly pertinent for the analysis of environmental policy. There may be both 'positive' and 'negative' externalities. Positive ones arise when other people benefit from activities without sharing the costs, negative ones involve unwanted consequences for these third parties. Much of the politics of environmental policy involves conflicts of interest between those affected by externalities and those whose activities produce them. The producers of positive externalities want the cost shared, those who suffer from negative ones want them to be prevented or to be compensated for them.

The creator of a positive externality is likely to resent the 'free riders' who will benefit from something they do not pay for. For example, if someone bears the entire costs of building a sea wall to protect their property from flooding, their neighbours are likely to share that benefit for free. There may, of course, in this case also be negative consequences somewhere else down the coast, in which case the combination of positive and negative effects further reinforces the case for collective action. Faced with a high-cost item, and the likelihood of free riders, an individual is likely to try to secure agreement for collective action (the sharing of the cost among the potential beneficiaries). As far as the community surrounding the builder of the hypothetical sea wall is concerned, the wall constitutes what is sometimes called a 'public good' – no one can be prevented from benefiting from it. There are other examples where the benefiting community may be very much larger, including (in the contemporary context) the international and global community. This notion of a public good is thus important in relation to the case for state action.

The problem of pollution provides the most obvious example of negative externalities. In the course of producing something, a manufacturer expels waste products up a chimney or into a water course. This action may have consequences for people, animals and land. While the worst effects are likely to be close to the emissions, effects may spread very widely. And of course, in the case of activities causing climate change, negative externalities are worldwide. Here, then, is a case for collective action to prevent environmental damage which its producer has no incentive to prevent, and where moreover, any individual suffering its effects is likely to lack the resources to take action alone.

It is relatively straightforward to develop policies to combat indiscriminate dispersal of waste products. Indeed, much of the anti-pollution activity of modern governments involves the encouragement (perhaps with coercion) of ways of absorbing, reusing or burying the by-products of production or the development of less polluting energy sources. But there is a wider issue to which the analysis of externalities draws attention. Hardin (1968) highlighted what has been called 'the tragedy of the commons'. This term was originally used to describe how 'rational' actors exploiting an unregulated common resource (such as grazing land) for their own gain and with no regard for others, will automatically contribute to the depletion of this common resource. While the examination of reasons why mediaeval villagers learnt to develop shared management of a small plot of land provides an instructive case study, what it should draw to our attention is the universality of this issue for the present. A global view on this was provided by Mahatma Gandhi in 1928, arguing that if India were to engage in the kind of economic exploitation undertaken by the West 'it would strip the world bare like locusts' (Gandhi quoted by Ghosh, 2016).

This consideration of externalities suggests how environmental policy issues have local, national, international and global dimensions. To some extent a function of developing science and developing internationalism, a shift of the policy agenda up through these dimensions has occurred. In the field of air pollution control in the UK for example, changes in the agenda from local to global can be observed over a comparatively short time. First, a concern about smoke abatement in the 1950s, an issue highlighted by local 'smogs' in London and other cities (Hall et al., 1975, Chapter 13). Second, a recognition that the process of expelling air-borne waste products out through high chimneys in this comparatively windy island led to forest and lake damage from acid rain not only in our own countryside but also in Scandinavia (Ashby and Anderson, 1981). Third, connected with work on this issue was the development of environmental policy in the EU as a whole, recognizing the interconnectedness of many pollution problems. And then finally the emergence of the issue of climate change on the global political agenda, an issue in which local implementation of global aspirations is essential for success.

Comparative approaches to environmental policy

Comparing states in terms of their environmental policies is a relatively undeveloped exercise in contrast to the multiplication of approaches to the comparative analysis of mainstream social policy. This is not surprising. There are various different issues with which environmental policy is concerned, and efforts to deal with them primarily take the form of regulation, which means that it involves relatively low public expenditure that is not easy to subject to comparative analysis. Much of the comparative analysis so far is one-dimensional, using the concept of 'environmental states' (Meadowcroft, 2005; Gough, 2016). This involves an echo of the idea of 'welfare states'. Gough's (2016) exploration of this topic starts with the following reservations about this parallel:

1. The extent to which, while it is domestic challenges that have driven welfare state developments, global threats and challenges are much more evident in environmental policy.
2. While regulation was a feature of early state welfare interventions this has developed in the direction of large-scale public financing, while on the other hand, as noted earlier, regulation rather than cash expenditure remains salient in environmental policy.
3. Environmental challenges 'are policy domains of great uncertainty and complexity compared with our understanding of threats to human nature' (Gough, 2016, p. 27).
4. Science and scientists play a much greater role in environmental policy than in mainstream social policy.

These four reservations rather underplay the parallels in specific policy areas at specific times and in specific places, and Gough's initial points here give particular attention to the most global and recent (in terms of recognition) issue: climate change. In his conclusions he emphasizes common themes that have been discussed in previous chapters – globalization, the increased power of international capital and the role of business. He does, however, suggest that differential environmental policy outputs and outcomes result from national variance in welfare regimes and related policy arrangements which produce country clusters that 'demarcate the Anglosphere from the EU' (Gough, 2016, p. 43). Gough's conclusion highlights two particular issues. One is that efforts to typologize countries with regard to environmental policy involve giving particularly strong attention to economic forces, particularly global ones. The other is that what seems to be indicated is a dichotomy: the Anglosphere/EU contrast that has much in common with the original form of varieties of capitalism theory (see Chapter 3). The studies reviewed here attempt to go beyond this simple dichotomy.

Perhaps the best way to compare countries, in any public policy, is in terms of outcomes, that is, actual achievements. In the case of the environment, cleaner air, cleaner water and so on offers a comparatively straightforward outcome measure. There are, however, two difficulties with this kind of comparison. One is that the causes of improvement may have nothing to do with government environmental policy and may result instead from changes to the economy. Recessions in particular involve the collapse of certain kinds of industrial activities and a consequent reduction in emissions. The other is the extent to which outcomes are geographically disbursed beyond individual nations, and are perhaps even global (as is the case with climate change).

The second difficulty can be to some extent avoided by attention to outputs rather than outcomes (what quantities of particular pollutants are discharged and where). Outcome approaches give attention to issues like air and river quality, but there have been efforts to put all the environmental issues together (see Fiorino, 2011, for a review). Özler and Obach (2009) use ecological footprints as the dependent variable in their study of the impact of capitalism and state economic policy on the environment, comparing a large sample of countries. The ecological footprint is a measure of environmental impact, expressed in terms of the additional land needed to compensate. Wackernagel and Rees (1996), using a measure of 'capitalism' developed from indices used by the right-wing Heritage Foundation, reach the conclusion that 'the more capitalist a state is, the greater its environmental impact is likely to be, even controlling for such factors as per capita GDP' (Özler and Obach, 2009, p. 103). Carbon footprints are also reported similarly, giving attention to the varied contributions to climate change.

An alternative approach to seeking outcome measures is to try to classify states in terms of their adoption of regulatory policies. This goes further towards unpacking the rather sweeping generalizations explored so far. Jänicke (2005), in trying to identify 'trend setters', and Liefferink et al.'s (2009) analysis of 'leaders and laggards', do this to some extent, although a broad US/EU division remains the key finding. Given the importance of the EU as a transnational developer of environmental policies, studies either have to look historically (as do Liefferink et al., 2009) or seek to trace variations in enthusiasm for regulation within the EU nations. The scholar who, so far, has come closest to developing an environmental policy 'regime' analysis is Duit (2016), who argues that environmental states may be identified in terms of four different 'faces' (see Table 11.1).

Table 11.1: The four 'faces' of environmental states

Regulation	Redistribution	Administration organization	Knowledge generation
The enactment of regulatory measures, classified in terms of date of origin into 'first' and 'second' generation	The use of redistributory mechanisms (taxes and subsidies)	The establishment of environmental policy agencies	The production and dissemination of relevant knowledge.

Source: Adapted from Duit (2016)

Duit then operationalizes these faces using two datasets which enable countries to be scored according to their approaches. Using cluster analysis, four clusters of states are identified (2016, pp. 84–5):

1. A group which 'set up an administrative structure quite early, use taxation to a large extent and have high levels of both first and second-generation policies and above average levels of Green research spending'. These are Austria, Denmark, Finland, France, Germany, the Netherlands, Sweden and the UK.
2. A group 'characterised by low levels of administrative capacity, the highest mean number of first generation policies, the second highest mean number of second-generation policies, the highest mean level of R&D spending and the second highest level of Green taxes'. These are Belgium, Hungary, Italy, Ireland, Norway and South Korea.
3. A group 'exhibiting the lowest average levels of administrative capacity, and slightly below average levels of knowledge production, policies and taxation'. This is a diverse group: Australia, Canada, Greece, Mexico, Poland, Spain, Slovakia, Switzerland and Japan.
4. A group with 'a weakly developed administrative capacity, few … regulations, little environment R&D spending and low levels of environment taxation'. This group consists of Argentina, Israel, New Zealand and US.

Duit points out the lack of correspondence with welfare state regime classifications (as do Koch and Fritz, 2014). EU members are spread between three of the four groups, but Northern European member states feature strongly in the top two groups. The identification of the Anglosphere as weak environmentalists is not entirely supported – possibly an EU influence on the UK and Ireland has an effect. Duit comments on the absence of two early pioneers of environmental policy – Japan and the US – in the 'top' groups, seeing this as 'largely a result of inertia'.

Typologizing in this way is very vulnerable to policy change over time and contrasts clearly with the relative stability of expenditure measures used in the classification of welfare states. In that respect Knill et al.'s (2012) study of some OECD nations, using similar methods, is pertinent since it identifies a somewhat different categorization – leaders, midfield and laggards, with countries allocated as shown in Table 11.2.

Table 11.2: Typology of 'environmental' states

Leaders	Midfield	Laggards
Austria	Finland	Bulgaria
Belgium	Japan	Denmark
France	Portugal	Ireland
Germany	Slovakia	United States
Hungary	Spain	
Italy	Sweden	
Netherlands	Norway	
Switzerland	United Kingdom	

Source: Adapted from Knill et al. (2012)

There is thus, in the work of both Duit (2016) and Knill et al. (2012), a classification of environmental states that is radically different from that of welfare regimes. Going beyond the OECD, with a classification that concerns carbon dioxide emissions that feature so significantly in global warming, Lamb et al. (2014) chart carbon emission data against average life expectancy. Like Wilkinson and Pickett's (2010) analysis of health inequalities, they find a relationship like an upturned letter 'L' in which, once attention is shifted from the nations where there are very low life expectancies, there is a flattening of the graph so that there are both very low emitter nations and very high emitter ones where life expectancies are much the same.

This tension between the identification of the most polluting nations, and their willingness to bear responsibility, continues to stall progress in many areas. While the SDGs make explicit the actions required by states and the public reporting of these, they are ultimately reliant on 'soft powers' rather than legal and/or regulatory frameworks.

Pollution, disease and death

It has been noted that life in environments which contribute to higher levels of mortality and morbidity is an important feature of analyses of contemporary health inequalities, but it is often difficult to separate out specific bad environmental effects from other disadvantages. An examination of early modern history shows environmental concerns to be among the first 'social policy' issues to arrive on the political agenda in the nineteenth century (see Fraser, 1975). Initially it was polluted water rather than impure air that received attention. McKeown's

(1980) influential text on the role of health services in the advancement of health stresses the role of environmental interventions for the improvement of health. In the twenty-first century the most dramatic illustrations of this point are seen in global health inequalities. Table 11.3 sets out figures for the WHO regions on deaths attributable to air pollution and to unsafe washing facilities – there are excess deaths in regions containing low- and middle-income countries compared to the rich global North. Data by country show that cross-national differences are far more pronounced than the regional figures indicate. The data on unsafe water are particularly striking: the death rate figure is close to zero in much of the world, but over 100 per 100,000 in Angola, the Democratic Republic of Congo and the Central African Republic, and close to that figure in Somalia, indicating extreme public health deficiencies in those countries.

By contrast, a number of large nations have very high levels of deaths caused by air pollution, notably China with 161.1 per 100,000 people and India with 133.7. The figure for Russia is 98.6 and in many Eastern European nations the figure is over 100 (including three EU members: Latvia, Hungary and Romania). At the other extreme, in only four nations is it below 1: Australia, Brunei, New Zealand and Sweden. The figure for the UK is 25.7. While the data in the WHO annual report come from 2012, a more recent source (WHO, 2018) states that air pollution is responsible for 6.5 million premature deaths annually, and that over 80 per cent of urban residents are exposed to air quality below the WHO recommended levels, with those in low- and middle-income countries most affected:

> The major outdoor pollution sources include vehicles, power generation, building heating systems, agriculture/waste incineration and industry. In addition, more than 3 billion people worldwide rely on polluting technologies and fuels (including biomass, coal and kerosene) for household cooking, heating and lighting, releasing smoke into the home and leaching pollutants outdoors.[1]

Table 11.3: Deaths per 100,000 people attributed to forms of pollution, 2012 by WHO region

	Deaths attributable to air pollution	Deaths attributable to unsafe washing facilities
Africa	80.2	2.8
The Americas	20.3	0.8
South East Asia	119.9	1.5
Europe	64.2	1.0
Eastern Mediterranean	58.2	1.4
Western Pacific	133.5	1.4
Global	92.4	1.5

Source: WHO (2017a, p. 100)

Clearly there are important connections between this evidence, which locates air pollution as a problem particularly linked to urbanization and industrialization, and issues relating to climate change, to be explored in the following section.

Climate change

Climate change is scientifically proven to be occurring. The essential issues are that climate change is occurring with complex effects, and that there is strong evidence that the primary contributor to this process is human activity. Most significant is the emission of gases as a consequence of fossil fuel consumption, where carbon dioxide (CO_2) emission is the major element. The rate of change is hard to predict, but the changes that have occurred so far are in themselves sufficient to have serious consequences for human welfare around the world. It may reasonably be argued that the continuing uncertainties involve risk assessments for which very high probabilities suggest that doing nothing is not an option. Climate change is thus a quintessential global issue and the externalities are global in character, but they are obviously affected by meteorological effects that are hard to pin down. There are, however, important questions both about causes and consequences, which need to be analyzed in terms of the roles of individual nation states inasmuch as global policies need national implementation and vary in their local effects.

There are three kinds of policy responses to the climate change issue. One, *geo-engineering* – a process of putting screening devices into the atmosphere – is unlikely because the science (let alone the politics) is still very complicated. The other two – *adaptation* and *mitigation* – are, however, fundamental for the politics of climate change (Dessler and Parson, 2010, p. 112):

> Adaptation measures target the impacts of climate change: they seek to adjust human society to the changing climate, to reduce the resultant harms. Examples include building sea walls or dikes to limit risks from higher sea levels or planting drought resistant crops to deal with drier summers ... Mitigation measures target the causes of climate change by reducing the emissions of greenhouse gases that are responsible.

These two kinds of responses are examined in separate subsections below.

Adaptation

Adaptation has the obvious political appeal that it does not seem to call for global action, but societies differ in terms of the impact of climate change. The key issues are variants on two themes: desertification and flooding. The Intergovernmental Panel on Climate Change (IPCC) offers a more elaborate identification of the key risks (see Box 11.1).

Box 11.1: IPCC identification of key risks associated with climate change

- 'Death, injury, ill health, or disrupted livelihoods' from flooding in coastal zones and small islands due to storms and rising sea-levels.
- 'Severe ill-health and disrupted livelihoods for large urban populations' from inland flooding.
- 'Systemic risks due to extreme weather events' affecting public services.
- 'Mortality and morbidity during periods of extreme heat' (to which risk of fire might be added).
- 'Food insecurity and breakdown of food systems' associated with warming, drought and flooding.
- 'Loss of rural livelihoods and income' due to lack of access to water.
- 'Loss of marine and coastal ecosystems'.
- 'Loss of terrestrial and inland water systems'.

Source: IPCC (2014, p. 13)

It does not require much imagination to identify that there will be major differences between nations in the extent to which these risks apply. Much attention is given to the particular vulnerability of Africa, where small-scale, rainfall-dependent agriculture remains predominant in a context of coexistent high levels of poverty, disease and insecurity (New Economics Foundation, 2005). Ghosh (2016) sees the current discourse as insufficiently concerned about the large number of people potentially affected in Asia, noting the presence of over 250 million people living around the Bengal Delta. At the same time desertification is an issue in India, Pakistan and China, with the melting of the Himalayan glaciers threatening to substantially reduce the flow of rivers on which many depend for water.

Of course the 'global' response could be that these are national problems calling for national responses. But the fact that their distribution is uneven, and that such unevenness may be a product of externally driven economic activities, indicates otherwise. Many of the dangers are in places where there is a lack of resources to deal with them, indeed in many cases places where international aid is already being used to mitigate poverty. The recognition that some of the problems identified may have cross-national implications, in that they may contribute to the movement of people, puts another issue high on the policy agenda. The impact of desertification is pertinent here, but perhaps the most extreme cases are those Pacific islands where rising sea levels are literally taking away the land.

Moreover, the fact that the problem is ultimately a product of the economic activity that has enriched the North, places a particular responsibility for assistance with adaptation issues upon these beneficiaries of uneven development. Indifference towards these risks is a characteristic of some of the responses to the problem of climate change in the richer countries of the world. Parenti offers a dystopian vision in his *Tropic of Chaos* (2012), writing of 'the politics of the armed lifeboat', and highlighting US intransigence on the way the problems of climate change play out differently across an unequal planet. Denial is accompanied by measures to protect US borders in an attempt to seal the country off from the world's problems. The election of Donald Trump in 2016 and his subsequent foreign and trade policy decisions, and most notably the US withdrawal from the Paris Agreement in 2017, have since brought much of this story to life.

Mitigation

The recognition by scientists of the human role in causation, and of the fact that the climate change problem was steadily widening, led to the recognition of the issue on the agenda of international organizations. Scientific collaboration began in the 1980s, but the crucial step towards global policy came with the Kyoto Protocol of 1997 which sought to impose specific emission targets for each industrial country. A sequence of conferences followed, leading up to one in Paris in December 2015 where it was agreed that all nations should work together to keep global temperature increases below 2 degrees Celsius beyond pre-industrial levels, and make efforts to keep them below 1.5 degrees. Since those limits were set *after* increases beyond pre-industrial levels had occurred, they implied an increase of little over 1 degree above 2015 levels. This is an ambitious target, reflecting the evidence of accelerating problems.

But an international agreement imposing obligations on individual nations leaves much to be accomplished. A key issue remains as to whether emission targets should be general, or whether the beneficiaries from past industrialization (the big polluters at the outset) should do more, giving the later industrializers more latitude so that their economic progress is not constrained. China is now the biggest emitter of CO_2, with the US coming second. But if figures are calculated per head of population, China is actually below several countries and Saudi Arabia and the US head the list (see Table 11.4).

The ease with which nations can change their emission patterns is affected by their fuel use. Both China and India, and for that matter Australia, are heavily dependent on the most polluting fuel: coal. The US, Canada and Saudi Arabia are producers of another of the more polluting fuels: oil. The issue of fuel use is central to the emergence of more optimistic scenarios for dealing with climate change, involving rapid development of solar and wind energy. To these could be added nuclear energy, but for continuing fears about the long-term implications of its use including safety, and the short-term issues about start-up costs.

What is clear is that – notwithstanding the (near) universal acceptance of the Paris Agreement – much still depends upon responses to the problem in individual countries. The US withdrawal will inevitably have long-term repercussions not only on the strength of commitment of other national signatories but also for the funding of both climate change-focused science programmes and the environmental aid to countries on whose economic progress the emissions targets have most impact. The opportunity presented to China to become the 'global

Table 11.4: CO_2 gas emissions: metric tonnes per capita, 2014

Country	CO_2 emissions
Saudi Arabia	19.5
US	16.5
Australia	15.4
Canada	15.1
Russia	11.9
Netherlands	9.9
Japan	9.5
Germany	8.9
China	7.5
UK	6.5
Spain	5.0
France	4.6
Brazil	2.6
India	1.7
Indonesia	1.6

Note: The last available date for these data is 2014, and so does not reflect the substantial changes and variations over time.

Source: World Bank (2019a), https://data.worldbank.org/indicator/EN.ATM.CO2E.PC

leader' on action on climate change and the subsequent EU–China statements emphasizing continuing political and economic commitments, indicate that efforts to tackle both the economic and natural problems will continue, but the disengagement of the US places further obstacles in the path of progress.

The size of the problem, and the rate at which it is intensifying, suggests that slow incremental policy changes will be insufficient. The two more fundamental alternatives involve, on the one hand, what may be called 'the green growth' strategy, and on the other hand, a recognition of the need for changes to the operation of the economy, which may involve giving much less attention to the goal of economic growth. The green growth (also termed 'clean growth') strategy involves seeing investment in change, for example the development of cleaner ways to generate energy, as to some extent a positive offset to costs that arise from curbing polluting activities. It may be optimistic to expect this offsetting process to be easy and cost free, and often, as is the case with 'fracking', energy-generation activities presented as new and/or clean have their own hazards and social impact. On the other hand, as suggested earlier in this chapter, if an approach to measuring growth that gave attention to the negative consequences of forms that depend upon pollution were adopted, this problem might be easier to solve. Chapter 12 returns to this theme – seeing aspects of what has been called a 'Green New Deal' as one of the more positive elements in contemporary discourse.

Before proceeding to a discussion of the politics of climate change it is appropriate to include a brief comment on the agricultural dimension, which has clear interdependencies with industry and transport and has been given increasing attention in the debate (IPCC, 2019). Agriculture is a source of greenhouse gases and can also play a significant role in the absorption of those gases (as a 'carbon sink'). Agriculture, as noted, is of course affected by climate change, and some of the most significant forms of consequent social harm are experienced by people whose livelihoods depend upon agriculture. A range of social policy issues thus follow on from, or are connected to, agriculture. At risk of simplification, a crude distinction can be made between (a) industrialized parts of societies where the main connection with agriculture involves issues about the marketing and consumption of products, (b) places where the agricultural industry is 'big business' but local population dependence upon it is low and (c) places where agriculture remains central to livelihoods. This illustrates the differences of interest and policy concerns that can be mapped globally.

For group (a) the issues concern almost all aspects of climate change. For example, trade in agricultural products is a huge source of pollution from transportation; 'carbon footprints' are not just a product of travel but also consumption practices. Attention to consumption has increased in the context of resource use in conversion of agricultural production into human consumption. This is key to policy interest in food consumption (see Holly, 2017, for a commentary on the social dimension). However, it cannot be expected that these issues can simply be addressed through human behaviour change since such change will have economic consequences, including increasing the costs of basic consumption goods which will therefore need political attention given the existing distribution of economic resources (see Fitzpatrick, 2014, on the intersection of poverty and climate change, for example).

Turning to groups (b) and (c), the earlier creation of zones of the world with high-intensity agricultural production lies close to the heart of many of the world's contemporary environmental problems. Desertification after extensive agricultural activity is by no means simply a modern problem. Such are the complications of climate change that some of its most dramatic manifestations are problems of flooding, many of them exacerbated by previous land use. What is also problematical is that until recently heavy use of fertilizers and pesticides was seen as the key to a 'green revolution' in many low-income countries. There is recognition of carbon capture opportunities from reforestation and changes in agriculture, yet the outstanding questions regarding the livelihoods of group (c) remain. A key question is how traditional agricultural activities that are low sources of pollution can be sustained. As noted earlier, the interactions between competing interests across the globe are daunting.

The politics of climate change mitigation

As the summary of the agricultural dimension indicates, issues about who gains and who loses from climate change policies need to be examined at many levels – globally, nationally and for communities and individuals. At the global level the issues are embodied in the questions to be asked about the figures in Table 11.4.

Fairness in the global context needs to have regard to the fact that the growth of China and India provides the most straightforward approach to raising standards of living in those societies, although that does not guarantee fairness within those societies. On the other hand, there is a very strong case for acceptance of cuts to growth (whatever that may mean) in the nations (the US and Europe) that were, until very recently, the main sources of atmospheric CO_2. Moreover, Gough (2017, p. 26) points out that there is an important distinction that should be made between 'production-based emissions' and 'consumption-based emissions'. He explains this point as follows:

> Consumption-based emissions of the OECD are higher than their territorial emissions, while those of the rest of the world are lower. This reflects the outsourcing of manufacturing and industry from the West to the East during the period of intense globalisation – and accompanying deindustrialisation in the West – since around 1980.

In short, in the contemporary globalized economy, pollution is often 'outsourced'.

The issues here about equity between nations then need to be supplemented by considerations about equity within nations. Gough (2013) shows from a review of European evidence that higher-income households contribute more to emissions in absolute terms, that lower-income households suffer more from environmental degradation, but that the main policy measures on the agenda burden lower-income households more. The crucial point is that favoured policies involve the use of pricing and taxing devices to curb fuel use, which tend to have regressive effects, particularly when applied to domestic heating costs for example.

In terms of popular support for action on climate change, this has become more apparent since the early 2010s, and by 2019 global protest in the form of 'climate strikes' largely led by school-age young people has indicated that governments and policy makers are increasingly having to account publicly for policy responses. Data suggest that opinion on the issue varies in ways that bear little relation to the strength of the evidence. For example a Gallup Poll in the US showed a division in public opinion following Trump's decision to pull out of the Paris Agreement – with 66 per cent of Democrats reporting worries about climate change as against 18 per cent of Republicans (Gallup, 2 June 2017). The difficulty facing efforts to focus attention on climate change lies in the fact that political agendas and public attitudes have tended to take a short-run view while dealing with climate change requires long-run attention. Historically, the pressures for action have been less urgent in the global North than in the South, but this may now be changing (see discussion in Chapter 12). Extreme weather events secure immediate attention but the political demands that arise tend to be for adaptation rather than mitigation: for strengthening sea walls, dredging rivers and reducing rates of water flow from river sources, for example, rather than essential changes to ways of living and producing.

Since the causes of climate change are multiple and the solutions may be seen as involving a variety of options, not all of which need to be adopted for ultimate success, there is a tendency for the political and popular debate to involve unhelpful segmentation of the issues. As environmental disasters vary in the extent to which they highlight particular aspects of the problem, or as new scientific reports give attention to particular pieces of the evidence, so attention shifts. Items on the long menu of things that could be done – less air travel, fewer cars, better ways of generating power, less wasteful uses of food and other resources and so on – and specific issues such as plastic use and plastic waste, fall in and out of political focus. The power of business groups to resist or reframe the issues in their own interests is also apparent in these debates. For example, the car industry has been able to invoke the long-run prospects of the shift to electric cars and thus limit immediate attention to car use per se. In this way the political agenda is rendered shapeless and fundamental issues are evaded.

Whatever the variations in willingness to accept the urgency of the situation, the underlying problem is the pressure for action on the 'catching up' nations, and need for the historical polluters to do more than clean up, all in the context of the still influential fossil fuel industries. The question is whether an incremental approach to this issue is feasible, or whether the changes needed are too great, and the barriers to embracing radical changes within the conventional democratic political agenda too difficult. Gough (2017, p. 194) sums up the core problem thus:

> the pursuit of social, egalitarian and sustainable goals must contend with a political economy driven fundamentally by greed and the pursuit of profit. … Indeed, capitalism is *the* systemic driver of climate change. Unless powerful countervailing forces are in play, it also leads to unacceptable levels of inequality and opportunities for predatory practices by the powerful.

Policies that can reduce the risk of flood, fire and crop devastation for many of the most vulnerable people in the world and call for changes in social redistribution have therefore to take a central place within the social policy agenda.

Environmental policy as social policy

Links between environmental issues and other social policy issues are manifest. Large numbers of people die unnecessarily because of preventable environmental problems, and many more suffer harmful consequences. The inequalities examined in other chapters interact with environmental inequalities directly and indirectly. This is most clearly evident with respect to health inequalities, but other inequalities – with respect to access to jobs or housing for example – contribute to or reinforce exposure to environmental problems. While this is a worldwide issue (apparent in unequal advanced economies, such as the US and the UK) it is particularly relevant in contexts of rapid urbanization in lower- and middle-income countries (see Chapter 8) and the health impact of poverty and environment in informal settlements (WHO, 2016b).

An important consideration, relevant in other fields of social policy, concerns the extent to which policies have the aim of preventing social problems that arise, rather than being responses to those that have already occurred (Gough, 2015). This recognizes that it is inadequate to see social policy simply as remedial action to deal with the casualties of a capitalist economy, and prevention is at the heart of environmental policy. However, it may be further argued that contemporary environmental policy issues are increasingly highlighting fundamental problems about how life is organized in capitalist societies, and raising debates about policy change that will have implications for policies such as income maintenance, employment and housing. These points are of special significance in debates about responses to climate change.

It is this connecting of environmental issues with wider questions about social development that makes it unsurprising that the main challenge to the status quo has emerged and continues to be articulated most directly by green movements. A statement made by a UN Secretary-General in 1971, long before climate change was on the mainstream political agenda, makes the crucial connection here:

> As we watch the sun go down, evening after evening, through the smog across the poisoned waters of our native earth, we must ask ourselves seriously whether we really wish some future universal historian on another planet to say about us: 'With all their genius and with all their skill, they ran out of foresight and air and food and water and ideas', or, 'They went on playing politics until their world collapsed around them'. (U Thant, quoted by Ghosh, 2016)

Many who suffer from environmental problems are not those contributing most to their creation, while elites who benefit most from polluting activities also have the financial and other resources to protect themselves from the worst effects. At the same time, those responsible for, and who benefit most from, environmentally degrading activities also challenge and sometimes deny the evidence for the damage to the planet that their activities have caused. But behind the arguments of the climate change 'deniers' lies a dominant discourse (explored earlier in relation to the concept of GDP), which prioritizes concerns about production, growth and competitiveness over those about their consequences.

Hence there is an important case for a more holistic vision which sets environmental policy as a core element of social policy, such as that offered by Gough (2017), combined with those that provide a critique of dominant economic thinking. Raworth (2017), for example, argues that growth in the world's population makes it essential that, contrary to the classical economic perspectives where 'land' is an infinitely available 'factor' in production, the use of the world's resources is recognized as requiring collective management and conservation.

Here, then, is the ultimate challenge to the view of social policy as a residual 'ambulance' system only called into play when the economy is malfunctioning.

Conclusion

The essential point with which this chapter began is that when exploring policies that influence social welfare it makes no sense to treat environmental policy as if it is different in its effects and implications to the other social policies explored in this book. Doing so necessitates a reconsideration of how economic progress is judged (particularly through the use of the concept of GDP) and a position on the extent to which the amelioration of welfare could be seen as a 'collective action problem'. Both of these issues apply to the analysis of many of the social policy issues covered in previous chapters. However, to introduce them here highlights two particular ways in which environmental policy links to other policies. In the case of the GDP measure, the fact that economic progress may produce adverse effects for the environment offers a particularly strong illustration of the wider dangers of the relentless pursuit of growth. In the case of collective action problems, the adverse impact of individual actions upon other individuals is similarly particularly evident if the North is effectively poisoning much of the rest of the world. In one sense this is a particularly strong example of the case against individualism in public policy, which could equally be made with regard to the other policy areas.

In discussing comparative studies it is again clear that a consideration of OECD countries alone does little more than highlight the 'deviant' case of the US. Beyond the OECD the crucial issues are about urgent problems with respect to air quality and its serious implications for health. It was suggested that the evidence on the impact of air pollution gives rise to further apprehension about the impact of industrial and urban growth, and leads to wider questions about climate change where national policies alone are no use. There are important respects in which it has been the single-minded pursuit of growth by the richer nations of the world that has been responsible for the problem, with the paradoxical consequence that the problem worsens as other nations are driven down the same economic path. Economic growth remains the central solution underpinning government promises for the development of public social policies, but if growth is part of the problem, then ways to deal with the adverse effects of industrial development, highlighted by the issues of climate change, make adherence to this position as unsustainable as its environmental consequences.

12

Conclusion:
A divided world of social policy?

Introduction

This book has approached its subject matter with a view that human welfare is a universal concern prompting a globally diverse range of social actions. It is also a comparative text, but not one that sees comparison as an add-on to the examination of issues in the UK, Europe or the OECD. Its comparative approach is located in the classic case for comparison as a method essential for those social sciences where experimentation is normally not possible.

It is recognized that an account of social policy of this kind cannot give encyclopaedic attention to all the variations across the many nations of the world. Because of this it has been necessarily guided by the increasing range of attempts to develop typologies of regimes and policies, but it does not offer a detailed examination of the methodologies on which those typologies are based. Furthermore, while it is informed by developments in what is called 'global social policy', its aim is to compare and contrast, noting global influences on national policies while not giving micro-level attention to the roles of the global institutions that contribute to social policy development. The chapter discussions also reflect the ways in which many key issues run across conventional policy divides, and have variously dealt with activities and processes that are fundamental to the impetus for, and design and operation of, social policies. Referring to a wide body of different literatures, chapters have also addressed the range of conflicts and competing demands that arise as policy fails to keep up with the realities of people's lives.

The preceding chapters have demonstrated that there have been significant advances in welfare over the last century, but that the benefits of these have been distributed unevenly between and across societies. Globally, there have been huge improvements in public health, provisions for older and retired people, accessibility of acute and primary health services, literacy and school enrolment beyond the primary years, protection of people unable to work and general housing conditions. All of these gains have resulted from political pressure applied to governments and international organizations by electorates and political and social movements, as well as the capacity of powerful individuals, groups and organizations to promote better welfare as an objective. However, in the 2020s the impulse for social progress is also the most fragile that it has been for a century, and alongside the established routes for social improvement, there are increasingly powerful forces that seek to alter the course of progress, restrict its benefits and return to an inward-looking, bordered view of welfare, where rewards are redistributed based on where people were born, and assumptions of self-interested individualism and the belief that people fully shape their own destinies take precedence.

Drawing on the book as a whole, the aim of this chapter is to consider social policy in the wider social, political and economic context. This is linked to the meaning of 'social' policy. It is often seen as a policy area that is subordinate to other policy areas, the subject of 'low politics' where the major concerns of states are the 'high politics' of, for example, preserving peace or managing the economy. But there is a paradox here. On the one hand, many specific social policies can be seen as unworkable without attention to the big issues, and an international survey inevitably brings attention to those societies where internal and external instability make many social policies a far off luxury. On the other hand, the inequalities and diswelfares that are so central to social policy analysis are fundamental to the explanation of social tensions, and what has been called 'ungovernability' across the world. This is why a key theme of the preceding chapters has been the inseparability of social and economic issues.

This concluding discussion returns to the theoretical 'worlds of welfare' and the disciplinary 'world' of social policy, and their relevance to the geographical world of similarity and difference. It will consider both the negatives and the positives that the exploration in the preceding chapters has identified in terms of the prospects for social policy design and practice, and our understanding of it. The first section concerns the extent to which universalism and diversity are both present and essential features of a global understanding. The second and third sections consider, respectively, the wider challenges and possibilities that represent the background conditions for contemporary policy making and how they are likely to shape future social policy developments.

Understanding social policy in a global context

In the introductory chapter it was noted that at the core of understanding social policy, in its global context, is the extent to which universalism and particularism operate both as underpinning principles in relation to human rights and social welfare and as features of policy design towards achieving these objectives. Titmuss (1974) had argued that social problems are fundamentally the same the world over, but are manifested and approached differently according to their socio-political, economic and historical context. However, while international study of social policy has focused both on the shared drivers of welfare state change and on the extent to which this signifies a linear convergence, as well as the diversity or uniqueness of particular social policy paths, cross-national comparative scholarship after Titmuss' time quickly moved to examining shared diversities and their explanations. Beyond simply confirming, refuting or expanding the 'three worlds' of Esping-Andersen (1990), and to shift thinking from a simple transplant of commodification, stratification and welfare mix as determining factors in all forms of welfare arrangements (although this may have merit), the continuing purpose of welfare state typologizing can be justified in terms of the need to discover whether these and/or different contextual factors or dynamics give rise to alternative frameworks for comparative social policy analysis, theories which ultimately have predictive capacity and can thus take us beyond a retrospective assessment of how we got here to a strategy for where we go from here.

Many of the chapters in this book have identified global processes such as financialization, as well as the role of global organizations and the power of their ideas as key factors in shaping the social policy development of many countries outside the OECD. They have also identified ways in which nation states still matter in blocking, adapting and shaping these ideas themselves. Although some capacity for resistance and adaptation is clear, the overall hegemony remains one that privileges free markets over social issues, and this is where, in policy terms, the ability to learn from experience particularly matters. And in social policy terms, the tools to ask the right questions, and the confidence to contribute convincing ideas as answers, also matter.

There is much evidence cited in the chapters relating to policy domains which indicates decline in the scope, generosity of and access to welfare provision, especially public provision, the limitations on policy tools employed to deal with social problems and the general shift away from redistribution as a policy goal. Some of these changes are regressive while others are due to a stalling of progress, some may have deeply embedded social and economic roots while others result from crisis conditions, but ultimately the responses to them are politically determined. Particularly at the macro level, it is impossible to disentangle politics from economics, hence the need for more fruitful analyses in the global political economy of welfare. But equally, it is impossible to sensibly separate the 'social' from either politics or economics.

It is also important to recognize that in exploring the world of social policy, much of the focus on comparative and international welfare arrangements is led by the theoretical frameworks developed in the North, and much of Michael Burawoy's (2016) critique of 'global' sociology applies equally to the globally cross-national study of social policy. From this perspective, social policy analysis is largely subject to the same national or Western academic coding of historical, political and social processes, even where the topic studied is 'development'. As discussed in Chapter 3, there have been numerous studies which apply the 'worlds of welfare' analytical framework to groups of countries outside the OECD. Comparisons undertaken between countries in the regions of East Asia (for example Kwon, 1997) and Latin America (for example Franzoni, 2008), and developing countries more widely (Abu Sharkh and Gough, 2010), all draw on the theoretical foundations of the welfare regimes approach.

The limitations of taking the experience of welfare state construction in the advanced economies and applying it to the welfare systems emerging in the

South are clear (Surender, 2013) and alternative approaches to analysis have been proposed recently which aim to better capture the specific historical and contemporary factors that shape emerging welfare arrangements outside the OECD countries. In the case of India, for example, Kapur and Nangia (2015) associate development with the notion of public goods, while Plagerson and Patel (2019) argue that the outcomes-focused capabilities approach widely used in development studies provides a route to a better understanding of global welfare regimes. The elaboration of better frameworks for analysis remains hinged, however, on fundamental questions around the emphasis given to individual, particularistic or collective and universal interests, and the extent to which welfare arrangements are assessed in terms of their capacity to meet measurable needs, or their capacity to deliver wider societal objectives that go beyond individual lives. These concerns have been highlighted by Mkandawire (2001, 2007) in his analyses of social policy in a development context and as a transformative project, where he points to the various economic and political uses of social policy instruments as well as the instrumentalism of social policy itself.

Exploring different worlds of social policy requires an examination of how the arrangements in other national contexts reflect specific national paths and the extent to which these are shaped by external forces, either historical, such as the influence of a colonial past, or contemporary, such as the influence of global organizations, powerful neighbours and so on.

In its early disciplinary form, 'social administration' was laced with the concerns of *British colonial* administration, as well as a strictly gendered notion of appropriate roles for women and men in the welfare state. Since the 1970s, and specifically with a comparative interest, the 1990s, the gendering of welfare states and welfare practice has been much more deeply interrogated, but, as noted in Chapter 3, considerations of 'race', ethnicity and racialized processes of social policy development have not featured so clearly in comparative analyses. Where issues of racial and ethnic divisions have been analyzed this has tended to be undertaken within the context of migration, 'immigration regimes' and the basis of citizenship (for example in Castles and Miller, 1993, and developed further in Castles et al., 2014).

Developing her work analyzing divisions of race, gender and class in the UK context (Williams, 1989), Fiona Williams (1995) argues that these need to be centred in comparative study to account for the ways in which nation, family and work shape particular welfare arrangements. As outlined in earlier chapters, family and work have indeed emerged as central components of comparative scholarship. 'Nation' remains a more limited dimension of analysis, albeit one that is highly significant in the changing post-2008 political landscape. The intersection of post-colonial studies and social policy is gaining academic attention (Bassel and Emejulu, 2018), and the turn to nationalist and more specifically nativist social politics in many countries in the 2010s has also provided a backdrop where studies that account for racialized processes and xenophobic practices as factors in social policy development are essential. This is particularly the case given the critique of 'methodological nationalism' (Wimmer and Schiller, 2003), which argues for more robust transnational theoretical frameworks to explain the movements of people and the social relations of race and ethnicity.

The climate emergency, coupled with unresolved military conflicts and deeply rooted global inequality, have all contributed to an increasing movement of people in a context of more general economic and political insecurity around the world. While threats to the future of welfare states in terms of political hostility and economic sustainability have been fairly constant since the 1970s, it is only in the decade since the 2008 crisis that opportunities have arisen for both antagonistic economic, and political forces to align in such a way that the previously identified factors of welfare state resilience have been challenged. The 2008 financial crisis has given way to a political and social crisis (Farnsworth and Irving, 2018c) that is manifested in a breakdown of trust in the state, a declining capacity to regulate capitalism and most importantly for social policy, an erosion of the recognition of solidarity as the keystone of social progress, as what Inglehart (2008) calls 'survival' values override those that recognize a global commons.

The decline of solidarities in the twenty-first century

Solidarity is arguably the most important and transformative force in the emergence of welfare provision. The recognition that interests are shared, giving a settlement for social goals and the measures required to achieve them, is essential for human progress. Solidarity is also the principle that has been most subjected to erosion in the twenty-first century, and all of the preceding chapters point to ways in which this has occurred. Halting the decline of recognized commonalities of interest is therefore a prerequisite for tackling the most pressing social policy challenges of the future. In the global context these concern the just distribution of power and resources, the tools necessary to effectively respond to the climate emergency and the recognition of the social rather than the economic elements of care as a fundamental human activity. Rather than being a fundamental policy challenge in itself, the involuntary movement of people is implicated as a symptom in all of these global problems.

The notion that solidarity is essential for progress has not been lost in the post-crisis political and policy sphere, and whether authentically or more cynically, it continues to frame many debates about social reform. The 2014 'No' campaign used 'better together' as its slogan in the Scottish independence referendum, and in 2016, Hilary Clinton's presidential campaign used the slogan 'stronger together'. Non-governmental organizations use titles that promote a principle of solidarity, such as 'More in Common' set up in 2017, to advance change in the narrative on identity and belonging in the wake of the refugee crisis. In her 2015 maiden speech, Jo Cox – a British Member of Parliament who was murdered by a right-wing extremist in 2016 during the UK Brexit referendum campaign – stated: 'We are far more united and have far more in common with each other than things that divide us.' This theme has since been taken up by other politicians, campaign groups and the UN, in a range of contexts, and is a belief to which evidence has been lent: in their international study of world social values, Hanel et al. (2019, p. 560) conclude that, 'In the course of making more than 168,000 comparisons, we found that similarities between any two groups of humans generally far outweigh the differences between them.' However, despite the various popular and academic ways in which solidaristic sentiments are presented and accepted, the reality is that there are currently more powerful forces which are reinforcing existing divisions and establishing new ones.

The age of austerity and its consequences

The age of austerity is at the heart of dissolving solidarities. In the wake of the 2008 financial crisis, austerity rapidly became established among both national governments and regional and international organizations such as the EU and the IMF, as the most economically 'logical' strategy for economic recovery. The decade of austerity from 2010 has seen public spending commitments plummet, with predictable consequences in terms of rising levels of economic hardship and social dislocation. Added to this, even where public debt has been reduced in the countries, such as Greece, Portugal, Spain and the UK, where the crisis wrought most financial damage, the GDP growth promised as an outcome of public belt-tightening has barely reached pre-crisis levels (see Figure 12.1).

Austerity measures are spread across spending cuts, fiscal arrangements and changes in social entitlements. Well-documented measures include cuts in discretionary public spending, public sector job cuts and wage freezes, removal of public subsidies on food and fuel, tax rises that affect those on lower incomes more such as VAT, and tax cuts that reduce the capacity for spending such as corporation tax (Ortiz et al., 2015). In addition to direct cuts, austerity has brought changes in eligibility for state support that remove universal entitlements and target them more narrowly, lower income and wealth thresholds for means-tested entitlements and the shaving of categories of people who previously qualified for services and benefits. Finally, austerity has enabled the wider access of private sector actors to participation in the provision of public and social welfare services, from the management of criminal justice to the information technology of benefit administration. These measures have not been introduced in isolation, and the packages of austerity applied in any particular country have varied, sometimes distinguishable by welfare regime type, sometimes by level of financial exposure in the crisis and sometimes by economic strength or weakness (Farnsworth and Irving, 2011). Many critics of austerity had predicted its failure (Blyth, 2013; Schui, 2014; Wren-Lewis, 2018), based on evidence of similar strategies adopted in the past, and in the failure of 'structural adjustment', the version of austerity advocated in development policies by the World Bank and IMF in the 1980s and 1990s in the global South. The lack of growth is also associated with increasing inequality in a negative cycle (Streeck, 2017), and is of course one reason why

Figure 12.1: Real GDP growth, annual percentage change, 2006–20

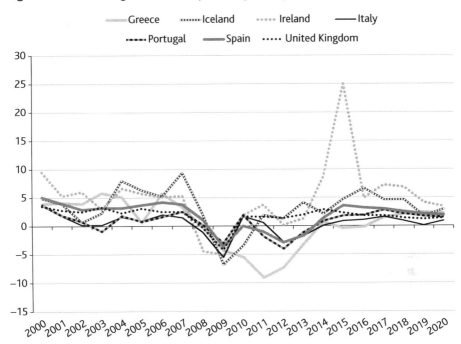

Note: The spike for Ireland in 2015 was reported as resulting from low corporation tax which attracted a number of multinational companies (including technology companies) to Ireland where their sales, especially based on intellectual property, are counted in GDP (OECD, 2016d).

Source: https://www.imf.org/external/datamapper/NGDP_RPCH@WEO/GRC/ISL/IRL/ESP/GBR/PRT/ITA?year=2019

international economic organizations such as the OECD and IMF have concerns about increasing inequalities (Cingano, 2014; IMF, 2017b).

The form of austerity is more complex and far-reaching than simple welfare retrenchment, however (Farnsworth and Irving, 2018b). In addition to austerity's material consequences, it has also changed public narratives on solidarity, recasting the twentieth-century welfare state as a hopelessly profligate dream and ushering in a new approach to social policy that frames it as an explicitly instrumental economic device, and in political terms, only of use for targeting the poorest. As an economic and political project, austerity has built increasing pressure to do less in terms of public welfare provision and rely more on private actors. In addition to this, austerity has also propagated and widened social divisions, setting generations in conflict with one another, and reinforcing social class differences within these. As real and perceived pressure on resources has become established since 2008, so has an exclusionary reaction, which has thrived in conditions where 'globalization' and its institutions can be cast by opponents as the villainous actors that have disempowered once dominant states, enfeebled once potent economies and diluted once majority culture (Mudde, 2007).

The shrinking of citizenship

The political ramifications of economic crises such as that experienced in 2008 pose an existential threat to the more open forms of social citizenship that comprehensive welfare states imply, and which the advanced welfare states had generally been moving towards by the 1990s through a combination of policies that supported greater economic equality as well as the expansion of equal rights to minority groups. The principle of universalism which was essential for the previous expansion of rights, has been directly undermined not just in economic terms through cost-cutting measures but also politically through the increasing electoral success of nationalist parties whose welfare policies are founded on nativist and socially conservative principles that limit social rights according to racialized notions of nationality and belonging, and gendered notions of rights and responsibilities in relation to work and family. In Europe, the US, Latin America and East Asia, many governments have hardened their positions on immigration and the treatment of asylum seekers in attempts to reduce the flow of migrants and limit or remove their entitlements to social support. In Hungary, physical borders have been constructed to advance and reinforce these policies, and the presence (or absence) of a 'wall' between the US and Mexico is a defining political meme of the Trump presidency.

Post-2008, the politics of nationalism has also fed into greater intolerance of ethnic minority groups within countries, rising levels of racially motivated hate crimes in the UK (Allen and Zayed, 2019) and the US (Eligon, 2018), and white nationalist terrorism in the US, New Zealand, Australia and across Northern Europe. The exclusionary social policy preferences exhibited by many far-right parties and governments are not necessarily antagonistic to greater economic equality, and this combination of redistributive sympathy with nativism is often described in academic literature as 'welfare chauvinism' (van der Waal et al., 2010; Lugosi, 2018). Social policy 'in the national interest' is not a new phenomenon, however, as welfare state building from the nineteenth century was very much aligned with nation state building. Early twentieth-century policies promoting child nutrition in the UK, post-war pro-natalist social security designed to favour larger family sizes in France, to the whole of the education system in any particular state (as discussed in Chapter 7) can be seen in the context of states advancing their own interests. As economic globalization occurred, so states reconfigured preferred areas of public spending to both maintain and redefine their national competitive advantages. The key difference in the contemporary age of austerity is that in contrast to the twentieth-century economic desire to attract and retain 'international' populations through the maintenance of colonial ties despite the independence of previously colonized states, advanced economies are now redefining what nationality means within their borders. For many countries the new politics of welfare now revolves around an imagined ethnically determined status, which does not include 'outsiders'. Again, this is not a new phenomenon: as Castles and Miller (1993) demonstrated in their categorization of 'immigration regimes', heritage, whether real or imagined, forms a clear driver in the forms of migration and consequent citizenship rights that are acceptable to national electorates.

The movement of people has always been part of the human condition, and a distinction between its voluntary and involuntary dimensions is traceable throughout history. Involuntary movement (and forced movement in the case of slavery) is also directly linked to the operation of trade and the development of capitalism. The contemporary relationship between global production and labour markets and patterns of migration therefore indicates that there is little likelihood that the demand for cheap and 'weak' (in the sense of having collective power) labour will abate. Set against the rising tide of exclusionary nationalism in the rich countries, the exploitation and criminalization of migrant workers is likely to degenerate further as their existing rights to residence, labour and social protection are further restricted. Equally, the lack of reduction in economic North–South inequalities and the differential impact of the climate emergency will continue to provide drivers for people to seek security and prosperity beyond the global South. Furthermore, the presence of increasingly restrictive immigration policies can only further entrench the patterns of migrant exploitation and human trafficking, and its profiteers, that have rapidly expanded in the twenty-first century (Bales, 2007; Kyle and Koslowski, 2011).

The rights and protection of migrants and refugees is undeniably a global social policy issue in the sense that all states are affected, but it is also one where states have consistently failed to either incorporate migrants into key agreements or to fulfil, in spirit, the responsibilities associated with the declarations to which they are signatories. Deacon (2013), for example, noted the restriction of the 2012 recommendations of the Social Protection Floor to 'residents', as defined by states, was a key weakness in an otherwise groundbreaking development in global social policy which had brought together all key IGOs and the G20 group of nations. More recently, the UN Global Compact for Safe, Orderly and Regular Migration endorsed by the UN General Assembly in late 2018 was not signed by certain countries, including the US, Australia, Poland and Denmark, despite it being a non-binding agreement that privileged national sovereignty in the interpretation of its provisions and terms. Clearly, the argument put forward in the early 2000s that so-called 'replacement migration' would be essential to offset the labour market pressures of an ageing population in the global North has been buried in the post-2008 context. Changes in the labour market are central to the perceived demand for international labour, and the future of work is a further area where traditional associations with social policy development are breaking down.

Changes to the essential relationship between social policy and work

Chapter 6 examined some of the long-term trends in employment policy and its relationship to work and the economy. Since 2008, many countries in Europe in particular have experienced recession, and increasing levels of unemployment. Where employment rates have stabilized, the jobs in which many people are employed have shifted further away from the industrial model of secure full-time jobs with prospects for upskilling, promotion and increased pay. In terms of job creation, this has occurred mainly in lower-skilled occupations, in services and in jobs with contracts that are less than full time, and in the case of the new platform economy in services, contracts which treat 'employees' as independent workers (Daugareilh et al., 2019).

In these new conditions of employment, the kinds of collective action that drove welfare struggles in the twentieth century are no longer possible. Union density (that is, the level of membership of trades unions as a proportion of employees) has declined rapidly in the period since the crisis in most world regions (see Table 12.1), although many countries in Latin America have seen an increase in union membership. Union density is one of the key indicators used to gauge the political power of labour vis-à-vis capital, and a weakening of unionization is therefore another sign that the traditional routes to improvements in welfare provision have changed. This also calls into question the kinds of measurements traditionally used to determine 'welfare stateness' in comparative study, since in the future, formal collectivization through trades unions may not be the route to social policy expansion.

In addition to these trends in the quantity and quality of work, there is an added threat in the form of automation which, it is argued, is likely to have a greater impact on mid-level skilled employees whose work lends itself to the advances in machine learning and robotics. There are various attempts to predict the employment and lifestyle consequences of such continuing technological

Table 12.1: World union density change, 2006–16 .

Region	Trade union density declined 2006–16 (or nearest year)	Trade union density increased 2006–16 (or nearest year)
Africa	Namibia, South Africa, Zambia, Tanzania, Ghana, Malawi	Egypt, Ethiopia, Cameroon
Americas	US, Argentina, Mexico	Bolivia, Uruguay, Chile, El Salvador, Panama, Dominican Republic, Peru
Asia and the Pacific	Malaysia, Philippines, Indonesia, New Zealand, Australia	Hong Kong, Singapore
Europe and Central Asia	Sweden, Finland, Belgium, Norway, Malta, Cyprus, Ukraine, Armenia, Luxembourg, Russian Federation, Austria, UK, Ireland, Romania, Greece, Netherlands, Germany, Portugal, Switzerland, Latvia, Poland, Slovakia, Czech Republic, Hungary, Lithuania, Estonia	Iceland, Israel, Turkey

Note: Data not available for all countries.

Source: ILO (2018, p. 25, figure 1.4)

change. All posit a dislocation of contemporary economic activity, but there are variations in the extent to which they suggest that there will be a substantial overall decline in the quantity of work (World Bank, 2016). However, there is a need to distinguish between predictions about single countries or specific groups of countries and those about the world as a whole – for example, job losses through automation in the North may be felt more acutely in low- and middle-income economies in the South where a consequent decline in the off-shoring of employment occurs (Carbonero et al., 2018).

Much of the dominant social policy discourse in the rich countries concerns adaptability and competitiveness. In response to this the arguments for new social policy measures such as universal basic income (see Chapter 5) see it as essential to compensate those deprived of work opportunities, but in the absence of collective pressure it is unlikely that a redistributive basic income, rather than one which simply supports a simpler and less generous administrative architecture, will emerge. The reality that the lack of economic competitiveness in the global economy is the underlying problem for work and social protection has yet to be accepted in politics. The bigger questions of inequalities in resource use, shortages and deficits in the global South, alongside extravagant consumption and waste in the North, are similarly underlying problems that are yet to be accepted unequivocally in national and international political arenas.

Social policy in a post-global world

Since the mid-2010s, progress in regulating international markets in labour and production, devising strategies to address climate change and control environmental pollution, and protecting displaced people has seen great losses, in what were at best minimal existing gains. While trust in states and political institutions has declined, the capacities of global governance institutions have also been compromised. The loss of momentum in global action in these areas presents a bleak prognosis on the adoption of positive changes to policy and practices.

The severity of the challenges identified above, in conjunction with the unsympathetic transformations of the political, economic and social landscape, gives little room for optimism. With such high degrees of uncertainty on a global scale, Wolfgang Streeck (2017, p. 12) suggests that 'traditional economic and sociological theories have today lost much of their predictive power'. Streeck's position is based on the view that systemically, capitalism has run out of ways to fix the problems that it creates, and that historically, the 'fixes' themselves then become the next problem. Social policy is one of the 'fixes' in the sense that it was the promise of state welfare provision that settled the conflicts between capital and labour in the mid-twentieth century, enabling a period of stable consumption until the financial crisis. Although state support was less generous from the 1970s, the availability of private credit to support welfare needs (especially housing) filled this gap. While the age of austerity has returned analysis to the fiscal crisis of the state and the sustainability of the welfare state, as suggested in the introduction to this book, the current global 'state of welfare' is also unsustainable. The prospects for welfare progress may seem dismal, but the history of social policy development also demonstrates that ideas lead to action and action leads to concrete change. The closing section of this book therefore considers some of the ideas that could and are advancing positive action on the re-envisioning of social policy in a divided age.

Concluding discussion

The core areas or challenges for social policy in the twenty-first century are located in the questions of environmental and economic security, the questions of how care is distributed and delivered and ultimately how this can be achieved in a way that advances fairness in the distribution of resources. The previous sections have set out a less than encouraging picture of the depth of problems requiring social policy attention and the deficit of solutions to address them. There are possibilities which can be glimpsed in the achievements and actions of those engaged in the policy battles and practical struggles for welfare in the twenty-first century.

While the climate emergency brings enormous challenges both in tackling the causes directly and in addressing the indirect outcomes, it also illustrates the potential of more creative social forces. From a position of power in the global North, there is a tendency towards 'victim blaming' in the face of environmental threats, with reference to individual lifestyle or consumption behaviour, or the failures of government in most at-risk countries. However, this position lacks perspective on both the pressures imposed by the massive imbalance between national economies and the fundamental importance of longer-term government-led collective action in the global North to address global problems and their disproportionate impact on the South. One of the obstacles in tackling environment-related problems is the tendency for policy makers to default to simple taxation measures (such as pollution taxes). However, not only do these impose the costs of remedial action on those least able to carry them, but they can be regarded as 'downstream' measures, when an upstream solution is needed that makes capitalism less exploitative of people and resources.

In the global North, this new approach is exemplified in thinking around the Green New Deal in the UK and the US for example. Commenting on the achievements and possibilities in making the Green New Deal a reality in the UK, through the use of public institutions to shape local capitalism (through new procurement practices in health and education services for example), Guinan and O'Neill (2018, p. 8) observe that 'None of this is about selling a fantasy. Real-world examples of democratic, participatory economic alternatives exist in communities across the globe.' The idea of participation is central to these developments, and there are clearly forces that are fighting back against 'climate denial' and the more subtle ways in which a lack of urgency on the issue of climate change is reflected in policy.

The 'School Strike for Climate' and 'Extinction Rebellion' movements of the late 2010s are the most recent examples of rapidly internationalizing projects which aim to use protest and civil disobedience for political change, but also demonstrate a global commonality of purpose. The impact of these movements is evident both in shifts in public attitudes, where polling indicates increasing concern with environmental issues above issues such as crime and immigration (for example in the UK),[1] and also in political outcomes (for example the electoral success of Green parties in the European Parliament elections in 2019). Although environmental movements have clear demands for the reduction of carbon emissions, the reining in of economic interests which operate to the detriment of the environment and a different form of democracy, their direct concerns with social policy in the traditional sense (rather than for example improvements in health gained from cleaner air), are less well articulated at present.

In the US, the Green New Deal incorporates a public works programme of job creation and a range of welfare guarantees related to health, housing and education, and is clearly purposively reminiscent of the original 'New Deal' established by President Roosevelt in the 1930s as a response to the economic crisis and depression of that period. The original required a sympathetic political alignment in the face of significant antipathy among economic interests, and although not systemically challenging, welfare gains were achieved. However, what is significantly different about the Green New Deal is that it is explicitly a response to a global problem.

Even while inequalities between nations may have been reduced on broad measures of income and assets, the inequalities within them are clearly rising. As the previous chapters have indicated (for example in health and housing), it is difficult to disentangle inequalities arising from failures in service provision from those that have other social and economic roots. Analyses like Piketty's (2014) indicate that the restraint of within-country inequalities has only occurred in the countries of the global North around the times of the two world wars, when massive public investment and redistributive taxation occurred. In peacetime, on the other hand, the continuing growth in returns to assets has inhibited equalizing forces, and it is argued that this tendency is increasing. Inasmuch as social policy discourse has been framed in terms of compensation for economic disadvantage, there is nothing new about saying that it makes a comparatively weak contribution in the face of the current economic forces that are contributing to inequality. While conventional political voices are being raised around the world about the need to counteract this trend, the policy interventions required to achieve this are massive, taking the politics of welfare way out of the domain of marginal incremental change and beyond what the New Deal achieved for the US.

In a context where advanced welfare states are less stable than they have ever been, social policy is also more open to possibilities than ever before, since the 'blueprints' advanced by the welfare states in the global North are themselves exposed as insufficient protection against twenty-first-century capitalism, and new interpretations of welfare commitments, economic and social guarantees, and the meaning of 'citizenship' are required. In order to develop ways in which these new interpretations can be transformed into workable policies that contribute to human welfare, ecological protection, social progress, distributive justice and a common good, it is necessary to gain a better understanding of how elements of all these aims have been achieved so far. It is in this endeavour that comparative, international and global perspectives are essential.

Notes

Chapter 1

1 Other than in China, where it is argued that increased income is the main driver.

Chapter 2

1 See especially the World Income Inequality Database, https://www.wider.unu.edu/ project/wiid-world-income-inequality-database, and the *World Income Inequality Report*, https://wir2018.wid.world.
2 An example is *The Pinch* (Willetts, 2010). Its subtitle is *How the Baby Boomers Took Their Children's Future – and Why They Should Give it Back.*

Chapter 5

1 That is, 13.3 people in the over 64 age group per 100 people in the working age group. See http://worldbank.org/indicator/SP.POP.DPND.OL.

Chapter 6

1 https://www.ilo.org/global/about-the-ilo/history/lang--en/index.htm.
2 That is, employment undertaken as an 'own-account' worker but in conditions where the worker is effectively dependently contracted to a single employer.
3 See OECD (2018a), table A, DOI: https://doi.org/10.1787/empl_outlook-2018-table64-en and 1, DOI: https://doi.org/10.1787/empl_outlook-2018-table68-en.
4 See http://mnregaweb4.nic.in/Netnrega/mpr_ht/nregampr_dmu_mis.aspx?fin_year=2015-2016&month=Latest&flag=1&page1=S&Digest=YNM1xjNNDz0MW PXC1L4hCQ.

Chapter 8

1 http://www.oecd.org/social/affordable-housing-database.htm.
2 https://www.bloomberg.com/news/articles/2018-08-21/u-k-experiences-largest-fall-in-home-ownership-in-the-eu-chart.
3 Authors' calculation from Table 678: Annual Social Housing Sales by Scheme for England, https://www.gov.uk/government/statistical-data-sets/live-tables-on-social-housing-sales#sale-of-local-authority-dwellings.
4 OECD, C3.1.1: Estimated number of homeless people, 2015 or latest year available.
5 Although figures for Denmark and Sweden are from 2013, and the UK, Germany and Sweden ones have some missing data. Source: PH3.1, http://www.oecd.org/social/affordable-housing-database.htm.
6 OECD data for HC1.2.1. Households' housing cost burden (mortgage and rent cost) as a share of disposable income, 2014 or latest year available.
7 https://www.selfbuildportal.org.uk.
8 In its General Comments No.4 (1991) and No.7 (1997).

9   https://assets.publishing.service.gov.uk/government/uploads/system/uploads/attachment_data/file/7812/138355.pdf.

10 https://unhabitat.org/wp-content/uploads/2015/04/Habitat-III-Issue-Paper-20_Housing-2.0.pdf.

Chapter 9

1   https://www.who.int/publications/almaata_declaration_en.pdf.

2   The 2018 update, Global Health Workforce Statistics, World Health Organization, Geneva, http://www.who.int/hrh/statistics/hwfstats/.

3   Approximately 15 per cent of the population, from 1989 to its implementation in 2014 when it fell below 10 per cent. See Center on Budget and Policy Priorities, https://www.cbpp.org/affordable-care-act-coverage-gains-driving-uninsured-rate-to-historic-low.

Chapter 11

1   http://www.who.int/airpollution/en/.

Chapter 12

1   YouGov polling in the UK over the months June to July 2019, https://d25d2506sfb94s.cloudfront.net/cumulus_uploads/document/7091t7u0ss/YG%20Trackers%20-%20Top%20Issues_W.pdf.

References

Aalbers, M. (2015) 'The Great Moderation, the Great Excess and the Global Housing Crisis', *International Journal of Housing Policy*, 15 (1): 43–60.

Aalbers, M. and Christophers, B. (2014) 'Centring Housing in Political Economy', *Housing, Theory and Society*, 31 (4): 373–94.

Abel-Smith, B. and Townsend, P. (1965) *The Poor and the Poorest*, London: Bell.

Abu Sharkh, M. and Gough, I. (2010) 'Global Welfare Regimes: A Cluster Analysis', *Global Social Policy*, 10 (1): 27–58.

Addey, C. and Sellar, S. (2018) 'Why Do Countries Participate in PISA? Understanding the Role of International Large-scale Assessments in Global Education Policy', in A. Verger, M. Novelli and H.K. Altinyelken (eds) *Global Education Policy and International Development*, 2nd edition, London: Bloomsbury Academic.

AfDB (African Development Bank) (2011) *The Middle of the Pyramid: Dynamics of the Middle Class in Africa*, Chief Economist Complex, Market Brief, April 20, African Development Bank. http://www.afdb.org/fileadmin/uploads/afdb/Documents/Publications/The%20Middle%20of%20the%20Pyramid_The%20Middle%20of%20the%20Pyramid.pdf.

Alcock, P. and Craig, G. (eds) (2001) *International Social Policy*, Basingstoke: Palgrave Macmillan.

Alcock, P., Glennerster, H., Oakley, A. and Sinfield, A. (eds) (2001) *Welfare and Wellbeing: Richard Titmuss's Contribution to Social Policy*, Bristol: Policy Press.

Allen, G. and Zayed, Y. (2019) *Hate Crime Statistics*, Briefing Paper No. 08537, 28 March 2019, London: House of Commons Library.

Altbach, P.G. and Knight, J. (2007) 'The Internationsalisation of Higher Education: Motivations and Realities', *Journal of Studies in International Education*, 11 (3/4): 290–305.

Ambler, J.S. (ed.) (1991) *The French Welfare State*, New York: New York University Press.

An, M.-Y. and Peng, I. (2016) 'Diverging Paths? A Comparative Look at Childcare Policies in Japan, South Korea and Taiwan', *Social Policy and Administration*, 50 (5): 540–58.

Anand, S., Segal, P. and Stiglitz, J.E. (eds) (2010) *Debates on the Measurement of Global Poverty*, Oxford: Oxford University Press.

Anttonen, A., Baldock, J. and Sipila, J. (eds) (2003) *The Young, the Old and the State: Social Care Systems in Five Industrial Nations*, Cheltenham: Edward Elgar.

Archer, M. (1979) *The Social Origins of Educational Systems*, Beverley Hills, CA: Sage.

Artaraz, K. and Hill, M. (2016) *Global Social Policy*, London: Palgrave.

Arts, W. and Gelissen, J. (2002) 'Three Worlds of Welfare Capitalism or More?', *Journal of European Social Policy*, 12 (2): 137–58.

Arts, W. and Gelissen, J. (2010) 'Models of the Welfare State', in F.G. Castles, S. Leibfried, J. Lewis, H. Obinger and C. Pierson (eds) *The Oxford Handbook of the Welfare State*, Oxford: Oxford University Press.

Ashby, E. and Anderson, M. (1981) *The Politics of Clean Air*, Oxford: Clarendon Press.

Ashford, D.E. (1986) *The Emergence of the Welfare States*, Oxford: Blackwell.

Atkinson, A. (2015) *Inequality: What Can Be Done?* Cambridge, MA: Harvard University Press.

Bahle, T., Pfeifer, M. and Wendt, C. (2010) 'Social Assistance', in F.G. Castles, S. Leibfried, J. Lewis, H. Obinger and C. Pierson (eds) *The Oxford Handbook of the Welfare State*, Oxford: Oxford University Press.

Baldwin, R. (2016) *The Great Convergence: Information Technology and the New Globalisation*, Cambridge, MA: Harvard University Press.

Baldwin, R. (2019) *The Global Upheaval: Globalisation, Robotics and the Future of Work*, London: Weidenfeld and Nicolson.

Bales, K. (2007) 'What Predicts Human Trafficking?', *International Journal of Comparative and Applied Criminal Justice*, 31 (2): 269–79.

Ball, S.J. (1990) *Politics and Policy Making in Education*, London: Routledge.

Ball, S.J. (1998) 'Big Policies/Small World: An Introduction to International Perspectives in Education Policy', *Comparative Education*, 34 (2): 119–30.

Ball, S.J. (2008) *The Education Debate*, Bristol: Policy Press.

Ball, S.J. (2017) *The Education Debate*, 3rd edition, Bristol: Policy Press.

Bambra, C. (2005) 'Worlds of Welfare and the Health Care Discrepancy', *Social Policy and Society*, 4 (1): 31–41.

Bambra, C. (2016) *Health Divides: Where You Live Can Kill You*, Bristol: Policy Press.

Barnett, M. and Finnemore, M. (2004) *Rules for the World: International Organizations in Global Politics*, Ithaca, NY and London: Cornell University Press.

Barr, N. (2001) *The Welfare State as Piggy Bank*, Oxford: Oxford University Press.

Barrientos, A. (2004) 'Latin America: Towards a Liberal-Informal Welfare Regime', in I. Gough, and G. Wood (eds) *Insecurity and Welfare Regimes in Asia, Africa and Latin America: Social Policy in Development Contexts*, Cambridge: Cambridge University Press.

Barrientos, A. and Hulme, D. (2008) *Social Protection for the Poor and Poorest*, Basingstoke: Palgrave Macmillan.

Bassel, L. and Emejulu, A. (2018) *Minority Women and Austerity*, Bristol: Policy Press.

Baumgartner, F. and Jones, B. (1993) *Agendas and Instability in American Politics*, Chicago: University of Chicago Press.

Baumgartner, F.R., Green-Pedersen, C. and Jones, B.D. (2006) 'Comparative Studies of Policy Agendas', *Journal of European Public Policy*, 13 (7): 961–63.

Beck, U. and Beck-Gernsheim, E. (2002) *Individualization: Institutionalized Individualism and its Social and Political Consequences*, London: Sage.

Becker, G.S. (2008) 'Human Capital', in D.R. Henderson (ed.) *The Concise Encyclopaedia of Economics*, Carmel, Indiana: Liberty Fund.

Béland, D. (2005) 'Ideas and Social Policy: An Institutionalist Perspective', *Social Policy and Administration*, 39 (1): 1–18.

Béland, D. (2007) 'The Social Exclusion Discourse: Ideas and Policy Change', *Policy and Politics*, 35 (1): 123–40.

Benson, M. and Hamiduddin, I. (eds) (2017) *Self-build Homes: Social Discourse, Experiences and Directions*, London: UCL Press.

Bettio, F. and Plantenga, J. (2004) 'Comparing Care Regimes in Europe', *Feminist Economics*, 10 (1): 85–113.

Bevan, A. (1952) *In Place of Fear*, London: Heinemann.

Beveridge, W. (1942) *Social Insurance and Allied Services*, London: HMSO, Cmd. 6404.

Birkland, T.A. (1998) 'Focusing Events, Mobilization, and Agenda Setting', *Journal of Public Policy*, 18 (1): 53–74.

Blackburn, R. (2002) *Banking on Death*, London: Verso.

Blank, R.H. and Burau, V. (2004) *Comparative Health Policy*, Basingstoke: Palgrave Macmillan.

Blaug, M. (1970) *The Economics of Education*, Harmondsworth: Penguin Books.

Blyth, M. (2002) *Great Transformations: Economic Ideas and Institutional Change in the Twentieth Century*, Cambridge: Cambridge University Press.

Blyth, M. (2013) *Austerity, the History of a Dangerous Idea*, Oxford: Oxford University Press.

Böhm, K., Schmid, A., Götze, R., Landwehr, C. and Rothgang, H. (2013) 'Five Types of OECD Healthcare Systems: Empirical Results of a Deductive Classification', *Health Policy*, 113: 258–69.

Bolderson, H. and Mabbett, D. (1991) *Social Policy and Social Security in Australia, Britain and the USA*, Aldershot: Avebury.

Bonal, X. (2002) 'Plus Ca Change … the World Bank Global Education Policy and the Post-Washington Consensus', *International Studies in Sociology of Education*, 12 (1): 3–22.

Bonoli, G. (1997) 'Classifying Welfare States: A Two-Dimensional Approach', *Journal of Social Policy*, 26 (3): 351–72.

Bonoli, G. (2005) 'The Politics of the New Social Policies: Providing Coverage Against New Social Risks in Mature Welfare States', *Policy and Politics*, 33 (3): 431–50.

Bonoli, G. (2010) 'Active Labor-Market Policy', *Politics and Society*, 38 (4): 435–57.

Bonoli, G. (2013) *The Origins of Active Social Policy: Labour Market and Childcare Policies in a Comparative Perspective*, Oxford: Oxford University Press.

Bonoli, G. and Shinkawa, T. (eds) (2005) *Ageing and Pension Reform Around the World*, Cheltenham: Edward Elgar.

Bonoli, G. and Reber, F. (2010) 'The Political Economy of Childcare in OECD Countries: Explaining Cross-national Variation in Spending and Coverage Rates', *European Journal of Political Research*, 49: 97–118.

Bourguignon, F. (2015) *The Globalisation of Inequality*, Princeton, NJ: Princeton University Press.

Bourguignon, F. and Morrisson, C. (2002) 'Inequality Among World Citizens: 1890–1992', *American Economic Review*, 92 (4): 727–44.

Bovens, M. and 't Hart, P. (1996) *Understanding Policy Fiascos*, Brunswick, NJ: Transaction Publishers.

Bowles, S. and Gintis, H. (1976) *Schooling in Capitalist America*, New York: Basic Books.

Bradshaw, J. and Richardson, D. (2009) 'Child Well-being in Europe', *Journal of Child Indicators Research*, 2 (3): 319–50.

Brock, C. and Alexiadou, N. (2013) *Education Around the World: A Comparative Introduction*, London: Bloomsbury.

Broome, A. and Seabrooke, L. (2012) 'Seeing Like an International Organisation', *New Political Economy*, 17: 1–16.

Burau, V. and Blank, R.H. (2006) 'Comparing Health Policy: An Assessment of Typologies of Health Systems', *Journal of Comparative Policy Analysis*, 8 (1): 63–76.

Burawoy, M. (2016) 'The Promise of Sociology: Global Challenges for National Disciplines', *Sociology*, 50 (5): 949–59.

Bureau of Labor Statistics (2018) *Fastest Growing Occupations, 2016 and Projected 2026* (Table 1.3), https://www.bls.gov/emp/tables/fastest-growing-occupations. htm.

Busemeyer, M.R. and Nicolai, R. (2010) 'Education', in F.G. Castles, S. Leibfried, J. Lewis, H. Obinger and C. Pierson (eds) *The Oxford Handbook of the Welfare State*, Oxford: Oxford University Press.

Butler, I. and Drakeford, M. (2003) *Scandal, Social Policy and Social Welfare*, Bristol: Policy Press.

Buzogány, A. and Varga, M. (2018) 'The Ideational Foundations of the Illiberal Backlash in Central and Eastern Europe: The Case of Hungary', *Review of International Political Economy*, 25 (6): 811–28.

Cahill, M. (1994) *The New Social Policy*, Oxford: Blackwell.

Cahill, M. (2002) *The Environment and Social Policy*, London: Routledge.

Cahill, M. (2010) *Transport, Environment and Society*, Maidenhead: Open University Press.

Cairney, P. and Jones, M.D. (2016) 'Kingdon's Multiple Streams Approach: What is the Empirical Impact of This Universal Theory', *Policy Studies Journal*, 44 (1): 37–58.

Carbonero, F., Ernst, E. and Weber, E. (2018) 'Robots Worldwide: The Impact of Automation on Employment and Trade', October, *Research Department Working Paper No. 36*, Geneva: International Labour Office.

Castles, F.G. (1985) *The Working Class and Welfare*, Sydney: Allen and Unwin.

Castles, F.G. (1989) 'Explaining Public Education Expenditures in OECD Countries', *European Journal of Political Research*, 17 (4): 431–48.

Castles, F.G. (1999) *Comparative Public Policy: Patterns of Post-war Transformation*, Cheltenham: Edward Elgar.

Castles, F.G. (2004) *The Future of the Welfare State*, Oxford: Oxford University Press.

Castles, F.G. and Mitchell, D. (1992) 'Identifying Welfare State Regimes: The Links Between Politics, Instruments and Outcomes', *Governance*, 5 (1): 1–26.

Castles, F.G. and Obinger, H. (2008) 'Worlds, Families, Regimes: Country Clusters in European and OECD Area Public Policy', *West European Politics*, 31 (1–2): 321–44.

Castles, F.G., Leibfried, S., Lewis, J., Obinger, H. and Pierson, C. (eds) (2010) *The Oxford Handbook of the Welfare State*, Oxford: Oxford University Press.

Castles, S. (1995) 'How Nation-States Respond to Immigration and Ethnic Diversity', *Journal of Ethnic and Migration Studies*, 21 (3): 293–308.

Castles, S. and Miller, M.J. (1993) *The Age of Migration*, Basingstoke: Palgrave Macmillan.

Castles, S. and Miller, M.J. (2003) *The Age of Migration*, 3rd edition, Basingstoke: Palgrave Macmillan.

Castles, S., de Haas, H. and Miller, M. (2014) *The Age of Migration: International Population Movements in the Modern World*, 5th edition, Basingstoke: Palgrave Macmillan.

Cerami, A. (2006) *Social Policy in Central and Eastern Europe: The Emergence of a New European Welfare Regime*, Berlin: LIT Verlag.

Cerami, A. and Stubbs, P. (2011) 'Post-communist Welfare Capitalisms: Bringing Institutions and Political Agency Back In', *EIZ Working Paper*, Zagreb, reprinted in M. Hill (ed.), *Comparative Public Policy* (2013), vol. 2, London: Sage.

Cingano, F. (2014) 'Trends in Income Inequality and its Impact on Economic Growth', *OECD Social, Employment and Migration Working Papers*, No. 163, Paris: OECD Publishing.

Clarke, J. (2005) 'Welfare States as Nation States: Some Conceptual Reflections', *Social Policy and Society*, 4 (4): 407–15.

Clasen, J. (ed.) (1997) *Social Insurance in Europe*, Bristol: Policy Press.

Cohen, M.D., March, J.G. and Olsen, J.P. (1972) 'A Garbage Can Model of Organizational Choice', *Administrative Science Quarterly*, 17: 1–25.

Coicaud, J.-M. and Zhang, J. (2011) 'The OECD as a Global Data Collection and Policy Analysis Organization: Some Strengths and Weaknesses', *Global Policy*, 2 (3): 312–17.

Collier, P. (2013) *Exodus: Immigration and Multiculturalism in the 21st Century*, Harmondsworth: Penguin Books.

Cook, S. and Lam, W. (2011) 'China's Response to Crisis: What Role for Social Policy?', in K. Farnsworth and Z. Irving (eds) *Social Policy in Challenging Times: Economic Crisis and Welfare Systems*, Bristol: Policy Press.

Copestake, J. (2015) 'Whither Development Studies? Reflections on its Relationship with Social Policy', *Journal of International and Comparative Social Policy*, 31 (2): 100–13.

Coyle, D. (2011) *The Economics of Enough*, Princeton, NJ: Princeton University Press.

Credit Suisse (2018) *Global Wealth Databook 2018*, October, Zurich: Credit Suisse AG Research Institute.

Crosland, C.A.R. (1956) *The Future of Socialism*, London: Cape.

Crouch, C. (2011) *The Strange Non-Death of Neoliberalism*, Cambridge: Polity.

Dahlgren, G. and Whitehead, M. (1991) *Policies and Strategies to Promote Social Equity in Health*, Stockholm: Institute for Futures Studies.

Daly, M. (2000) *The Gender Division of Welfare*, Cambridge: Cambridge University Press.

Daly, M. (2015) 'Parenting Support as Policy Field: An Analytical Framework', *Social Policy and Society*, 14 (4): 597–608.

Daly, M. and Rake, K. (2003) *Gender and the Welfare State*, Cambridge: Polity.

Da Roit, B. and Le Bilan, B. (2010) 'Similar and Yet So Different: Cash for Care in Six European Countries' Long-term Care Policies', *The Millbank Quarterly*, 88 (3): 286–309.

Daugareilh, I., Degryse, C. and Pochet, P. (2019) *The Platform Economy and Social Law: Key Issues in Comparative Perspective*, Working Paper 2019.10, Brussels: European Trade Union Institute.

De Wispelaere, J. and Haagh, L. (2019) 'Themed Section: Basic Income in European Welfare States: Opportunities and Constraints', *Social Policy and Society*, 18 (2): 237–332.

De Wispelaere, J. and Stirton, L. (2012) 'A Disarmingly Simple Idea? Practical Bottlenecks in the Implementation of a Universal Basic Income', *International Social Security Review*, 65: 103–21.

Deacon, B. (1983) *Social Policy and Socialism*, London and Sydney: Pluto Press.

Deacon, B. (1997) *Global Social Policy*, London: Sage.

Deacon, B. (2005) 'The Governance and Politics of Global Social Policy', *Social Policy and Society*, 4 (4): 437–45.

Deacon, B. (2007) *Global Social Policy and Governance*, London: Sage.

Deacon, B. (2013) *Global Social Policy in the Making: The Foundations of the Social Protection Floor*, Bristol: Policy Press.

Deacon, B. and Stubbs, P. (2013) 'Global Social Policy Studies: Conceptual and Analytical Reflections', *Global Social Policy*, 13 (1): 5–23.

Deacon, B., Macovei, M., Van Langehove, L. and Yeates, N. (eds) (2010) *World-Regional Social Policy and Global Governance: New Research and Policy Agendas in Africa, Asia, Europe and Latin America*, London: Routledge.

Dean, H. (2010) *Understanding Human Need*, Bristol: Policy Press.

Deaton, A. (2002) 'Policy Implications of the Gradient of Health and Wealth', *Health Affairs*, 21: 13–30.

Deaton, A. (2013) *The Great Escape: Health, Wealth and the Origin of Inequality*, Princeton, NJ: Princeton University Press.

Dessler, A. and Parson, E.A. (2010) *The Science and Politics of Global Climate Change*, Cambridge: Cambridge University Press.

Dewey, J. (1976) *Democracy and Education*, New York: Free Press.

Doern, G.B. and Phidd, R.W. (1983) *Canadian Public Policy*, Agincourt, Ontario: Methuen.

Dolowitz, D. and Marsh, D. (1996) 'Who Learns What from Whom: A Review of the Policy Transfer Literature', *Political Studies*, 44: 343–57.

Dolowitz, D. and Marsh, D. (2000) 'Learning from Abroad: The Role of Policy Transfer in Contemporary Policy Making', *Governance*, 13 (1): 5–24.

Doyal, L. and Gough, I. (1991) *A Theory of Human Need*, Basingstoke: Palgrave Macmillan.

Duit, A. (2016) 'The Four Faces of the Environmental State: Environmental Governance in 28 Countries', *Environmental Politics*, 25 (1): 69–91.

Durkheim, E. (eds) (1982) *The Rules of Sociological Method and Selected Texts on Sociology and its Method*, London: Macmillan.

Eardley, T., Bradshaw, J., Ditch, J., Gough, I. and Whiteford, P. (1995) *Social Assistance in OECD Countries: Synthesis Report*, Department of Social Security Research Report No. 46, London: HMSO.

Economist, The (2016) 'The Trouble with GDP', 30 April.

EHRC (2016) *Healing a Divided Britain – The Need for a Comprehensive Race Equality Strategy*, Equality and Human Rights Commission, https://www.equalityhumanrights.com/sites/default/files/healing_a_divided_britain_-_the_need_for_a_comprehensive_race_equality_strategy_final.pdf.

Eligon, J. (2018) 'Hate Crimes Increase for the Third Consecutive Year, F.B.I. Reports', *New York Times*, 13 November.

Emmanuel, D. (2017) 'Utilising Social Housing During the Post-2009 Crisis: Problems and Constraints in the Case of Greece', *Critical Housing Studies*, 4 (2): 76–83.

Emmenegger, P., Kvist, J., Marx, P. and Petersen, K. (2015) 'Three Worlds of Welfare Capitalism: The Making of a Classic', *Journal of European Social Policy*, 25 (1): 3–13.

Engels, F. (1848/1958) *The Condition of the Working Class in England in 1844*, Oxford: Blackwell.

Esping-Andersen, G. (1990) *Three Worlds of Welfare Capitalism*, Cambridge: Polity Press.

Esping-Andersen, G. (ed.) (1996) *Welfare States in Transition*, London: UNRISD/Sage.

Esping-Andersen, G. (1999) *Social Foundations of Post-industrial Economies*, Oxford: Oxford University Press.

Esping-Andersen, G. (ed.) (2002) *Why We Need a New Welfare State*, Oxford: Oxford University Press.

Estevan-Abe, M., Iversen, T. and Soskice, D. (2001) 'Social Protection and the Formation of Skills: A Reinterpretation of the Welfare State', in P. Hall and D. Soskice (eds) *Varieties of Capitalism: The Institutional Foundations of Comparative Advantage*, Oxford: University Press.

Fahey, T. and Norris, M. (2010) 'Housing', in F.G. Castles, S. Leibfried, J. Lewis, H. Obinger and C. Pierson (eds) *The Oxford Handbook of the Welfare State*, Oxford: Oxford University Press.

Farmer, P. (2014) 'Who Lives and Who Dies', *London Review of Books*, 36 (20): 38–39.

Farnsworth, K. (2012) *Social versus Corporate Welfare*, Basingstoke: Palgrave Macmillan.

Farnsworth, K. (2014) 'Business and Global Social Policy', in N. Yeates (ed.) *Understanding Global Social Policy*, 2nd edition, Bristol: Policy Press.

Farnsworth, K. and Irving, Z. (eds) (2011) *Social Policy in Challenging Times: Economic Crisis and Welfare Systems*, Bristol: Policy Press.

Farnsworth, K. and Irving, Z. (eds) (2015) *Social Policy in Times of Austerity*, Bristol: Policy Press.

Farnsworth, K. and Irving, Z. (2018a) 'Who Benefits and Who Pays?', in J. Millar and R. Sainsbury (eds) *Understanding Social Security*, Bristol: Policy Press.

Farnsworth, K. and Irving, Z. (2018b) 'Deciphering the International Monetary Fund's (IMFs) Position on Austerity: Incapacity, Incoherence and Instrumentality', *Global Social Policy*, 18 (2): 119–42.

Farnsworth, K. and Irving, Z. (2018c) 'Austerity: Neoliberal dreams come true?', *Critical Social Policy*, 38 (3): 461–81.

Fenger, M. (2018) 'The Social Policy Agendas of Populist Radical Right Parties in Comparative Perspective', *Journal of International and Comparative Social Policy*, 34 (3): 188–209.

Ferrara, M. (1996) 'The "Southern Model" of Welfare in Social Europe', *Journal of European Social Policy*, 6 (1): 17–37.

Finch, J. and Groves, D. (eds) (1983) *A Labour of Love*, London: Routledge and Kegan Paul.

Fiorino, D.J. (2011) 'Explaining National Environmental Performance: Approaches, Evidence, and Implications', *Policy Sciences*, 44: 367–89.

Fitzpatrick, T. (2014) *Climate Change and Poverty: A New Agenda for Developed Nations*, Bristol: Policy Press.

Fitzpatrick, T., Kwon, H.-J., Manning, N., Midgley, J. and Pascall, G. (2010) *International Encyclopaedia of Social Policy*, volumes 1 and 2, London: Routledge.

Flora, P. (ed.) (1986) *Growth to Limits*, Berlin: De Gruyter.

Flora, P. and Alber, J. (1984) 'Modernization, Democratization and the Development of Welfare States in Western Europe', in P. Flora and A.J. Heidenheimer (eds) *The Development of Welfare States in Europe and America*, New Brunswick: Transaction Books.

Flora, P. and Heidenheimer, A.J. (eds) (1981) *The Development of Welfare States in Europe and America*, New Brunswick, NJ: Transaction Books.

Förster, M.F. and Tóth, I.G. (2015) 'Cross-Country Evidence of the Multiple Causes of Inequality Changes in the OECD Area', in A. Atkinson and F. Bourguignon (eds) *Handbook of Income Distribution*, vol. 2B, Amsterdam: Elsevier.

Franzoni, J.M. (2008) 'Welfare Regimes in Latin America: Capturing Constellations of Markets, Families, and Policies', *Latin American Politics and Society*, 50 (2): 67–100.

Fraser, D. (1975) *The Evolution of the British Welfare State*, London: Macmillan.

Fraser, N. (1997) *Justice Interruptus: Critical Reflections on the 'Postsocialist' Condition*, London: Routledge.

Freeman, R. and Rothgang, H. (2010) 'Health', in F.G. Castles, S. Leibfried, J. Lewis, H. Obinger and C. Pierson (eds) *The Oxford Handbook of the Welfare State*, Oxford: Oxford University Press.

Friedman, S. and Laurison, D. (2018) *The Class Ceiling: Why it Pays to be Privileged*, Bristol: Policy Press.

Fulbrook, J. (1978) *Administrative Justice and the Unemployed*, London: Mansell.

Galbraith, J.K. (1963) *American Capitalism*, Harmondsworth: Penguin Books.

Gamble, A. (2016) *Can the Welfare State Survive?* Cambridge: Polity.

Ghosh, A. (2016) *The Great Derangement: Climate Change and the Unthinkable*, Chicago: University of Chicago Press.

Giddens, A. (2009) *The Politics of Climate Change*, Cambridge: Polity Press.

Gietel-Basten, S., Scherbov, S. and Sanderson, W. (2015) 'Remeasuring Ageing in Southeast Asia', *Asian Population Studies*, 11 (2): 191–210.

Gilardi, F. (2014) 'Methods for the Analysis of Policy Interdependence', in I. Engeli and A.C. Rothmayr (eds) (2014) *Comparative Policy Studies: Conceptual and Methodological Challenges*, Basingstoke: Palgrave Macmillan.

Ginsburg, N. (1992) *Divisions of Welfare*, London: Sage.

Glasby, J. and Littlechild, R. (2016) *Direct Payments and Personal Budgets*, 3rd edition, Bristol: Policy Press.

Goldin, I., Cameron, G. and Balarajan, M. (2011) *Exceptional People*, Princeton, NJ: Princeton University Press.

Goldstein, H. (2016) Letter to *The Guardian*, 8 December.

Goldthorpe, J. (2013) 'Understanding – and Misunderstanding – Social Mobility in Britain: The Entry of the Economists, the Confusion of Politicians and the Limits of Education Policy', *Journal of Social Policy*, 42 (3): 431–50.

Golinowska, S., Henstenberg, P. and Żukowski, M. (eds) (2009) *Diversity and Commonality in European Social Policy: The Forging of a European Social Model*, Warsaw: Friedrich-Ebert-Stiftung.

Gough, I. (1979) *The Political Economy of the Welfare State*, London: Macmillan.

Gough, I. (2013) 'Carbon Mitigation Policies, Distributional Dilemmas and Social Policy', *Journal of Social Policy*, 42 (2): 191–214.

Gough, I. (2015) 'The Political Economy of Prevention', *British Journal of Political Science*, 45 (2): 307–27.

Gough, I. (2016) 'Welfare States and Environmental States: A Comparative Analysis', *Environmental Politics*, 25 (1): 24–47.

Gough, I. (2017) *Heat, Greed and Human Need*, Cheltenham: Edward Elgar.

Gough, I. and Wood, G. (eds) (2004) *Insecurity and Welfare Regimes in Asia, Africa and Latin America: Social Policy in Development Contexts*, Cambridge: Cambridge University Press.

Gough, I., Bradshaw, J., Ditch, J., Eardley, T. and Whiteford, P. (1997) 'Social Assistance in OECD Countries', *Journal of European Social Policy*, 7 (1): 17–43.

Green, A. (1990) *Education and State Formation*, Basingstoke: Macmillan.

Green, A. and Janmaat, J.G. (2011) *Regimes of Social Cohesion, Societies and the Crisis of Globalisation*, Basingstoke: Palgrave Macmillan.

Grek, S. (2009) 'Governing by Numbers: The PISA "Effect" in Europe', *Journal of Education Policy*, 24 (1): 23–37.

Greve, B. (ed.) (2013) *The Routledge Handbook of the Welfare State*, London: Routledge.

Guinan, J. and O'Neill, M. (2018) 'The Institutional Turn: Labour's New Political Economy', *Renewal, A Journal of Social Democracy*, 26 (2): 5–16.

Gusfield, J.R. (1981) *The Culture of Public Problems: Drinking-driving and the Symbolic Order*, Chicago: University of Chicago Press.

Hacker, J.S. and Pierson, P. (2010) *Winner-Take-All Politics*, New York: Simon and Schuster.

Hall, A. and Midgley, J. (2004) *Social Policy for Development*, London: Sage.

Hall, P., Land, H., Parker, R. and Webb, A. (1975) *Change, Choice and Conflict in Social Policy*, London: Heinemann.

Hall, P.A. (1986) *Governing the Economy: The Politics of State Intervention in Britain and France*, Cambridge: Polity Press.

Hall, P.A. (1993) 'Policy Paradigms, Social Learning and the State: The Case of Economic Policy Making in Britain', *Comparative Politics*, 25 (3): 275–96.

Hall, P.A. and Taylor, R.C.R. (1996) 'Political Science and the Three New Institutionalisms', *Political Studies*, 44 (5): 936–57.

Hall, P.A. and Soskice, D. (eds) (2001) *Varieties of Capitalism: The Institutional Foundations of Comparative Advantage*, Oxford: Oxford University Press.

Hall, S., Murie, A. and Knorr-Siedow, T. (2005) 'Large Housing Estates in their Historical Context', in R. van Kempen, K. Dekker, S. Hall and I. Tosics *Restructuring Large Housing Estates in Europe*, Bristol: Policy Press.

Hanel, P.H.P., Maio, G.R. and Manstead, A.S.R. (2019) 'A New Way to Look at the Data: Similarities between Groups of People are Large and Important', *Journal of Personality and Social Psychology*, 116 (4): 541–62.

Hardin, G. (1968) 'The Tragedy of the Commons', *Science*, 162: 1243–8.

Hastings, T. and Heyes, J. (2018) 'Farewell to Flexicurity? Austerity and Labour Policies in the European Union', *Economic and Industrial Democracy*, 39 (3): 458–80.

Hay, C. and Wincott, D. (2012) *The Political Economy of European Welfare Capitalism*, Basingstoke: Palgrave Macmillan.

Heclo, H. (1985) *The Welfare State in Hard Times*, Washington, DC: American Political Science Association.

Hega, G.M. and Hokenmaier, K.G. (2002) 'The Welfare State and Education: A Comparison of Social and Educational Policy in Advanced Industrial Societies', *German Policy Studies*, 2 (1): 143–73.

Heidenheimer, A.J., Heclo, H. and Adams, C.T. (1990) *Comparative Public Policy*, 3rd edition, New York: St. Martin's Press.

Hemerijck, A. (2015) 'The Quiet Paradigm Revolution of Social Investment', *Social Politics: International Studies in Gender, State and Society*, 22 (2): 242–56.

Henderson, D.R. (ed.) (2008) *The Concise Encyclopaedia of Economics*, Carmel, Indiana: Liberty Fund.

Higgins, J. (1981) *States of Welfare*, Oxford: Blackwell.

Hill, M. (2006) *Social Policy in the Modern World*, Oxford: Blackwell.

Hill, M. (2007) *Pensions*, Bristol: Policy Press.

Hill, M. and Hupe, P. (2014) *Implementing Public Policy*, 3rd edition, London: Sage.

Hill, M. and Irving, Z. (2009) *Understanding Social Policy*, 8th edition, Oxford: Wiley-Blackwell.

Hill, M. and Varone, F. (2016) *The Public Policy Process*, 7th edition, London: Routledge.

Hills, J. (1993) *The Future of Welfare: A Guide to the Debate*, York: Joseph Rowntree Foundation.

Hinrichs, K. and Lynch, J. (2010) 'Old Age Pensions', in F. G. Castles, S. Leibfried, J. Lewis, H. Obinger and C. Pierson (eds) *The Oxford Handbook of the Welfare State*, Oxford: Oxford University Press.

Hochschild, A.R. (2000) 'Global Care Chains and Emotional Surplus Value', in W. Hutton and A. Giddens (eds) *On the Edge: Living with Global Capitalism*, London: Jonathan Cape, pp. 130–46.

Holliday, I. (2000) 'Productivist Welfare Capitalism: Social Policy in East Asia', *Political Studies*, 48 (4): 706–23.

Holliday, I. (2005) 'East Asian Social Policy in the Wake of the Financial Crisis: Farewell to Productivism? *Policy and Politics*, 33 (1): 145–62.

Holly, G. (2017) 'Climate Change and Food: A Green Social Work Perspective', *Critical and Radical Social Work*, 5 (2): 145–62.

Holzinger, K. and Knill, C. (2005) 'Causes and Conditions of Cross-National Policy Convergence', *Journal of European Public Policy*, 12 (5): 775–96.

Hood, C. (1986) *The Tools of Government*, Chatham, NJ: Chatham House.

Hood, C. (2007) 'Intellectual Obsolescence and Intellectual Makeovers: Reflections on the Tools of Government after Two Decades', *Governance*, 20 (1): 127–44.

Howlett, M., Ramesh, M. and Perl, A. (2009) *Studying Public Policy*, Oxford: Oxford University Press.

Huber, E. and Bogliaccini, J. (2010) 'Latin America', in F. G. Castles, S. Leibfried, J. Lewis, H. Obinger and C. Pierson (eds) *The Oxford Handbook of the Welfare State*, Oxford: Oxford University Press.

Huby, M. (1998) *Social Policy and the Environment*, Buckingham: Open University Press.

Hüfner, K., Meyer, J.W. and Naumann, J. (1987) 'Comparative Education Policy Research: A World Society Perspective', in M. Dierkes, H.N. Weiler and A.B. Antal (eds) *Comparative Policy Research: Learning from Experience*, Aldershot: Gower.

Humphries, R. (2013) *Paying for Social Care*, London: The King's Fund.

Hunter, D. (2003) *Public Health Policy*, Cambridge: Polity Press.

Huo, J., Nelson, M. and Stephens, J.D. (2008) 'Decommodification and Activation in Social Democratic Policy: Resolving the Paradox', *Journal of European Social Policy*, 18 (1): 5–20.

IFS (Institute for Fiscal Studies) (2017) *The IFS Green Budget, February 2017*, London: Institute for Fiscal Studies.

Illich, I. (1977) *Limits to Medicine*, Harmondsworth: Penguin.

ILO (International Labour Organization) (2014) *Minimum Wage Systems*, International Labour Conference, 103rd Session, 2014, General Survey of the Reports on the Minimum Wage Fixing Convention, 1970 (No. 131), and the Minimum Wage Fixing Recommendation, 1970 (No. 135), Geneva: International Labour Office.

ILO (2015) *ILO Global Estimates of Migrant Workers and Migrant Domestic Workers: Results and Methodology*, Geneva: ILO.

ILO (2016) *World Employment and Social Outlook: Transforming Jobs to End Poverty*, Geneva: International Labour Office.

ILO (2017a) *World Employment and Social Outlook*, Geneva: International Labour Office.

ILO (2017b) *World Social Protection Report 2017–19*, Geneva: International Labour Office.

ILO (2018) *World Employment and Social Outlook: Trends 2018*, Geneva: International Labour Office.

IMF (International Monetary Fund) (2017a) World Economic Outlook Datamapper, https://www.imf.org/external/datamapper/NGDP_RPCH@WEO/OEMDC/ADVEC/WEOWORLD.

IMF (2017b) *Fiscal Monitor: Tackling Inequality*, October, Washington, DC: International Monetary Fund.

Inglehart, R. (2008) 'Changing Values Among Western Publics from 1970 to 2006', *West European Politics*, 31 (1–2): 130–46.

IPCC (Intergovernmental Panel on Climate Change) (2014) *Climate Change 2014 – Impacts, Adaptation and Vulnerability. Part A: Global and Sectoral Aspects*. Working Group II contribution to the Fifth Assessment Report of the Intergovernmental Panel on Climate Change, New York: Cambridge University Press.

IPCC (2019) *Climate Change and Land*, August 2019, WMO/UNEP, https://www.ipcc.ch/site/assets/uploads/2019/08/Fullreport-1.pdf.

Irving, Z. (2015) 'Transformation and Persistence in the Gender Division of Work', in V. Robinson and D. Richardson (eds) *Introducing Gender and Women's Studies*, 4th edition, Basingstoke: Palgrave Macmillan.

Irving, Z., Fenger, M. and Hudson, J. (eds) (2015) *Social Policy Review 27: Analysis and Debate in Social Policy*, Bristol: Policy Press.

Iversen, T. and Stephens, J.D. (2008) 'Partisan Politics, the Welfare State and Three Worlds of Human Capital Formation', *Comparative Political Studies*, 41 (4/5): 600–37.

Jackson, T. (2009) *Prosperity Without Growth*, London: Earthscan.

Jänicke, M. (2005) 'Trend-setters in Environment Policy: The Character and Role of Pioneer Countries', *Environmental Policy and Governance*, 15 (2): 129–42.

Jensen, C. (2011) 'Capitalist Systems, Deindustrialisation and the Politics of Public Education', *Comparative Political Studies*, 44 (4): 412–35.

John, P. (1998) *Analysing Public Policy*, London: Pinter.

Jones, C. (ed.) (1993) *New Perspectives on the Welfare State in Europe*, London: Routledge.

Kaasch, A. (2015) *Shaping Global Health Policy: Global Social Policy Actors and Ideas about Health Care Systems*, Basingstoke: Palgrave Macmillan.

Kaasch, A. and Stubbs, P. (eds) (2014) *Transformations in Global and Regional Social Policies*, Basingstoke: Palgrave Macmillan.

Kaasch, A. and Martens, K. (eds) (2015) *Actors and Agency in Global Social Governance*, Oxford: Oxford University Press.

Kangas, O. (1994) 'The Politics of Social Security: On Regressions, Qualitative Comparisons and Cluster Analysis', in T. Janoski and A.M. Hicks (eds) *The Comparative Political Economy of the Welfare State*, Cambridge: Cambridge University Press.

Kapur, D. and Nangia, P. (2015) 'Social Protection in India: A Welfare State Sans Public Goods?', *India Review*, 14 (1): 73–90.

Kasza, G.J. (2002) 'The Illusion of Welfare Regimes', *Journal of Social Policy*, 31 (2): 271–89.

Kemeny, J. and Lowe, S. (1998) 'Schools of Comparative Housing Research: From Convergence to Divergence', *Housing Studies*, 13 (2): 161–76.

Kennett, P. (ed.) (2004) *A Handbook of Comparative Social Policy*, Cheltenham: Edward Elgar.

Keynes, J.M. (1936) *The General Theory of Employment Interest and Money*, London: Macmillan.

King, D. (1999) *In the Name of Liberalism: Illiberal Social Policy in the USA and Britain*, Oxford: Oxford University Press.

Kingdon, J.W. (2013) *Agendas, Alternatives and Public Policies*, 3rd edition, New York: Addison, Wesley, Longman.

Klant, J.J. (1984) *The Rules of the Game: The Logical Structure of Economic Theories*, Cambridge: Cambridge University Press.

Klugman, J., Rodríguez, F. and Choi, H.-J. (2011) 'The HDI 2010: New Controversies, Old Critiques', *Journal of Economic Inequality*, 9 (2): 249–88.

Knill, C. and Liefferink, D. (2007) *Environment Politics in the European Union*, Manchester: Manchester University Press.

Knill, C., Heichel, S. and Ardnt, D. (2012) 'Really a Front-runner, Really a Straggler? Of Environmental Leaders and Laggards in the European Union and Beyond – a Quantitative Policy Perspective', *Energy Policy*, 48: 36–45.

Knoepfel, P. and Weidner, H. (1982) 'Formulation and Implementation of Air Quality Control Programmes: Patterns of Interest Consideration', *Policy and Politics*, 10 (1): 85–109.

Knoepfel, P., Larrue, C., Varone, F. and Hill, M. (2007) *Public Policy Analysis*, Bristol: Policy Press.

Koch, M. and Fritz, M. (2014) 'Building the Eco-Social State: Do Welfare Regimes Matter?', *Journal of Social Policy*, 43 (4): 679–703.

Korpi, W. and Palme, J. (1998) 'The Paradox of Redistribution: Welfare State Institutions and Poverty in the Western Countries', *American Sociological Review*, 63 (5): 661–87.

Krugman, P. (2012) *End This Depression Now*, New York and London: Norton.

Ku, Y.-W. (1997) *Welfare Capitalism in Taiwan: State, Economy and Social Policy*, Basingstoke: Macmillan.

Kuhn, T.S. (1970) *The Structure of Scientific Revolutions*, 2nd edition, Chicago: University of Chicago Press.

Kwon, H.-J. (1997) 'Beyond European Welfare Systems: Comparative Perspectives on East Asian Welfare Systems', *Journal of Social Policy*, 26 (4): 467–84.

Kwon, H.-J. (1999) *The Welfare State in Korea: The Politics of Legitimation*, New York: St. Martin's Press.

Kyle, D. and Koslowski, R. (eds) (2011) *Global Human Smuggling, Comparative Perspectives*, 2nd edition, Baltimore: The Johns Hopkins University Press.

Lallement, M. (2011) 'Europe and the Economic Crisis: Forms of Labour Market Adjustment and Varieties of Capitalism', *Work, Employment and Society*, 25 (4): 627–641.

Lamb, W.F., Steinberger, J.K., Bows-Larkin, A., Peters, G.P., Roberts, J.T. and Wood, F.R. (2014) 'Transitions in Pathways of Human Development and Carbon Emissions', *Environment Research Letters*, 9, 014111.

Lascoumes, P. and Le Gales, P. (2007) 'Introduction: Understanding Public Policy Through its Instruments – from the Nature of Instruments to the Sociology of Public Policy Instrumentation', *Governance*, 20 (1): 1–21.

Leibfried, S. (1992) 'Towards a European Welfare State', in Z. Ferge and J.E. Kolberg (eds) *Social Policy in a Changing Europe*, Frankfurt am Main: European Centre for Social Welfare Policy and Research.

Leisering, L. and Barrientos, A. (2013) 'Social Citizenship for the Global Poor? The Worldwide Spread of Social Assistance', *International Journal of Social Welfare*, 22 (S1): 50–67.

Leung, J. (1994) 'Dismantling the "Iron Rice Bowl": Welfare Reforms in the People's Republic of China', *Journal of Social Policy*, 23 (3): 341–62.

Leung, J.C.B. and Xu, Y. (2015) *China's Social Welfare*, Bristol: Policy Press.

Lewin, L., Lewin, B., Bäck, H. and Westin, L. (2008) 'A Kindler, Gentler Democracy? The Consensus Model and Swedish Disability Politics', *Scandinavian Political Studies*, 31 (3): 291–310.

Lewis, J. (1992) 'Gender and the Development of Welfare Regimes', *Journal of European Social Policy*, 2 (3): 159–73.

Lewis, J. (ed.) (1993) *Women and Social Policies in Europe: Work, Family and the State*, Aldershot: Edward Elgar.

Lewis, J. (1997a) 'Gender and Welfare Regimes: Further Thoughts', *Social Politics*, Summer, 160–77.

Lewis, J. (ed.) (1997b) *Lone Mothers in European Welfare Regimes*, London: Jessica Kingsley.

LGiU and Mears (2017) *The Human Cost of Cut-Price Care*, https://www.lgiu.org.uk/report/paying-for-it-the-human-cost-of-cut-price-care/.

Liefferink, D., Arts, B., Kamstra, J. and Ooijevaar, J. (2009) 'Leaders and Laggards in Environmental Policy: A Quantitative Analysis of Domestic Policy Outputs', *Journal of European Public Policy*, 16 (5): 677–700.

Lijphart, A. (1999) *Patterns of Democracy*, New Haven, CT: Yale University Press.

Lindblom, C.E. (1977) *Politics and Markets*, New York: Basic Books.

Linder, S.H. and Peters, B.G. (1991) 'The Logic of Public Policy Design: Linking Policy Actors and Plausible Instruments', *Knowledge in Society*, 4: 15–51.

Lingard, B., Martino, W. and Rezai-Rashti, G. (2013) 'Testing Regimes, Accountabilities and Education Policy: Commensurate Global and National Developments', *Journal of Education Policy*, 28 (5): 539–56.

Lohmann, H. and Zagel, H. (2016) 'Family Policy in Comparative Perspective: The Concepts and Measurement of Familization and Defamilization', *Journal of European Social Policy*, 26 (1): 48–65.

Lohmann, H. and Marx, I. (2018) *Handbook on In-Work Poverty*, Cheltenham: Edward Elgar.

LoVuolo, R. (2012) 'Prospects and Challenges for the Basic Income Proposal in Latin America', *Basic Income Studies*, 7 (1): 1–17.

Lowe, S. (2011) *The Housing Debate*, Bristol: Policy Press.

Lugosi, N. (2018) 'Radical Right Framing of Social Policy in Hungary: Between Nationalism and Populism', *Journal of International and Comparative Social Policy*, 34 (3): 210–33.

Macmillan, M. (2008) *The Uses and Abuses of History*, London: Profile Books.

Malpass, P. and Murie, A. (1994) *Housing Policy and Practice*, Basingstoke: Macmillan.

Mansell, J. and Beadle-Brown, J. (2010) 'Deinstitutionalisation and Community Living: Position Statement of the Comparative Policy and Practice Special Interest Group of the International Association for the Scientific Study of Intellectual Disabilities', *Journal of Intellectual Disability Research*, 54 (2): 104–12.

Marx, K. and Engels, F. (1848) [2002] *The Communist Manifesto*, Harmondsworth: Penguin Books.

May, P.J. (2015) 'Implementation Failures Revisited: Policy Regime Perspectives', *Public Policy and Administration*, 30 (3–4): 277–99.

McBride, S., Mahon, R. and Boychuk, G.W. (2015) *After '08: Social Policy and the Global Financial Crisis*, Vancouver: University of British Columbia Press.

McDaniel, S. and Zimmer, Z. (ed.) (2016) *Global Ageing in the Twenty-First Century: Challenges, Opportunities and Implications*, London: Routledge.

McGoey, L. (2015) *No Such Thing as a Free Gift*, London: Verso.

McGrew, A.G. and Lewis, P. (1992) *Global Politics: Globalization and the Nation State*, Cambridge: Polity Press.

McKeown, T. (1980) *The Role of Medicine*, Blackwell: Oxford.

Meadowcroft, J. (2005) 'From Welfare State to Eco-State', in J. Barry and R. Eckersley (eds) *The State and the Global Ecological Crisis*, Cambridge, MA: MIT Press.

Meadows, D.H. (1999) 'Sustainable Systems', lecture at the University of Michigan, https://www.youtube.com/watch?v=HMmChiLZZHg.

Meadows, D.H., Meadows, D.L. and Randers, J. (1972) *The Limits to Growth*, New York: Universe Books.

Meyer, H.-D. and Benavot, A. (eds) (2013) *PISA, Power and Policy: The Emergence of Global Educational Governance*, Oxford: Symposium Books.

Meyer, T., Bridgen, P. and Reidmüller, B. (eds) (2007) *Private Pensions versus Social Inclusion: Non-state Provision for Citizens at Risk in Europe*, Cheltenham: Edward Elgar.

MHCLG (2018a) *English Housing Survey, Private Rented Sector 2016–17*, Ministry of Housing, Communities and Local Government, https://assets.publishing.service.gov.uk/government/uploads/system/uploads/attachment_data/file/723880/Private_rented_sector_report.pdf.

MHCLG (2018b) *Statutory Homelessness and Prevention and Relief*, January to March (Q1) 2018, England, Ministry of Housing, Communities and Local Government, Housing Statistical Release, 29 June 2018, https://assets.publishing.service.gov.uk/government/uploads/system/uploads/attachment_data/file/721285/Statutory_Homelessness_and_Prevention_and_Relief_Statistical_Release_Jan_to_Mar_2018_-_REVISED.pdf.

MHCLG (2018c) *Rough Sleeping Statistics*, Autumn 2017, England (Revised), Ministry of Housing, Communities and Local Government, Housing Statistical Release, 16 February 2018 (Revised), https://assets.publishing.service.gov.uk/government/uploads/system/uploads/attachment_data/file/682001/Rough_Sleeping_Autumn_2017_Statistical_Release_-_revised.pdf.

Midgley, J. (1995) *Social Development: The Development Perspective in Social Welfare*, London: Sage.

Milanovic, B. (2012) 'Global Inequality: From Class to Location, from Proletarians to Migrants', *Global Policy*, 3 (2): 125–34.

Milanovic, B. (2016) *Global Inequality: A New Approach for the Age of Globalization*, Cambridge, MA: Harvard University Press.

Millar, J. and Bennett, F. (2017) 'Universal Credit: Assumptions, Contradictions and Virtual Reality', *Social Policy and Society*, 16 (2): 169–82.

Mishra, R. (1998) 'Beyond the Nation State: Social Policy in an Age of Globalization', *Social Policy and Administration*, 32 (5): 481–500.

Misra, J., Woodring, J. and Merz, S.N. (2006) 'The Globalization of Care Work: Neoliberal Economic Restructuring and Migration Policy', *Globalizations*, 3 (3): 317–32.

Mitchell, D. (1991) *Income Transfers in Ten Welfare States*, Aldershot: Avebury.

Mkandawire, T. (2001) *Social Policy in a Development Context*, Social Policy and Development Programme Paper, Number 7, June, Geneva: United Nations Research Institute for Social Development (UNRISD).

Mkandawire, T. (2007) 'Transformative Social Policy and Innovation in Developing Countries', *The European Journal of Development Research*, 19 (1): 13–29.

Mkandawire, T. (2016) *Colonial Legacies and Social Welfare Regimes in Africa: An Empirical Exercise*, UNRISD Working Paper, No. 2016-4, Geneva: United Nations Research Institute for Social Development.

Mommsen, W.J. (ed.) (1981) *The Emergence of the Welfare State in Britain and Germany*, London: Croom Helm.

Monaghan, M. (2011) *Evidence versus Politics: Exploiting Research in UK Drug Policy*, Bristol: Policy Press.

Moran, M. (1994) 'Health Care Policy', in J. Clasen and R. Freeman (eds) *Social Policy in Germany*, Hemel Hempstead: Harvester Wheatsheaf.

Moran, M. (2000) 'Understanding the Welfare State: The Case of Health Care', *British Journal of Politics and International Relations*, 2 (2): 135–60.

Morris, P. (2015) 'Comparative Education, PISA, Politics and Educational Reform: A Cautionary Note', *Compare: A Journal of Comparative and International Education*, 45 (3): 470–4.

Mudde, C. (2007) *Populist Radical Right Parties in Europe*, Cambridge: Cambridge University Press.

Murie, A. (2014) 'The Housing Legacy of Thatcherism', in S. Farrell and C. Hay (eds) *The Legacy of Thatcherism*, Oxford: Oxford University Press.

Murphy, H. and Kellow, A. (2013) 'Forum Shopping in Global Governance: Understanding States, Business and NGOs in Multiple Arenas', *Global Policy*, 4 (2): 139–49.

New Economics Foundation (2005) *Africa Up in Smoke*, London: New Economics Foundation.

Norris, M. and Byrne, M. (2015) 'Asset Price Keynesianism, Regional Imbalances and the Irish and Spanish Housing Booms and Busts', *Built Environment*, 41 (2): 227–43.

O'Brien, R., Goetz, A.M., Scholte, J.A. and Williams, M. (2000) *Contesting Global Governance: Multilateral Economic Institutions and Global Social Movements*, Cambridge: Cambridge University Press.

O'Connor, J. (1973) *The Fiscal Crisis of the State*, New York: St Martin's Press.

O'Connor, J.S. (1996) 'From Women in the Welfare State to Gendering Welfare State Regimes', *Current Sociology*, Special Issue, 44 (2): 1–130.

OECD (Organisation for Economic Co-operation and Development) (1987) *Financing and Delivering Health Care: A Comparative Analysis of OECD Countries*, Paris: OECD.

OECD (2004/5) 'Is GDP a Satisfactory Measure of Growth?', *OECD Observer*, no. 246/7.

OECD (2006) *Starting Strong*, Paris: OECD.

OECD (2011a) *An Overview of Growing Income Inequalities in OECD Countries: Main Findings*, Paris: OECD.

OECD (2011b) *Help Wanted? Providing and Paying for Long-term Care*, Paris: OECD.

OECD (2015) *In it Together: Why Less Inequality Benefits All*, Paris: OECD.

OECD (2016a) *Education at a Glance*, Paris: OECD.

OECD (2016b) 'Singapore Tops Latest OECD PISA Global Education Survey', press release, 6 December, https://www.oecd.org/newsroom/singapore-tops-latest-oecd-pisa-global-education-survey.htm.

OECD (2016c) *OECD Pensions Outlook 2016*, Paris: OECD.

OECD (2016d) *Irish GDP up by 26.3% in 2015?* OECD Statistics and Data Directorate, Paris: OECD, http://www.oecd.org/sdd/na/Irish-GDP-up-in-2015-OECD.pdf.

OECD (2016e) Affordable Housing Database, http://www.oecd.org/social/affordable-housing-database.htm

OECD (2017a) *Education at a Glance*, Paris: OECD.

OECD (2017b) 'Long-term Care Expenditure', in *Health at a Glance 2017: OECD Indicators*, Paris: OECD.

OECD (2017c) *Basic Income as a Policy Option: Can it Add Up?* Paris: OECD.

OECD (2017d) *Health at a Glance 2017*, Paris: OECD.

OECD (2017e) *OECD Employment Outlook*, Paris:OECD.

OECD (2017f) *Preventing Ageing Unequally*, Paris: OECD.

OECD (2017g) *Pensions at a Glance*, Paris: OECD.

OECD (2018a) *Public Expenditure Database (SOCX)*, https://www.oecd.org/social/expenditure.htm.

OECD (2018b) *OECD Employment Outlook 2018*, Paris, OECD.

OECD (2018c) *Education at a Glance*, Paris: OECD.

OECD (2019) *Social Expenditure Update 2019, Public Social Spending is High in Many OECD Countries*, Paris: OECD.

Ohmae, K. (1990) *The Borderless World*, London: Collins.

Opus Restructuring LLP and Company Watch (2017) *Domiciliary Care Finances Report*, March, http://www.opusllp.com/wp-content/uploads/2017/03/DOC-170317-NRH-domiciliary-care-finances-report-v2.pdf.

Orloff, A.S. (1993) 'Gender and the Social Rights of Citizenship: State Policies and Gender Relations in Comparative Research', *American Sociological Review*, 58 (3): 303–28.

Ortiz, I., Cummins, M., Capaldo, J. and Karunanethy, K. (2015) *The Decade of Adjustment: A Review of Austerity Trends 2010–2020 in 187 Countries*. Extension of Social Security Working Paper No. 53, Geneva: International Labour Office.

Orton, M. and Rowlingson, K. (2007) 'A Problem of Riches: Towards a New Social Policy Research Agenda on the Distribution of Economic Resources', *Journal of Social Policy*, 36 (1): 59–77.

Oxfam (2015) *Wealth: Having it All and Wanting More*, Oxfam Issue Briefing, January 2015, Oxford: Oxfam International.

Oxley, M. (1991) 'The Aims and Methods of Comparative Housing Research', *Scandinavian Housing and Planning Research*, 8 (2): 67–77.

Özler, I. and Öbach, B.K. (2009) 'Capitalism, State Economic Policy and Ecological Footprint: An International Comparative Analysis', *Global Environmental Politics*, 9 (1): 79–108.

Palmer, G.R. and Short, S.D. (1994) *Health Care and Public Policy: An Australian Analysis*, 2nd edition, South Melbourne: Macmillan.

Pampel, F.C. and Williamson, J.B. (1989) *Age, Class, Politics and the Welfare State*, Cambridge: Cambridge University Press.

Papadopoulos, T. and Roumpakis, A. (2017) 'Family as a Socio-Economic Actor in the Political Economies of East and South-East Asian Welfare Capitalisms', *Social Policy & Administration*, 51 (6): 857–75.

Parenti, C. (2012) *Tropic of Chaos: Climate Change and the New Geography of Violence*, New York: Nation Books.

Pascall, G. and Manning, N. (2000) 'Gender and Social Policy: Comparing Welfare States in Central and Eastern Europe and the Former Soviet Union', *Journal of European Social Policy*, 10 (3): 240–66.

Pearson, H. (2015) *The Life Project*, Harmondsworth: Penguin Books.

Pechar, H. and Andres, L. (2011) 'Higher-Education Policies and Welfare Regimes: International Comparative Perspectives', *Higher Education Policy*, 24 (1): 25–52.

Pedersen, A.W. and Kuhnle, S. (2017) 'The Nordic Welfare State Model', in I. Knutsen and P. Oddbjørn (eds) *The Nordic Models in Political Science: Challenged, but Still Viable?* Bergen: Fagbokforlaget.

Peet, R. (2009) *Unholy Trinity: The IMF, World Bank, and WTO*, London: Zed Books.

Pierson, P. (1994) *Dismantling the Welfare State*, Cambridge: Cambridge University Press.

Pierson, P. (2000) 'Increasing Returns, Path Dependence and the Study of Politics', *American Political Science Review*, 92 (4): 251–67.

Pierson, P. (ed.) (2001) *The New Politics of the Welfare State*, Oxford: Oxford University Press.

Pierson, P. (2005) 'The Study of Policy Development', *Journal of Policy History*, 17 (1): 34–51.

Piketty, T. (2014) *Capital*, Cambridge, MA: Harvard University Press.

Pilling, D. (2018) *The Growth Delusion*, London: Bloomsbury.

Piven, F.F. and Cloward, R.A. (1972) *Regulating the Poor*, London: Tavistock.

Plagerson, S. and Patel, L. (2019) 'Welfare Regimes in the Global South: Does the Capability Approach Provide an Alternative Perspective?', *Journal of Poverty and Social Justice*, 27 (1): 23–40.

Polanyi, K. (1944) *The Great Transformation*, Boston: Beacon Press.

Pollitt, C. and Bouckaert, G. (2009) *Continuity and Change in Public Policy and Management*, Cheltenham: Edward Elgar.

Powell, M. (2016) 'Citation Classics in Social Policy Journals', *Social Policy and Administration*, 50 (6): 648–72.

Pralle, S.B. (2009) 'Agenda-Setting and Climate Change', *Environmental Politics*, 18 (5): 781–99.

Preston, S. (1975) 'The Changing Relation between Mortality and Level of Economic Development', *Population Studies*, 29 (2): 231–48.

Ramesh, M. (2004) *Social Policy in East and Southeast Asia: Education, Health, Housing and Income Maintenance*, London: Routledge Curzon.

Raworth, K. (2017) *Doughnut Economics: Seven Ways to Think Like a 21st Century Economist*, London: R.H. Business Books.

Razavi, S. (2007) *The Political and Social Economy of Care in a Development Context: Conceptual Issues, Research Questions and Policy Options*, Gender and Development Programme Paper, 3, Geneva: United Nations Research Institute for Social Development.

Rhodes, R.A.W. (1994) 'The Hollowing Out of the State', *Political Quarterly*, 65 (2): 138–51.

Rimlinger, G. (1971) *Welfare Policy and Industrialisation in Europe, America and Russia*, New York: Wiley.

Ronald, R., Kadi, J. and Lennartz, C. (2015) 'Home-ownership Based Welfare in Transition', *Critical Housing Analysis*, 2 (1): 52–64.

Rose, R. (1993) *Lesson Drawing in Public Policy*, Chatham, NJ: Chatham House.

Rothgang, H., Cacace, M., Grimmeisen, S. and Wendt, C. (2005) 'The Changing Role of the State in Healthcare Systems', *European Review*, 13 (1): 187–212.

Rowntree, B.S. (2000) *Poverty: A Study of Town Life*, Bristol: Policy Press.

Sabatier, P.A. (ed.) (1999) *Theories of the Policy Process*, Boulder, CO: Westview Press.

Sabatier, P.A. and Weible, C. (eds) (2014) *Theories of the Policy Process*, 3rd edition, Boulder, CO: Westview Press.

Sainsbury, D. (1993) 'Dual Welfare and Sex Segregation of Access to Social Benefits: Income Maintenance Policies in the UK, the US, the Netherlands and Sweden', *Journal of Social Policy*, 22 (1): 69–98.

Sainsbury, D. (ed.) (1994) *Gendering Welfare States*, London: Sage.

Sainsbury, D. (1996) *Gender Equality and Welfare States*, Cambridge: Cambridge University Press.

Scheve, K. and Stasavage, D. (2016) *Taxing the Rich*, Princeton, NJ: Princeton University Press.

Schlager, E. (1997) 'A Response to Kim Quaile Hill's "In Search of Policy Theory"', *Policy Currents*, 7: 14–15.

Schmidt, V.A. (2009) 'Putting the Political Back into Political Economy by Bringing the State Back in Yet Again', *World Politics*, 61 (3): 516–46.

Schneider, A.L. and Ingram, H. (1997) *Policy Design for Democracy*, Lawrence: University Press of Kansas.

Schröder, M. (2009) 'Integrating Welfare and Production Typologies: How Refinements of the Varieties of Capitalism Approach Call for a Combination of Welfare Typologies', *Journal of Social Policy*, 38 (1): 19–43.

Schubert, R., Hegelich, S. and Bazant, U. (2009) *The Handbook of European Welfare Systems*, London: Routledge.

Schui, F. (2014) *Austerity: The Great Failure*, New Haven, CT: Yale University Press.

Schut, F.T. and van den Berg, B. (2011) 'Sustainability of Comprehensive Universal Long-term Care Insurance in the Netherlands', in J. Costa-Font (ed.) *Reforming Long-term Care in Europe*, Chichester: Wiley-Blackwell.

Schwartz, H.M. and Seabrooke, L. (2008) 'Varieties of Residential Capitalism in the International Political Economy: Old Welfare States and the New Politics of Housing', *Comparative European Politics*, 6 (3): 237–61.

Scruggs, L. and Allan, J. (2006) 'Welfare-state Decommodification in 18 OECD Countries: A Replication and Revision', *Journal of European Social Policy*, 16 (1): 55–72.

Seelkopf, L. and Starke, P. (2019) 'Social Policy by Other Means: Theorizing Unconventional Forms of Welfare Production', *Journal of Comparative Policy Analysis: Research and Practice*, 20 (3): 219–34.

Seldon, A. (1990) *Capitalism*, Oxford: Blackwell.

Sen, A. (1985) *Commodities and Capabilities*, Elsevier: Amsterdam.

Serra, N. and Stiglitz, J. (2008) *The Washington Consensus Reconsidered, Towards a New Global Governance*, Oxford: Oxford University Press.

Sharkh, M.A. and Gough, I. (2010) 'Global Welfare Regimes: A Cluster Analysis', *Global Social Policy*, 10 (1): 27–58.

Shin, D.-M. (2003) *Social and Economic Policies in Korea: Ideas, Networks and Linkages*, London: Routledge Curzon.

Siaroff, A. (1994) 'Work, Welfare and Gender Equality: A New Typology', in D. Sainsbury (ed.) *Gendering Welfare States*, London: Sage.

Sklair, L. (2000) 'The Transnational Capitalist Class and the Discourse of Globalisation', *Cambridge Review of International Affairs*, 14 (1): 67–85.

Skocpol, T. (1995) *Protecting Soldiers and Mothers: The Political Origins of Social Policy in the United States*, Cambridge, MA: Harvard University Press.

Sørensen, N.N. (2012) 'Revisiting the Migration–Development Nexus: From Social Networks and Remittances to Markets for Migration Control', *International Migration*, 50 (3): 61–76.

Sorsa, V.-P. (2016) 'Public-private Partnerships in European Old-Age Pension Provision: An Accountability Perspective', *Social Policy and Administration*, 50 (7): 846–74.

Standing, G. (2008) 'How Cash Transfers Promote the Case for Basic Income', *Basic Income Studies*, 3 (1), online, doi:10.2202/1932-0183.1106.

Standing, G. (2011) *The Precariat: The New Dangerous Class*, London: Bloomsbury.

Standing, G. (2014) 'The Precariat: From Denizens to Citizens', *Polity*, 44 (4): 588–608.

Steinmo, S., Thelen, K. and Longstreth, F. (eds) (1992) *Structuring Politics: Historical Institutionalism in Comparative Analysis*, Cambridge: Cambridge University Press.

Stevens, T. (2017) 'Turning the Theory into Reality', in M. Benson and I. Hamiduddin (eds) *Self-build Homes: Social Discourse, Experiences and Directions*, London, UCL Press.

Stiglitz, J. (2016) *The Great Divide*, London: Penguin.

Stiglitz, J., Sen, A. and Fitoussi, J. (2009) *Report by the Commission on the Measurement of Economic Performance and Progress*, Paris: OECD.

Stone, D. (2008) 'Global Public Policy, Transnational Policy Communities and Their Networks', *Policy Studies Journal*, 36 (1): 19–38.

Streeck, W. (2014) *Buying Time: The Delayed Crisis of Democratic Capitalism*, London: Verso.

Streeck, W. (2017) *How Will Capitalism End? Essays on a Failing System*, London: Verso.

Streeck, W. and Thelen, K. (eds) (2005) *Beyond Continuity: Institutional Change in Advanced Political Economies*, Oxford: Oxford University Press.

Stuckler, D. and Basu, S. (2013) *The Body Economic: Eight Experiments in Economic Recovery from Iceland to Greece*, London: Penguin Books.

Sung, S. and Pascall, G. (2014) *Gender and Welfare States in East Asia: Confucianism or Gender Equality?* Basingstoke: Palgrave Macmillan.

Surender, R. (2013) 'The Role of Historical Contexts in Shaping Social Policy in the Global South', in R. Surender and R. Walker (eds) *Social Policy in a Developing World*, Cheltenham: Edward Elgar.

Surender, R. and Walker, R. (eds) (2013) *Social Policy in a Developing World*, Cheltenham: Edward Elgar.

Szikra, D. (2014) 'Democracy and Welfare in Hard Times: The Social Policy of the Orbán Government in Hungary Between 2010 and 2014', *Journal of European Social Policy*, 24 (5): 486–500.

Tallberg, J. and Jönsson, C. (eds) (2010) *Transnational Actors in Global Governance: Patterns, Explanations, and Implications*, London: Palgrave Macmillan.

Taylor-Gooby, P. (ed.) (2001) *European Welfare States under Pressure*, London: Sage.

Taylor-Gooby, P. (2002) 'The Silver Age of the Welfare State: Perspectives on Resilience', *Journal of Social Policy*, 31 (4): 597–622.

Taylor-Gooby, P. (ed.) (2004) *New Risks, New Welfare: The Transformation of the European Welfare State*, Oxford: Oxford University Press.

Taylor-Gooby, P. (2013) *The Double Crisis of the Welfare State and What We Can Do About it*, Basingstoke: Palgrave Macmillan.

Thévenon, O. (2011) 'Family Policies in OECD Countries: A Comparative Analysis', *Population and Development Review*, 37 (1): 57–87.

Titmuss, R.M. (1974) *Social Policy: An Introduction*, London: Allen and Unwin.

Townsend, P. (ed.) (1970) *The Concept of Poverty*, London: Heinemann.

Townsend, P. (1993) *The International Analysis of Poverty*, Hemel Hempstead: Harvester Wheatsheaf.

Trifilletti, R. (1999) 'Southern European Welfare Regimes and the Worsening Position of Women', *Journal of European Social Policy*, 9 (1): 49–64.

UNDESA (2015) *World Population Ageing 2015* (ST/ESA/SER.A/390), United Nations, Department of Economic and Social Affairs, Population Division.

UNDESA (2018) *World Urbanization Prospects: The 2018 Revision* (ST/ESA/SER.A/420), United Nations, Department of Economic and Social Affairs, Population Division.

UNDP (United Nations Development Programme) (2010) *Human Development Report 2010, 20th Anniversary Edition, the Real Wealth of Nations: Pathways to Human Development*, Basingstoke: Palgrave Macmillan.

UNESCO (2016) *Leaving No One Behind: How Far on the Way to Universal Primary and Secondary Education?* Global Education Monitoring Report, Policy Paper 27/Fact Sheet 37, July ED/GEMR/MRT/2016/PP/27 REV. 4, United Nations Education, Scientific and Cultural Organisation.

UN-Habitat (2011a) *A Policy Guide to Rental Housing in Developing Countries*, Quick Policy Guide Series, volume 1, Kenya: UN-HABITAT.

UN-Habitat (2011b) *Enabling Shelter Strategies: Design and Implementation Guide for Policymakers*, Quick Policy Guide Series, volume 2, Kenya: UN-HABITAT.

UN-Habitat (2014) *The Right to Adequate Housing, Fact Sheet No. 21 (Rev. 1)*, GE.14-80125-May 2014-2,000, Geneva: UN-HABITAT.

UN-Habitat (2015) *World Atlas of Slum Evolution*, Working Document, December, Nairobi: United Nations Human Settlements Programme.

UNHCR (2017) *Global Trends, Forced Displacement 2017*, Geneva: United Nations High Commission for Refugees.

United Nations (1995) *Beijing Declaration and Platform for Action/Beijing+5 Political Declaration and Outcome*, reprinted by UN Women (2014), New York: UN Women.

United Nations (2017) *Population Facts*, no. 5, December.

Unterhalter, E. (2019) 'The Many Meanings of Quality Education: Politics of Targets and Indicators in SDG4', *Global Policy*, 10 (S1): 39–51.

Van Gent, W. (2010) 'Housing Policy as a Lever for Change? The Politics of Welfare, Assets and Tenure', *Housing Studies*, 25 (5): 735–53.

Van Kersbergen, K. and Vis, B. (2014) *Comparative Welfare State Politics*, Cambridge: Cambridge University Press.

Van der Waal, J., Achterberg, P., Houtman, D., de Koster, W. and Manevska, K. (2010) '"Some Are More Equal Than Others": Economic Egalitarianism and Welfare Chauvinism in the Netherlands', *Journal of European Social Policy*, 20 (4): 350–63.

Verger, A., Novelli, M. and Altinyelken, H.K. (2018) *Global Education Policy and International Development*, 2nd edition, London: Bloomsbury Academic.

Vlandas, T. (2013) 'Mixing Apples with Oranges? Partisanship and Active Labour Market Policies in Europe', *Journal of European Social Policy*, 23 (1): 3–20.

Wackernagel, M. and Rees, W. (1996) *Our Ecological Footprint*, Gabriola Island, BC: New Society Publishers.

Wacquant, L. (2009) *Punishing the Poor*, Durham, NC and London: Duke University Press.

Waite, L., Lewis, H., Dwyer, P. and Hodkinson, S. (2015) 'Precarious Lives: Refugees and Asylum Seekers' Resistance within Unfree Labouring', *ACME: An International Journal for Critical Geographies*, 14 (2): 479–91.

Walker, A. (2018) 'Why the UK Needs a Social Policy on Ageing', *Journal of Social Policy*, 47 (2): 253–73.

Walker, A. and Wong, C.-K. (2004) 'The Ethnocentric Construction of the Welfare State', in P. Kennett (ed.) *A Handbook of Comparative Social Policy*, Cheltenham: Edward Elgar.

Walker, R. (2005) *Social Security and Welfare: Concepts and Comparisons*, Maidenhead: Open University Press.

Weale, A. and Clark, S. (2010) 'Co-payments in the NHS: An Analysis of the Normative Arguments', *Health Economics, Policy and Law*, 5 (2): 225–46.

Weaver, R.K. (1986) 'The Politics of Blame Avoidance', *Journal of Public Policy*, 6 (4): 371–98.

Welch, A.R. (1993) 'Class, Culture and the State in Comparative Education: Problems, Perspectives and Prospects', *Comparative Education*, 29 (1): 7–27.

Wendt, C. (2014) 'Changing Healthcare System Types', *Social Policy and Administration*, 48 (4): 864–82.

Wendt, C., Frisina, L. and Rothgang, H. (2009) 'Healthcare System Types: A Conceptual Framework for Comparison', *Social Policy and Administration*, 43 (1): 70–90.

Wheelock, J. (1999) 'Fear or Opportunity: Insecurity in Employment', in J. Vail, J. Wheelock and M. Hill (eds) *Insecure Times*, London: Routledge.

Whitehead, M., Dahlgren, G. and Gilson, L. (2001) 'Developing the Policy Response to Inequities in Health: A Global Perspective', in T. Evans, M. Whitehead, F. Diderichsen, A. Bhuiya and M. Wirth (eds) *Challenging Inequities in Health: From Ethics to Action*, Oxford: Oxford University Press.

WHO (World Health Organization) (1978) *Alma-Ata Declaration*, https://www.who.int/publications/almaata_declaration_en.pdf.

WHO (2016a) *Global Strategy on Human Resources for Health: Workforce 2030*, Geneva: World Health Organization.

WHO (2016b) *Global Report on Urban Health*, Geneva: World Health Organization.

WHO (2017a) *World Health Statistics*, Geneva: World Health Organization.

WHO (2017b) 10 Facts on Dementia, updated April 2017, http://www.who.int/features/factfiles/dementia/en/.

WHO (2018) Ambient (Outdoor) Air Quality and Health, Fact Sheet No.313, May 2018, https://www.who.int/en/news-room/fact-sheets/detail/ambient-(outdoor)-air-quality-and-health.

Wilensky, H.L. (1975) *The Welfare State and Equality*, Berkeley: University of California Press.

Wilensky, H.L. and Lebaux, C.N. (1965) *Industrial Society and Social Welfare*, Glencoe, IL: Free Press.

Wilkinson, R. and Pickett, K. (2010) *The Spirit Level: Why Equality is Better for Everyone*, Harmondsworth: Penguin.

Willetts, D. (2010) *The Pinch: How the Baby Boomers Took Their Children's Future – and Why They Should Give it Back*, London: Atlantic Books.

Williams, F. (1989) *Social Policy: A Critical Introduction – Issues of Race, Gender, and Class*, Cambridge: Polity Press.

Williams, F. (1995) 'Race, Ethnicity, Gender and Class in Welfare States', *Social Politics: International Studies in Gender, State and Society*, 2 (1): 127–59.

Williams, F. (2015) 'Towards the Welfare Commons: Contestation, Critique and Criticality in Social Policy', in Z. Irving, M. Fenger and J. Hudson (eds) *Social Policy Review 27: Analysis and Debate in Social Policy*, Bristol: Policy Press.

Williams, F. (2016) 'Critical Thinking in Social Policy: The Challenge of Past, Present and Future', *Social Policy and Administration*, 50 (6): 628–47.

Wimmer, A. and Schiller, N.G. (2003) 'Methodological Nationalism, the Social Sciences, and the Study of Migration: An Essay in Historical Epistemology', *International Migration Review*, 37 (3): 576–610.

Wimo, A., Gauthier, S. and Prince, M. (2018) *Global Estimates of Informal Care*, London: Alzheimer's Disease International, https://www.alz.co.uk/adi/pdf/global-estimates-of-informal-care.pdf.

Wincott, D. (2013) 'The (Golden) Age of the Welfare State: Interrogating a Conventional Wisdom', *Public Administration*, 91 (4): 806–22.

Wolf, A. (2002) *Does Education Matter?* London: Penguin Books.

World Bank (1994) *Averting the Old Age Crisis*, Oxford: Oxford University Press.

World Bank (2016) *World Development Report 2016: Digital Dividends*, Washington, DC: World Bank.

World Bank (2019a) 'CO_2 Gas Emissions: Metric Tonnes Per Capita, 2014', The World Bank Group, https://data.worldbank.org/indicator/EN.ATM.CO2E.

World Bank (2019b) 'Population Aged 65+, 2017', The World Bank Group, https://data.worldbank.org/indicator/SP.POP.DPND.OL

World Commission on Environment and Development (1987) *Our Common Future*, Oxford: Oxford University Press.

World Economic Forum (2018) *The Global Gender Gap Report 2018*, Insight Report, Geneva: World Economic Forum.

Wren-Lewis, S. (2018) *The Lies We Were Told*, Bristol: Bristol University Press.

Yeates, N. (2002) 'Globalization and Social Policy: From Global Neoliberal Hegemony to Global Political Pluralism', *Global Social Policy*, 2 (1): 69–91.

Yeates, N. (2004) 'Global Care Chains', *International Feminist Journal of Politics*, 6 (3): 369–91.

Yeates, N. (2007) 'The Social Policy Dimensions of World-Regionalism', *Global Social Policy*, 7 (3): 251–2.

Yeates, N. (2012) 'Global Care Chains: A State-of-the-Art Review and Future Directions in Care Transnationalization Research', *Global Networks*, 12 (2): 135–54.

Zhou, J. and Ronald, R. (2017a) 'The Resurgence of Public Housing Provision in China: The Chongqing Programme', *Housing Studies*, 32 (4): 428–48.

Zhou, J. and Ronald, R. (2017b) 'Housing and Welfare Regimes: Examining the Changing Role of Public Housing in China', *Housing, Theory and Society*, 34 (3): 253–76.

Index